LOOSE CONNECTIONS

LOOSE CONNECTIONS
Joining Together in America's Fragmented Communities

ROBERT WUTHNOW

HARVARD UNIVERSITY PRESS
Cambridge, Massachusetts / London, England / 1998

Library of Congress Cataloging-in-Publication Data

Wuthnow, Robert.
  Loose connections : joining together in America's fragmented
communities / Robert Wuthnow.
      p. cm.
  Includes bibliographical references and index.
  ISBN 0-674-53903-6 (alk. paper)
  1. Social participation—United States. 2. Social networks—
United States. 3. Community organization—United States.
I. Title.
HN59.2.W87   1998
302'.14'0973—dc21   98-14519

Contents

Preface

WHEN I WAS A CHILD my father talked about participating in threshing circles with his father and other farmers in the neighborhood. As an adult he took part in farmers' cooperative meetings and helped with fundraising drives for local charities, and my mother belonged to sewing circles and attended missionary society meetings. Compared to the close-knit community in which they lived, my own ties have been more long-distance and ephemeral. Some observers would argue that these changes are symptomatic of a large-scale breakdown in the fabric of community in America. My own view is that our involvement in our communities is changing, rather than simply declining. But this raises important questions of how and why it is changing.

The idea of examining these questions in a book grew out of conversations with Peter Berger, who graciously supported its writing through a grant from the Bradley Foundation to the Institute for the Study of Economic Culture at Boston University. This support made it possible for a small group of scholars to assemble on several occasions to discuss work in progress on aspects of civic culture and civil society. I am particularly grateful to Peter Berger and to the other members of the group, John Boli, Brigitte Berger, Anton Zijderveld, and Robert Hefner, for their insights and suggestions.

The research on which this book is based is of three kinds. Between 1995 and 1997 several associates and I designed and conducted in-depth qualitative interviews with approximately 250 people in a wide variety of communities across the country to find out about the civic organizations in which people are involved, how these organizations are changing, and how Americans understand their participation in their communities. In 1997 I commissioned a national survey of approximately 1,500 randomly selected respondents to gather descriptive information about Americans' attitudes toward and activities in their communities. Finally, I reanalyzed data from more than a dozen other surveys, spent time in libraries in several states culling through newspapers and local histories of civic organizations, and pieced together as much as I could about larger social conditions from census data and other studies.

The research was funded by grants from the Lilly Endowment and the Pew Charitable Trusts. I thank Craig Dykstra and Paul C. Light at these foundations for their interest and support. Field work for the national survey was performed by the Gallup Organization. Much of the qualitative research was carried out by Academic Research Services. I am especially grateful to Natalie Searl, and to Sylvia Kundrats, Leah Flickinger, Karen Myers, Brian Steensland, and Brad Verter, for their important contributions to the research, and to Geter Hicks and Cindy Gibson for administrative support.

Several related experiences contributed to the thinking that went into this book. One was an earlier collaborative project on civil society that was also sponsored by Peter Berger at the Institute for the Study of Economic Culture at Boston University. Interaction with several members of that project, especially Adam Seligman, John A. Hall, Daniel Chirot, and José Casanova, shaped some of my early ideas about civic involvement. A second was an opportunity to interact with the research team assembled by John A. Coleman in Berkeley to study the relationships between citizenship and discipleship in church-based community organizations. A third was an invitation to deliver the 1996 Rockwell Lectures at Rice University, which I devoted to the topic of Christianity and Civil Society. At the invitation of Robert Putnam, I also participated in a comparative project on the decline of social capital under the sponsorship of the Bertelsmann Science Foundation. Interaction with Robert Putnam, Theda Skocpol, Peter A. Hall, Claus Offe, Volker Then, and other members of this project was especially helpful. Paul Light hosted an informative gathering to discuss research on trust, and William Galston and Robert Fullinwider made it possible for me to participate in some of the work of the National Commission on Civic Renewal. Finally, the project on Common Values and Social Diversity at the Center for Advanced Study in the Behavioral

Sciences under the direction of Neil Smelser and Jeffrey Alexander provided an occasion to reflect on some of the underlying theoretical issues.

Readers of my earlier work will recognize this book's indebtedness to longstanding interests in religion, the nonprofit sector, volunteerism, community service, support groups, and personal values. Here I develop some of those themes further, but with emphasis on civic activities that contribute directly to the good of the community and that have implications for the ways in which citizenship is defined and put into practice.

Joyce Seltzer at Harvard University Press played an active and constructive role as my editor. I am also indebted to many students and colleagues both at Princeton and elsewhere for their insights. My wife, Sara, and my children, Robyn, Brooke, and Joel, all have connections of their own that they have shared with me, and they are above all my primary community.

LOOSE CONNECTIONS

Introduction

ELAINE SANBORN IS DEEPLY CONCERNED about the problems she sees in her community. She is a married mother in her early fifties who teaches high school English in a suburb of a northeastern city. "I see families in disarray," she says. "I see children coming to school abused." She thinks people are having to work too hard to pay the mortgage and are spending too many evenings watching television rather than taking part in community activities. "There's a void in a lot of people's lives. There's something really missing. It's that feeling we used to have in small cohesive hometowns where everybody knew everyone. People are missing that sense of community."

These sentiments are echoed again and again. In Cleveland a human services worker complains about how preoccupied people in her community are with "themselves, their job, and their children." She thinks most people "have very little energy to expend on a larger vision." In Chicago a Haitian immigrant who lives in a low-income neighborhood says, "You live every day wondering if you're going to make it." Instead of feeling solidarity with his neighbors, he describes his neighborhood as "scary" and "harsh." In downtown Louisville an African American woman complains that people in her neighborhood "just don't respect each other the way they used to." In a small town in Maine a young mother describes the factions that divide her community and laments, "You feel like there is a center of town, but there is nothing really drawing people together in that center."

Such concerns have become widespread. A sizable majority of Americans believe that our community-mindedness is eroding. Equally high proportions express concern about the breakdown of families and the degree to which selfishness prevails. Fewer than half believe their fellow citizens genuinely care about others.[1]

As social observers have tried to make sense of these concerns, many have come to focus on questions about the nature and extent of civic involvement. Are Americans no longer as interested in working for the good of their communities as they once were? Are people withdrawing into themselves to pursue private rather than public concerns? Have ties to community groups really become shallow and inconstant?

Some argue that civic involvement is declining, leaving the nation with fewer engaged citizens to help solve such problems as crime, drug abuse, joblessness, and the deterioration of public schools. In this view, democracy itself may be in jeopardy, especially if citizens are giving up their responsibilities to the few who would wield power. It seems that acrimony and mistrust are causing citizens to retreat from efforts to promote the common good. Others argue that civic involvement is changing in ways that cause uncertainty and concern, but not necessarily declining. They are generally less than sanguine about the prospects for American democracy, but they disagree about the nature of the changes taking place and the reasons for them.[2]

The view that civic involvement is in decline has been popularized by the work of the political scientist Robert Putnam. Putnam has examined trends in social and political participation in the United States using a variety of evidence from polls, election surveys, and membership reports. He concludes that Americans in the 1990s are less civic-minded than their counterparts in the 1960s and early 1970s, both in the degree to which they join civic organizations and in their propensity to vote, to engage in campaign activities, and to express confidence in public leaders. Putnam suggests that the nation is now experiencing a crisis similar to the one it faced at the end of the nineteenth century, when agriculture and small towns were being replaced by industry and cities. He wonders whether it will be possible to reinvent solutions, such as the Progressive reforms, the settlement houses, and the service clubs, that saved America's sense of civic order and community a century ago.[3]

The opposing view has been voiced by those who, while perhaps agreeing that much is not right with America, question the empirical basis of the claims about the decline of civic involvement. The public opinion analyst Everett Ladd, for example, challenges Putnam's assertions about diminishing group memberships, voting, and trust, and cites other surveys that point to more stable levels of involvement. Similarly, the political scientist Sidney Verba and two colleagues present evidence that casual kinds of social and political involvement were often as strong in the late 1980s as in the 1960s.[4]

There is in fact much evidence that America's communities are suffering serious problems. Violent crime is rampant, despite swollen prison populations, and drug use continues to be a national scandal.[5] Acts of terrorism are perpetrated by individuals and groups who live by their own asocial conceptions of morality. Poverty has increased, especially in urban areas and among children and the elderly.[6] Racial tensions persist.[7] Yet, at the same time, federal cutbacks are placing more responsibilities on communities to solve their own problems. And if citizens' willingness to become involved in their communities is uncertain or weak, then there is ample reason for concern.

If we look to the past for guidance, those who take a pessimistic view of the present appear to be on solid ground. Earlier in this century millions of Americans joined service clubs, veterans' organizations, and ladies' auxiliaries to contribute to the improvement of their communities. Immigrant farmers participated in threshing circles for the benefit of all and held community meetings at one-room schools to share common problems; their offspring belonged to farmers' co-ops and attended neighborhood gatherings in church basements. Millions of other Americans joined trade associations and fraternal organizations. Through these enduring relationships, people connected with their communities and fulfilled their civic responsibilities. In so doing, they contributed to the strength of American democratic society.

Today in contrast, sizable numbers of Americans have withdrawn from service clubs, labor unions, and churches, apparently believing it makes little difference whether they engage in civic activities or not. Some evidence suggests that a growing number of people regard their neighbors as inherently untrustworthy (especially if they are of a different race or nationality) and as alien to their idea of a like-minded community. It is easy to infer from such evidence that many Americans are turning their backs on the general welfare and pursuing their own interests as single-mindedly as possible. Given such inferences, it is hardly surprising that the passivity and narcissism of contemporary Americans are recurrent themes in thoughtful social analyses.[8]

Although it is easy to render impassioned judgments about Americans' lack of civic involvement, it is by no means clear what has provoked this apparent retreat from public life. Nor should we conclude too readily that civic involvement has been declining as uniformly or as dramatically as some have suggested. Indeed, one of the most important consequences of the current debate is that it forces us to think harder about what we mean by civic involvement. No longer can it be assumed that membership in Rotary or Kiwanis, attendance at political rallies, or even voting is its defining characteristic. These activities may be in decline, but we cannot know how to interpret the changes unless we consider newly emerging alternatives and the reasons for them.

To examine the shifting character of civic participation in relation to the deeper social changes of recent decades, we must pay close attention to the ways in which Americans themselves understand and experience these changes. People who remain outside community organizations have stories to tell about what has alienated them. People who are more actively involved have poignant stories to tell about their triumphs, their frustrations, and their struggles to adapt to changing social circumstances. These stories help us understand the contemporary meanings of community ties and civic engagement.

We cannot understand the apathy that afflicts so much of the public if we view it in isolation without taking into account the complex circumstances in which people live. The innovative ways in which many Americans are reaching out to one another tell us a great deal about American society at the end of the twentieth century. The decay of some forms of civic participation is accompanied by the gradual emergence of new ways of relating to communities, and there are signs that some of the nation's most venerable civic organizations are adapting to new social realities. We cannot grasp the dynamic of civic participation today without viewing it in relation to the broader changes in families, communities, corporate structures, and government.

During the past thirty years, as our nation has expanded economically, politically, and socially, becoming more complex and diversified, virtually all of our institutions have been transformed in their organization and accessibility. The result is a climate of unsettledness that is deeply influencing the daily lives of Americans. For many, it means spending longer years gaining a specialized education to meet an increasingly demanding labor market, postponing family and community responsibilities because it is unclear where and when they will find a stable job. For working Americans, the struggle to stay ahead frequently means moving farther away from parents and kin, sinking shallower roots into particular communities, and negotiating compromises with a spouse who has equally demanding employment arrangements. Family schedules become enormously complicated, especially for single parents and in two-career households. Not surprisingly, the proportions of Americans who say they experience stress and "always feel rushed" have risen substantially in recent years.[9] It is little wonder that civic responsibilities get shunted aside.

Many Americans are troubled by the lack of communal ties and activities. They are worried that the moral values they wish to communicate to their children cannot be sustained unless we strengthen the social relationships that tie individuals, families, friends, and neighbors together. Nationally, seven in ten believe that people in their own community do not care enough for one another. And this concern is closely associated (as closely as worries about crime) with how people feel about their community as a whole (see Methods, especially Table 1). Few express trust and respect for the larger society.

Some Americans have begun to search for ways to combat their isolation and to connect with neighbors and like-minded people. They are trying to identify workable ways to help their friends and to receive help from them, to be responsible members of their neighborhoods, and to contribute to the betterment of their communities. They are experimenting with looser, more sporadic, ad hoc connections in place of the long-term memberships in hierarchical organizations of the past. Many people find it hard to join community groups that demand years of commitment, and so busy men and women do the best they can, giving a little of their time, seeking to be responsible citizens in small ways, and being creative in the ways they relate to their neighbors and the nation.

The changing character of civic participation relates to the increasing *porousness* of social institutions. As the population has expanded and become more diverse, and as environmental and informational technologies have become more complex, institutions have adapted by developing less rigid boundaries that allow goods, ideas, and people to flow in and out more easily. Many institutions have been reconfigured in the process. In most realms these new loosely confederated structures are better able to adapt to the challenges of uncertain and complex circumstances. These permeable structures also shape the ways in which individual Americans live and relate to one another, dictating greater flexibility and limited commitment. Personal schedules become less certain and relationships shift more often, and some people are simply unable to find or create their niche.

Some argue that the problems in America's communities can be traced to some moral failure, such as too much individualism, too little willingness to participate in civic organizations, or too much emphasis on personal rights at the expense of social responsibilities.[10] Although there is much to be said for this claim, it doesn't help us understand the institutional realities with which people are confronted. A close look at the porousness of contemporary institutions and its effects on individuals' lives and energies can tell us much more about democratic society today and about its potential for the future than can a call for moral reform.

Living with fragmented institutions, many Americans are altering their ways of carrying out their civic responsibilities, if they carry them out at all. People who live within ambiguous social spaces are less likely to feel that long-term memberships in civic organizations are a meaningful option. Their view may be short-sighted, but it is not irrational. And yet fragmented communities increase the need for people to seek intentional relationships with others, and these relationships can lead to innovative forms of civic participation.

A balanced assessment of how well the United States is prepared to face the next century requires a careful look at new forms of civic involvement. In the past, changes in social conditions were always associated with new forms of cooperation. The national benevolent associations and temperance societies that Tocqueville observed in the United States in the 1830s were recent developments, replacing some older civic groups such as craft guilds and town meetings and responding to the increasing integration of the country as a single nation. Labor unions emerged slowly during the next century as the economy gradually developed its industrial base. Settlement houses and urban missions were relatively unknown until the expansion of cities at the end of the nineteenth century made them an obvious form of civic involvement. Many of the civic associations that are now declining emerged largely in small towns and among shopkeepers and merchants.

Implicitly, the current debate about civil society has recognized the changing influence of social conditions, but consideration of these conditions has often taken on partisan overtones. For example, some observers attribute the shrinking of traditional civic associations to the growth of big government between the 1930s and the 1970s. They point out that special-interest groups, political action committees, and single-issue organizations have been inevitable responses to this growth in centralized government. Yet, besides the special-interest groups that can be dismissed as send-a-check organizations, thousands of community groups are searching for—and finding—new ways to enlist people who may not have the time or the inclination to participate in more established organizations.

As historical examples suggest, specific forms of civic involvement tend to evolve within specific social and historical environments. The labor movements and socialist labor parties that emerged in Europe between 1870 and 1914 appeared within an economic system that brought large numbers of workers together to work in heavy industry.[11] The way civic involvement manifests itself within a particular social environment will depend on the availability of and competition for scarce resources among various organizations, groups, and movements. Citizens have always had limited time and energy. Peasant-landlord relationships and kin networks were effective ways of mobilizing civic participation in early modern Europe. Cycling clubs, brass bands, and student groups became the means for mobilizing recruits to the Nazi party in Germany following World War I.[12] Over a period of years, the organizations that manage to carve out a niche for themselves and are able to extract resources from their environment will not only survive but also come to resemble the particular features of their environment.

Broadly conceived, civic involvement consists of participation in social activities that either mediate between citizens and government or provide ways for citizens to pursue common objectives with or without the help of government. These activities are purposive, but their objectives can range from putting pressure on the government to pass a particular bill, to ensuring that the local schools operate effectively, to helping people who have no other means of support. Some of these activities may be performed alone (taking soup to a needy neighbor is an example). But most require people to work together, and even those that are ostensibly solitary (like voting) are generally the result of organized efforts.

As Americans sense the fragmentation of their communities, many are now talking seriously about making connections with other people. They talk of coming together for the good of their communities, either in informal personal networks or through larger and more formal organizational partnerships. But these connections are often looser than was true in the past. Instead of cultivating lifelong ties with their neighbors, or joining organizations that reward faithful long-term service, people come together around specific needs and to work on projects that have definite objectives.[13]

These loose connections apparently suit many Americans today because of the permeable institutions in which we live. To understand how these newer forms of civic involvement work—and how they differ from older kinds of community organizations—we need to consider some examples.

1

Breaking Apart, Coming Together

HOW DO AMERICANS REACH OUT to others nowadays? How do they involve themselves in their communities? Some are still active in traditional organizations, such as men's and women's service clubs, fraternal orders, and volunteer firefighting units. Others are being drawn into newer forms of involvement, such as violence-prevention networks, coalitions to help the needy, and self-help groups. Comparing the two kinds of civic involvement will help us understand the differences between them and the social conditions that lead people to choose one kind rather than the other.

In the past, one of the most common ways in which Americans participated in their communities was through service clubs and organizations. Many of these—Rotary, Kiwanis, Lions, Jaycees—were founded near the beginning of the twentieth century, and their memberships were limited to men. They were dedicated to helping the needy, promoting better health and education, encouraging international exchanges, and supporting local charities and youth organizations. But it has become harder for some of these organizations to attract members and secure their active participation. The social changes to which local chapters are having to adapt are clearly evident in the experiences of Jack Schmidt.

Jack Schmidt is a silver-haired man in his early seventies who lives with his wife in an older East Coast suburb composed of moderately expensive colonial-style houses. A retired manager who worked for many years at a pharmaceutical firm, he is now serving a term as district governor of Rotary International. He joined Rotary more than twenty years ago, shortly after the youngest of his three children left home for college. A friend invited him to attend one day. Jack knew it was an honor to be invited. At the luncheon he recognized some of the prominent men in the community. They sang, ate a nice lunch, listened to a speaker, and did some networking. Jack decided to join, intrigued mostly by the prestige the club seemed to offer. Over the years Rotary has become the main activity that gets him out of the house (especially since he retired). It puts him in contact with other men with whom he enjoys sharing a few jokes, and it makes him feel useful. He is quite proud of the services Rotary has rendered to the community.

He boasts that one of the clubs in his district built a nursing home and is now expanding it to include 140 more beds. Another built a laundromat in an inner-city neighborhood and collected computers for a nearby school. His own club has done everything from purchasing a fire truck for one of the local volunteer fire companies, to volunteering at a center for children from dysfunctional families, to operating a drug and substance abuse prevention program. The clubs also contribute to district-wide efforts, such as collecting used books for school libraries, raising money to send students to college, and supplying professional expertise for agricultural and irrigation projects in developing countries.

Jack knows the history of Rotary well enough to take some pride in being able to tell it. He knows that Rotary was founded in 1905 by the Chicago lawyer Paul Harris and four business associates who wanted to replicate some of the community values they had known growing up in small towns. The name was chosen because luncheon meetings were held on a rotating basis at its members' offices. From its inception, it included a broad range of business and professional men, and thus it grew as the numbers of middle managers and professionals swelled, especially after World War II. Official estimates place its worldwide membership at approximately 1.2 million, making up some 27,000 local clubs.

Jack gives the impression that Rotary is flourishing. Despite his enthusiasm, however, a study of the history of men's service clubs in the United States suggests that they are "hanging on through sheer social inertia, attracting a hard core of dedicated members but few others, ending with even their public insignias unintelligible except to the initiated."[1]

Jack Schmidt may be one of those who are hanging on from inertia. Neither of his sons-in-law has chosen to join. But he doesn't see it that way. From his perspective, Rotary International has fared better than other established service clubs and fraternal lodges. Shriners' membership, for instance, peaked at 942,000 in 1978 and is now at 609,000; the Benevolent and Protective Order of Elks has experienced a similar decline.[2] Moose,

Lions, and Kiwanis have shrunk as well. In comparison, Rotary has held its own, counting approximately 460,000 members in the United States, 10 percent of whom are now women, who, with Asian Americans, account for enough growth in recent years to offset earlier declines.[3]

As district governor, Jack Schmidt spends at least three full evenings a week on Rotary activities. Some weeks he puts in seven evenings. He also spends entire days at training sessions and conferences. Soon after returning from a four-day "zone conference" (a meeting of all the district governors in a several-state region), he was expecting to spend a week at a meeting for district governors from around the world. He was also planning a day-long training session for presidents of the clubs in his district, to make sure they understood Rotary's current rules and goals, to show them how to initiate new programs, and to start them thinking about strategic planning. He stays active in his local club as well, serving as an ad hoc member of all seventeen of its committees. For him, in short, Rotary is like a part-time job. For the moment, as long as his health continues, Jack is able to travel at Rotary's expense, make important decisions, and occupy a prestigious position, much as he did when he was employed. It satisfies many of his personal needs while it connects him to other men like himself both in and beyond his community.

Of course the time demands are not as great for rank-and-file members, but Rotary requires high levels of commitment from them too. Besides luncheons and committee meetings, members are expected to set aside time to participate in major projects, and these projects are often impossible for people with inflexible schedules. For instance, Jack worked hard to arrange an exchange program between Rotarians in the United States and in Sweden. With financial assistance from the Rotary Foundation, four U.S. businessmen were sent to live for five weeks with Rotarians in Sweden.

The activities of many men's service clubs were better geared to an earlier time than they are to the present. Clubs that accepted only men or only women were more common in the past. But Rotary has tried to adapt to changing social conditions. The change in bylaws that made it possible for women to join was one example. New projects have also been initiated. In Jack Schmidt's district, less attention is being devoted to beautifying the local streets and more to such problems as drug use and child abuse than would have been imagined a generation ago. In hope of attracting younger members, some of the clubs sponsor softball games and Little League teams. Organizational arrangements have also changed. Although the clubs still emphasize hands-on projects, these projects now often require more sophisticated knowledge of building codes and other government regulations; they require more cooperation with trained professionals, such as drug counselors and family therapists; and they include partnerships with a wider variety of nonprofit agencies. Many of Rotary's newer projects are temporary, involving working for a few weeks or months with a community development corporation, a school, or a mayor's commission.

These adaptations notwithstanding, Rotary has found itself struggling to maintain the old level of commitment among members. The largest club in Jack's district, centered in the heart of the city, grew to approximately 600 members in the early 1970s; today it has only 200. Jack blames much of this decline on corporate relocations. As companies have moved to suburbs and exurbs, central-city clubs have been depopulated. But suburban clubs have also been having difficulty.

Jack laments the fact that people live in one suburb, work in another suburb, perhaps attend church in yet another, and shop elsewhere; the result is that Rotary has trouble knowing where to locate its clubs. If it locates them where people work, they may come to luncheon meetings but not to evening functions, and neighborhood clubs do less well at drawing on networks among co-workers. Some clubs have had to disband entirely because their memberships have dropped below the required minimum. Some members have also become disillusioned, feeling that the club no longer puts them in contact with important people, or that its projects are uninteresting. Companies that used to provide support for local Rotary projects no longer do, Jack complains, and part of the problem is that these companies now have weaker ties to local communities.

Another serious problem is Rotary's cumbersome hierarchy. It has taken Jack two decades to work up to his position as district governor. Rotary rewards seniority by requiring members to serve on as many as six different committees, then to devote a year each to chairing these various committees, and then to move through various elected offices at the club level (including secretary, treasurer, vice-president, president-elect, and president) before assuming positions at higher levels of the organization. Not every member aspires to these positions, of course, but younger men and women often feel impatient and think they can make a difference more quickly by working in other organizations.

Jack himself is reluctant to criticize Rotary's hierarchy. He says the most frustrating aspect of being a district governor is the "impasse" in getting younger people involved.[4] He acknowledges that Rotary may need to change if this impasse is to be resolved, but hopes it will not compromise its traditions. In the meantime, he worries most that people are finding it easier to give excuses than to get involved: "I believe this honestly, as the older generation passes on, we're turning a whole nation over to people that's looking at what's in it for me?" He hopes more people will start thinking about their children. "How well are you preparing them," he asks, "if you're not willing to help your community?"

Men like Jack Schmidt worry that the vision of community involvement that led men of their generation to organizations such as Rotary will not be transmitted to younger men and women. Younger generations seem unable to fit traditional community service groups into their lifestyles and jobs. This is as true for women as for men. Organizations like Rotary that were originally established for men have always been complemented by the work of women in women's and mixed-gender organizations. In fact, women have traditionally borne more than their share of the burden of volunteering and community service. But more and more American women have joined the labor force, giving them less time and fewer incentives to connect with other people through voluntary organizations.[5]

Elizabeth Meade exemplifies the human dilemmas created by women's changing relation to community service. She is an upper-middle-class woman in her late fifties, short, with graying brown hair, who lives in a beautiful stone house nestled among rolling hills on the outskirts of a large city. Her two children are grown, so she is free to travel with her husband, a successful self-employed businessman whose work takes him on periodic trips outside the United States. Elizabeth has never worked outside the home. The League of Women Voters has been her abiding interest.

Elizabeth joined the League thirty years ago, shortly after she and her husband moved to the community. Her son was less than a year old, and Elizabeth knew hardly anyone in the community. Her husband was interested in politics, and one evening they got a babysitter and went to a seminar on politics at the local community college. Over coffee, one of the other women at the seminar asked Elizabeth if she'd like to join the League. Elizabeth knew very little about what the League did, and she disliked politics, but she agreed to attend a meeting in hope of meeting some of her neighbors. The League's membership chairwoman helped her find a babysitter.

"It was a chance to get out and be with other women," Elizabeth recalls. "And they were very actively studying the school district at that time, so I started being involved in the committee. I got to know people, and I learned a lot about the community both from the real League studies, but also just from talking over coffee around the kitchen table. Most of these women were older." Elizabeth lived some distance from her mother, so the League women became a valuable source of advice about raising her family. "All of them were older than I was, so their kids were further through the school system. I learned a lot about what to expect, not only about the school, but what's a ten-year-old like. So a lot of it was social."

As a young mother with a liberal arts education but no practical skills gained from working at a job, Elizabeth also appreciated the opportunities the League offered: "I learned a lot. Whatever skills I have, I learned from the League, whereas most people nowadays learn them from being in the workplace. I've never been in the workplace, so my adult education has come from what I've done in the League."

The chapter to which she belonged was typical of League chapters across the country, drawing its energies mostly from educated middle-class women. The League's aim is to promote citizens' participation in government and to do this mostly through education. It prints and distributes a voters' guide, hosts debates and other gatherings at which citizens can meet candidates, and studies local issues. Although it is nonpartisan and does not support particular candidates, it does take positions on issues.

One of the more ambitious projects Elizabeth Meade's chapter undertook was a study of library facilities in the county. After securing the cooperation of other chapters, its members conducted a study of the branch libraries to determine how many books were available and how accessible they were to the county's growing population. After months of study, it recommended that branch libraries meet Library Association standards, that a new branch be opened, that it be within walking distance of people in the village, and that it have adequate parking (and a book drop) for those who drove in from new developments. Elizabeth is proud that the new library has recently opened and that it meets all the League's criteria.

But Elizabeth is also discouraged at the trend she sees at League meetings. Like Jack Schmidt, she worries about diminishing participation. Nationally, membership in the League of Women Voters dropped by 42 percent between 1969 and 1994.[6] During that period, participation shrank dramatically in Elizabeth's county as well. There used to be four chapters; several years ago they agreed to consolidate into one, which now draws about as many active members as each of the four used to attract.

One reason for the decline is that general-purpose organizations like the League are facing increased competition from special-interest groups that have clearer goals and pursue them more aggressively. Elizabeth admits, "There's many single-interest groups, and it's easier now [than 25 years ago] to get into a single-issue organization. You're all focused on one thing, and you accomplish something or at least you've got that goal ahead of you." In contrast, the League confuses some people with its multiple missions: "Every problem known to man was on our plate, and so sometimes you think, 'Oh! You know, we haven't done a thing.' We'd say, 'Well, our real mission is citizen education, so let's drop all the studies. Let's just do voters' guides.' But then it was the studies that really interested people. So we were scattered. I don't know what will happen."

Consolidation of chapters, while a rational move at the time, has also contributed to the League's decline. The county-wide chapter can address county-level issues more easily than the separate chapters could in the past, but the county is an artificial jurisdiction that means little to most members. They care about their local villages and townships more than about the entire county. Some also recognize the importance of addressing regional issues spanning a six-county area, but feel the League is ill-suited to do so compared with special-interest groups.

In this particular case, consolidation also reduced the likelihood of women from more diverse segments of the community becoming involved in the League. When there were four chapters, two catered largely to upper-middle-class women like Elizabeth while the other two included lower-middle-class and working-class women. Now that there is only one chapter, the upper-middle-class women dominate. When pushed, Elizabeth acknowledges the problem: "We're concerned that we tend to be white, middle class, relatively well educated, and we would like to involve more young people and more people at all levels of society and it's just difficult."

The most significant reason for diminishing participation, however, is time. When most of the League's members were housewives or employed only part time, meetings could be scheduled more easily. As Elizabeth points out, there used to be twenty-five possible meeting times during the week: early mornings, late mornings, early afternoons, late afternoons, and evenings, five days a week. Now there are only five: evenings. Most members have family obligations on Friday evenings. And she finds it increasingly difficult to schedule regular meetings on the other evenings. It isn't that members have no free time; it's that their free time doesn't coincide with that of other members.

As Elizabeth gets older, she wonders how much longer she will be able to participate in League activities. In her early fifties, she is in perfect health and expects to be energetic for many years. But it is one thing to drive a mile or two in the morning or afternoon to attend a local chapter meeting, quite another to drive ten miles to the county seat in the evening: "I don't mind going at 10 o'clock in the morning, but at night when there might be frozen ice patches, I'm not so keen on it. I probably won't drop my membership, but I don't think I'm going to be as active."

Whereas Rotary and the League of Women Voters have been organized nationally and have tried to attract well-educated members of the middle class, many traditional civic organizations have been more local in character and have appealed more to a working-class membership. Frank Purelli provides an example of this kind of involvement. He is a tall, muscular, thirty-year-old 200-pounder who wears his hair short (except for a ponytail), has a mustache, and wears an earring in one ear. Although Frank is a member of the younger generation that Jack Schmidt worries about, he is trying to do something positive for his community. His form of involvement is also fairly traditional, and it brings into sharp relief some of the problems that younger people face when they try to sustain such commitments.

Frank is an Italian Catholic who has lived in the same township all his life. Both his father and his grandfather grew up there as well. After high school Frank worked for three years doing landscaping for a local nursery. His days consisted mostly of spreading mulch, planting trees and bushes, building trellises, and laying flagstone. He enjoyed being outdoors, but the wages were meager. After marrying his high school sweetheart, Frank switched to working at a small print shop that specialized in fliers and greeting cards. He's learned how to operate all the machines and is now in charge of production scheduling. He has known the boss since he was a boy and finds the company a good, low-pressure place to work.

In his spare time Frank visits his parents, who live just down the street. He socializes with the neighbors (one of whom was in his class in high school), goes hunting, and generally tries to be a good neighbor. He likes to talk about local politics with the guys at the barbershop, and he serves on the volunteer fire squad. Frank especially enjoys being a volunteer fireman, finding it more exciting than his job at the print shop. He spends between five and ten hours a week at the fire station, and works longer hours each spring during the annual fundraising drive and pancake feed. His boss lets him off work whenever there is a fire, and sometimes Frank takes the occasion to check out calls for the rescue squad as well. He says it is thrilling to be a fireman and he loves to sit around the firehouse and chew the fat with the other guys.[7]

Frank is one of about 800,000 men and women (mostly men) in the United States who serve as volunteer firefighters. Organized into approximately 25,000 local companies, they make up an estimated 80 percent of the total U.S. firefighting force.[8] They also represent one of the oldest continuing forms of civic participation. In colonial America firefighting was entirely volunteer but was seldom organized in formal brigades. The structure of present-day fire companies dates largely from the early nineteenth century, when villages and towns started to erect buildings to house horse-drawn pump wagons and enlisted volunteers to maintain the equipment.[9] The company Frank Purelli belongs to was organized in 1890, soon after his community became an official municipality.

National evidence suggests that membership in volunteer fire companies may have declined by as much as 20 percent in the past decade, although some companies appear to be thriving. Whatever the case, members of many volunteer companies complain that it has become increasingly difficult to enlist new recruits, especially in suburban areas, where loyalties to the community may be weaker than in small towns. Professional companies make up a growing share of the nation's firefighting force: the number of career firefighters has grown by approximately 11 percent over the past decade, to approximately 210,000.[10]

For men like Frank Purelli, serving on the volunteer fire squad is partly a way of holding on to a sense of community that is rapidly receding from their grasp. He says his township has a population of 44,000, approximately 500 of whom serve as volunteers on one of the ten fire companies or on the rescue squads or police auxiliaries that operate in conjunction with them. The fact that even this many people are involved is a matter of pride with him. Part of him feels that people care about the welfare of the community and that the community is a good place to live.

His sense of ownership in the community stems mostly from the fact that his father and grandfather were also volunteer firemen in the same township. At present, Frank's brother and two of his uncles are also volunteer firemen. Frank joined the company as soon as he was eighteen (the minimum age), after having "hung around here a lot as a kid," and he is now president of the unit. "Typical story," he observes, "little kid goes down to the firehouse, sits in the truck, wants to be a fireman." He is not particularly reflective about his motives, saying only that "I like to do things for people" and "I've always enjoyed it." He likens it to the rock band he used to play in, saying that it gives him something to do in the evenings.

The trouble now is that he and his wife have two young children and she works at a full-time job. Frank feels guiltier than before about leaving the house. So he eases his guilt by trying to be on call for the squad during working hours more than in the evenings, but he is unable to avoid evening calls entirely. He also tells himself that he needs to feel worthwhile, a feeling he seldom gets at work. If he didn't do his printing job, somebody else would step in and do it. He's not so sure the fire company could exist without him.

Being a fireman is a skill that has been passed on from generation to generation in Frank's family, giving him a sense of his place in history, and it is part of the Purellis' image in the community. As the community has changed, maintaining this image has become all the more important. Frank jokingly describes himself as a blue-collar, working-class man, and he occupies a lower rung in the social hierarchy than the professionals and managers who have moved into the township in recent years. Even in comparison with his father, who attained a white-collar, middle-management position at a large firm, Frank is lower in social status.

Being a fireman is Frank's way of saying to himself and to his peer group that he is a member of one of the established, respected families in the township. Fire companies have a culture all their own, giving Italian Catholics like Frank a feeling that they are paying something back to the community, just as their parents and grandparents did. Indeed, he is rather scornful of the newcomers and of those who move into and out of the community instead of settling down. He doesn't much like to socialize with them because they don't share his values. He is afraid the community will go downhill if too many of these people move in. Frank's ties to the community are strong and deeply felt, but changes in its nature and population as well as in his own household are challenging the maintenance of those ties.

Although Jack Schmidt, Elizabeth Meade, and Frank Purelli are still involved with their community organizations, all talk about the problems the organizations are having. Memberships have been falling and it is harder to secure active involvement from members than it was a generation ago. In its own way, each organization is struggling to adapt to new social realities, and only time will tell how effective these efforts may be. Meanwhile, other organizations and activities have emerged to better meet the needs of contemporary life, and through them civic participation is being reinvented.

Grace Bishop, forty-seven, is the assistant director of human services at the county level in a metropolitan area that has become increasingly divided along racial, ethnic, and income lines. She has a masters degree in social work, is married, and is the mother of a teenage son and daughter. Three years ago she received a phone call from a high school principal asking if someone in her office could help resolve the problem of violence among teenagers. The call was precipitated by an incident in which several teenagers had been injured at the school, and now there was growing tension between the members of two rival gangs. The principal was worried that someone might be seriously hurt—a concern that proved accurate within the following year when a teenager in the community was stabbed and nearly died.

After the principal's call Grace talked with her supervisor about the problem and he formed an interdepartmental committee to discuss it. The committee met several times over a period of months, but it accomplished little because nobody was able to take on the additional work needed to move from ideas to action. Feeling frustrated, Grace decided to form a new organization that would enlist both voluntary and professional effort to tackle the problem.

The organization she started is called Partners for Peace. Now in its third year, it is a network of approximately twenty-five people from the county Department of Human Services, schools, local hospitals, law enforcement, and the community at large. Its goal, Grace says, is "to build a culture of nonviolence, particularly with young people." She and the four other founders of Partners for Peace defined its mission as generating information that could be useful to people interested in fighting violence in their own ways. There were "little pockets of conversation," as she terms them, in scattered parts of the community as a result of an occasional incident in the schools of students carrying weapons, or an altercation that got out of hand, or a student being intimidated on the way home from school. "We wanted to bring the awareness [of the problem] up a bit," she says, "and at the same time begin to offer some ways of addressing it."

Grace decided that two kinds of information might be useful: greater awareness of the problem and ideas about what to do about it (so that people didn't just wring their hands and feel hopeless). As a way to provide both kinds of information, she aimed to bring together people from the schools, churches, police, and social welfare agencies, who already had partial knowledge of the problem. Instead of calling another meeting (like the ones that hadn't worked), she opted for a "conference" with an outside speaker who would offer fresh energy and insights.[11]

After the conference Grace and her group met several times to talk about what they had learned. Since then Partners for Peace has developed wider social networks through which practical information about violence prevention can flow. Some of these networks have helped link people from communities throughout the state. For example, Partners for Peace sponsored a conference of mayors and county executives that brought a number of leaders together. To promote awareness of the possibilities for preventing violence, the conference included a demonstration by one of the elementary schools that had initiated a successful program.

Because it is not part of a national federation, Partners for Peace cooperates with other organizations through what Grace terms "partnering." For example, she worked with a regional organization that was concerned with drug problems in schools. It was a good partnership because Grace was able to put on a workshop and the other organization was able to pay for people to attend through a federal grant it had received. On another occasion Partners for Peace collaborated with the YMCA on a violence-prevention campaign. The YMCA's national office ran a publicity campaign on television and provided "organizer kits," and Grace Bishop and her fellow volunteers did most of the work.

Partners for Peace illustrates some of differences between the new efforts to help with community problems and the established civic organizations. Rather than aiming to carve out an entirely distinct niche for itself, Partners for Peace forms loose alliances with the many other groups already working in the community, including government-funded organizations such as schools and police departments as well as voluntary organizations such as churches. Partners for Peace has relatively little administrative structure of its own; its five-member planning committee has intentionally been kept small. Volunteers are drawn in to work on specific projects, such as putting on a symposium, rather than being asked to maintain the organization itself. They can more easily schedule one evening to work on a project than commit themselves to a regular program of activities. They also make greater use of paid professionals. Grace Bishop herself is not clear about how much of her involvement in Partners for Peace is part of her job and how much is volunteer effort. The time she devotes to it during lunch breaks and after work blends almost imperceptibly with the phone calls she makes as part of her job.

The main limitation of Partners for Peace is that it is ephemeral. Grace is thinking of stepping down and turning her attention to something else. If she does, it is unclear whether the organization will survive. It is also unclear whether violence in the schools will truly be prevented or whether the public's interest will prove transient. In a community that is changing rapidly, transience itself is often the most enduring reality. Nevertheless, Partners for Peace is one of thousands of such violence-prevention networks that have been founded in recent years and that now enlist some 8.6 million Americans as volunteers.[12]

Whereas an organization like Partners for Peace is recognizable as a new form of civic participation, other changes may be less obvious. Coalitions among local organizations are an important manifestation of these changes. These coalitions are often more stable than the ad hoc relationships Grace Bishop cultivates. But they permit people to become involved in their communities in more flexible ways than may have been true in the past. Glen Wilson's experiences provide a vivid illustration.

At sixty-five, Glen Wilson is taking life easy. He is a retired accountant whose four children are grown. He and his wife devote much of their time to puttering around their modest middle-class house; the mortgage was paid off years ago. They are in good health, make periodic pilgrimages to see their grandchildren, and go to a Protestant church where there are other couples their age. Several years ago Glen agreed to devote a few hours a week to the church's effort to feed the hungry.

Throughout their history, Christian churches have tried to follow Jesus's command to "heal the sick, feed the hungry, and clothe the naked." In earlier centuries helping the hungry generally involved congregants' giving alms directly to the poor or bringing a portion of their fruits and vegetables to the church for the use of widows and orphans. Twentieth-century efforts have included massive campaigns to fight hunger around the world. But the local congregation has remained the front line for most food-distribution activities. Parishioners donate canned goods on designated Sundays or deacons establish small funds that the pastor can draw from when one of the church families is in need.

The kind of activity in which Glen Wilson is involved is thus about as traditional as one can imagine. Indeed, approximately 39 million Americans participate in food-distribution efforts of some kind, and 83 percent of all church members say their congregation helps sponsor such efforts.[13] Glen Wilson certainly did not regard himself as an innovator when he agreed to serve. But the Food Place, as it is called, provides a perfect example of the way civic activities are being reprogrammed to take account of changing social conditions. Although it relies almost completely on volunteer labor (and is thus different from Grace Bishop's anti-violence project), the Food Place is part of a loose network of organizations that draws on a wide variety of community resources.

The Food Place came into existence about a decade ago. Before that, local churches mostly took care of the hungry in their separate ways, and referred more serious needs to the county's welfare department. The decision to set up a single food-distribution facility to which the churches would contribute was necessitated by the fact that social welfare services were being cut, leaving more families without provisions, and by a decline in the memberships and finances of the older churches. Banding together was a way to make better use of limited resources.

Ten churches are part of the coalition that supports the Food Place. Each church agreed to staff it one month of the year. They had hoped to enlist two other churches, but have been unable to, so a couple of the larger churches have tried to fill in the gaps. The Food Place is open three days a week from ten in the morning until one in the afternoon. That means twelve volunteers are needed each month and each volunteer must be willing to put in a three-hour shift.

Glen Wilson and another man are extras. Each puts in about four hours a week making sure everything runs smoothly. The aim is to make food available on an emergency basis to low-income families who suddenly find themselves without cash. To qualify, recipients must earn less than 150 percent of the official poverty level for a family of their size. They must fill out a card giving their name and address and explain why they are in need. They must be local residents. And they cannot come in more than six times a year. If they meet these criteria, they are given a three-day supply of food. Only nonperishable items are available, and recipients have no choice as to what they are given.

About 500 families make use of the Food Place at least once during the year, receiving a total of approximately five tons of food. Making this happen requires ingenuity, not only to be sure volunteers are there, but also to pay the rent and secure the food. The Food Place is housed in a warehouse known as the County Building Annex. At first the county provided the space free of charge, but recently it has been charging $1,000 a year, which is about what it takes to cover the heat and electricity. To raise this amount, the Food Place co-sponsors the annual CROP walk, a widely used fundraiser in which children, teenagers, and any adults who can be persuaded to participate walk about five miles with an agreement from sponsors to contribute a certain amount for each mile walked. The Food Place receives a quarter of the proceeds, or about $2,500.

After the rent is paid the money left over is used to purchase food. Several years ago Glen discovered a federal program that permits nonprofit organizations like the Food Place to buy surplus food in bulk for only a few cents a pound. Once or twice a year he arranges to have food delivered from the warehouse. Most of the food, however, is contributed by schoolchildren. Each year the students in the local schools are asked to collect canned goods (from their parents in most cases) and bring them to school. Each grade is assigned a different item, thus ensuring an appropriate variety.

It is a complicated system, but the Food Place does supply food to a number of needy people. Rather than simply closing shop when they started to lack volunteers, the churches found a new way to do what they could. People are still reluctant to volunteer, Glen says, but this way they can do something without committing themselves to more than a few hours a year. As a separate organization, the Food Place is better positioned to work with CROP, through the schools, and with the county and federal government than if it were part of a single church. The biggest problem is an inadequate supply of food. But most of the people who come for food are only temporarily in need: the line one morning included a man who had just moved to town and started a job but would not receive his first paycheck for another week, a woman caught short because her rent had to be paid that day, and another woman whose husband was late on his child-support payments.

For Glen Wilson, helping at the Food Place has its ups and downs. It makes him feel good about himself to be involved and to be helpful to those in need. But there are also frustrations. After the first few times, the work started to get boring. He hates to ask people to volunteer and hates it even worse when they fail to show up. His wife worries that he'll injure himself lifting cartons of food. He's not at all sure this is the best way to take care of community needs. Most of the recipients seem genuinely needy, but there are others who just come in as often as they can. Glen wishes he didn't have to deal with these people. Though he is committed to helping feed the hungry, Glen's connection to the Food Place is just for now as he questions how long the organization will be able to survive.

It is evident that the involvement of Grace Bishop and Glen Wilson — flexible though it may be — is directed toward the wider needs of people in the community, rather than being mainly for their own benefit. A more controversial form of civic involvement is the so-called self-help group, such as Alcoholics Anonymous and similar groups that follow AA's "twelve steps" to recovery. Currently, somewhere between 10 and 15 million Americans take part in self-help groups, at least 7 million of these in "anonymous" recovery groups.[14] Unlike the Rotary or Kiwanis chapters, which specifically seek to place "service above self," recovery groups focus attention almost entirely on the self, encouraging members to work through their addictions or to examine the effects of dysfunctional backgrounds on their personalities. These organizations do not engage in projects, such as building a park or taking wheelchairs to the elderly, but encourage people to sit at meetings and talk about themselves with others similarly troubled. Members are discouraged from discussing what is going on in the community or their views on politics, which may distract them from their primary purpose. Because the participants seek anonymity, they are unlikely to enlist each other in community projects. Some observers do not consider these gatherings "groups" at all, and suggest that their popularity is compelling evidence that Americans are becoming obsessively self-interested and turning away from the larger community.[15]

Few would deny that Alcoholics Anonymous and similar groups perform a positive function for society insofar as they do help some people recover from addictions that might otherwise make them unable to hold a

job or to drive safely. Approximately 14 million Americans—11 percent of all men and 4 percent of all women—are estimated to be afflicted with problems of alcohol abuse and substance dependence, and many of those who participate regularly in AA have been able to keep their addictions in check.[16] The concern that has been expressed is more aptly directed to AA's various spin-off groups, such as Al-Anon, Adult Children of Alcoholics (ACOA), and Co-Dependents Anonymous (CODA). Participants in these groups may show no evidence of debilitating chemical addictions, and yet many attend faithfully for an hour or more a week over a period of years. Even some observers who might grant that these groups help participants to overcome anxiety or other personal maladjustments wonder if there is something in American culture that leads people to be so deeply concerned about their family problems and so little concerned about the health of their communities.

The same conditions that have made it harder for Americans to be involved in anything but loosely connected activities are among the factors that have produced twelve-step groups as a popular way of dealing with personal problems. People attend these groups because they have lost other attachments to communities, such as those through family or church, that give them a satisfactory definition of themselves. Before they can be effective citizens, they have to relearn how to be effective persons. To be sure, the very groups they join may perpetuate their obsession with themselves, rather than directing their energies toward serving others. Many of the participants are nevertheless the casualties of a society that tears communities and families apart, and the groups to which they turn are places to regain some of the interpersonal support that they need to function effectively.

Raymond Harper, a longtime member of an ACOA group who is not chemically addicted, provides a useful illustration of how society contributes to the problems that have led to the popularity of such groups. Raymond is a man in his late forties who grew up in a Catholic family in a small town in Ohio, went away to college at a large state university, and then attended another large university where he earned his Ph.D. in theater. During the next decade he held four different academic jobs in four different parts of the country. Each time, he says, "I've never had a choice; I've never been offered more than one job at a time; it was just 'here's a job' and so we'd move."

It was during the third of these jobs, he remembers, that "everything I

had become in the first thirty years of my life fell apart and just didn't work anymore." Intensely anxious and unhappy, Raymond began seeing a therapist and kept an extensive journal about his feelings, but nothing he heard or read was helpful. One day his eye fell on an article in a magazine that listed the symptoms associated with having grown up in an alcoholic family. Raymond recognized the symptoms as his own and immediately started attending ACOA meetings. He acknowledges that there was no tangible evidence, other than the list of symptoms, that either of his parents had been an alcoholic, and yet he would object to any suggestion that he had simply found a convenient way of making sense of the anxieties that many people experience as they go through life. He has learned in ACOA that parents can hide their alcoholism so completely that one cannot expect to find proof of its existence.

When Raymond was a junior in high school he tried out for a part in the school play and got the part. Being in the play gave him something to be proud of; more important, it gave him the sense of community he had been missing: "I discovered that being in the cast of a play was like having an extended family, and that's what I've been doing ever since. Basically since my junior year in high school I've been in one show after another." From the first he felt "a sense of belonging, a sense of being important to other people that I probably hadn't had anywhere else."

As it has for many people, a profession became Raymond's primary source of identity and his only source of community. To pursue his interest in acting, he moved five hours away from his hometown to attend college, and to gain the credentials he needed, he left the state to go to graduate school, and then moved again and again to find jobs in his profession. Although he married, he maintained only perfunctory contact with any of his own relatives, including his parents, lost all contact with his hometown, quit going to church, and moved in and out of different theater companies and academic departments so that he had few lasting friendships even with people in his profession. The one source of continuity was his career: "Since my junior year in high school, there was always the next show. It was all seamless from high school to college, to graduate school, to teaching."

Yet it was not that Raymond was literally alone, nor that he had become a loner. To keep his identity together, he in fact stayed in groups as much as possible. He describes his undergraduate and graduate experiences as "the golden years" because he was always with a circle of friends, and he

continued to interact intensively with people he knew after he started teaching. When he started to have anxiety attacks, he went to the counseling center and asked if there was a therapy *group* he could attend. "I was entirely a people person," he says. Only in the last few years has he been able to stand being alone, and he thinks this is a sign that he is finally coming to terms with who he is, rather than having to depend so much on friends.

The third job Raymond took was "the big move," because it was at a more prestigious university and in a part of the country he enjoyed. When he did not receive tenure, the bottom fell out of his career, and the self he had become "didn't work anymore." Attending ACOA meetings ever since has been Raymond's way of reconstructing an identity that works. He admits he has been dependent on the group, just as he was on his friends in the theater, but the important difference is that ACOA is *not* theater and therefore not part of his career.

As he talks about his struggle to reconstruct his identity, Raymond unwittingly exudes the kind of narcissism that makes observers critical of twelve-step groups. But it is also evident that he has benefited from the group. He is able to make it through the day now without being completely distracted by anxiety, and he has been able to settle into a new job and to pursue it with a greater sense of balance in his life, rather than being preoccupied with success in his career. He appears to have gained an understanding of personal integrity, a quality he always admired in others but felt lacking in his own fragmented personality, and he has experienced enough anguish in his personal life that he shows signs of being able to express compassion toward others.

We can only speculate how things might have been different for Raymond had he been able to fit comfortably into the extended family that his parents enjoyed in Ohio, or had he been able to stay in one community rather than moving repeatedly to find jobs, or had he been able to spend shorter days pursuing his career and thus had time to spend evenings at church or in civic organizations. Had he derived some of his identity from civic activities or family or his neighborhood, he might not have experienced such a catastrophic personal crisis when he was denied tenure. The fluidity of American communities and the uncertain demands of the labor force impose conditions on individuals like Raymond that make it hard for them to imagine living in any other way.

Under such circumstances, self-help groups may provide some people with an opportunity to refashion their identity so that they can function more effectively as spouses and parents and citizens. Even though such groups do not change the circumstances in which people live, they convey the message that people are not "just victims," as Raymond says, but can take greater responsibility for their lives. Raymond is still a long way from feeling at home in his community. In fact, he says the thing he likes best about his neighborhood is that it is close to the on ramp of the freeway. He and his wife escape early each morning, hoping to beat the rush-hour traffic as they commute in different directions to their jobs. When asked if he is involved in any civic activities, he admits he does virtually nothing, although he did volunteer this year to staff the phones for a campaign to raise funds for the public radio station he listens to on his way to work. But he and his wife have been having intense discussions about their need for "connectiveness" and to be part of a geographic community. "There was a time when I couldn't even think about such things," he admits. "I'm beginning to get more interested in what I can do for the community now, and I think it's likely I will be involved in something before very long."

Only time will tell, but across the nation many people who have participated in twelve-step groups have become involved in helping other people or working on civic projects. As Raymond does, they go out for coffee or ice cream together after their meetings, and in this informal context talk about social issues and politics. They do not remain in twelve-step groups for a lifetime, but move on, just as people in other kinds of groups do. Some of them follow the twelve steps to the point that they can look more honestly at their dependence on their careers or at the extent to which their identity is wrapped up in having people in the community who think they are special.

All six of the people I have described are most concerned about whether or not what they are doing really matters. The problems in their communities seem to be getting worse, the number of volunteers is either shrinking or becoming harder to maintain, and they are clearly becoming disillusioned. They don't come right out and say so, but their own commitment to their communities is beginning to wear thin. Jack Schmidt feels he's served long enough; there isn't much higher for him to climb in Rotary. Elizabeth Meade isn't sure the icy roads are worth driving over just to stay active in the League of Women Voters. Frank Purelli wonders if he shouldn't be spending more time at home with his children than at the firehouse with the guys. Grace Bishop is thinking about quitting her job at the human services bureau, or at least cutting to half time. Glen Wilson figures he will have done his bit for the Food Place in another year or so. Raymond Harper fears that his ACOA group is falling apart.

We may ask whether these people, even through their civic involvement, illustrate just how serious the malaise in America has become. Not that they are typical. But it is interesting that one is a man near the end of his life and another is one of the declining number of women who have time to volunteer because they are not in the labor force. The fact that Grace Bishop is a paid professional raises the question of whether volunteering itself may be anachronistic. Frank Purelli's breed of risk-seeking firefighters may be harder to sustain in upscale communities like the one his is becoming. And if religious organizations are the best hope for civic involvement, as some enthusiasts argue, then Glen Wilson's struggles to find volunteers for the Food Place should be a sobering lesson.

These people are probably not very different from many other Americans. They are aware of the troubles facing their communities, families, and nation. They don't quite know what to do about these troubles. There have been long periods in all their lives when they did nothing much at all, other than raise their children and keep peace with their neighbors. At other times they have been drawn into community activities by friends or because the activities were part of their jobs.

But these people are also products of the society in which they live. Their definitions of meaningful civic involvement reflect understandings they have gained from reading the newspaper, watching television, growing up in certain kinds of families, and interacting with friends. Jack Schmidt was predisposed to see joining Rotary as a good way to serve his community. Raymond Harper would never have considered joining Rotary. His parents or grandparents would never have considered joining something like his ACOA group. Understandings of service have been changing. They are still in flux, so much so that the very idea of civic involvement is being transformed.

Despite their own involvement, none of these people think they are saving the world. They are connecting with fellow citizens because they have time on their hands, because they feel an obligation to a friend who invited them to join a civic organization, because they like to network with influential people, because they see civic activities as stepping-stones to a better career, and because their own children benefit from their activities. For these reasons, they are reaching out in small ways to other people, and they are connecting to their communities through a bewildering array of organizations. Some of the older, established organizations in which they are involved are declining; others appear to be thriving on innovation.

One point on which these people agree is that civic participation is having to adapt to changing conditions. Time pressures are not going away; stronger appeals will not be effective by themselves. Durable memberships are giving way to looser connections. Ad hoc arrangements focusing on specific projects are becoming more common. Civic activity is becoming more diverse than an earlier generation of Americans might have imagined.

2

The Changing Meanings
of Involvement

PEOPLE LIKE JACK SCHMIDT, ELIZABETH MEADE, AND FRANK PURELLI who participate in well-established civic organizations are following models in the culture that tell them how to be useful in their communities. People like Grace Bishop, Glen Wilson, and Raymond Harper are also following models from the society that influence how people think about civic involvement. But the latter's understandings are different from, and less traditional than, the former's. What it means to be involved in one's community has been changing dramatically during the past half-century.

In the 1950s a common way for men to relate to their communities was as an organization man. Although the organization man is an image that pertains especially to the bureaucratic style of middle-class work in that period, it is also an apt description of a prominent understanding of civic involvement. The organization man performed his civic responsibilities by joining a lodge, such as the Masons or Odd Fellows, or by belonging to a service club, such as Rotary or Kiwanis.[1] In the 1950s the large number of World War I and World War II veterans also belonged to the American Legion or VFW. Others belonged to Jaycees or Optimists clubs. The common thread in all this civic participation was that it assumed an implicit link between service and belonging. Indeed, decency itself was thought to be at stake; as Sinclair Lewis had observed a generation earlier, "It was required that [a decent man] should belong to one, preferably two or three, of the innumerable 'lodges' and prosperity-boosting lunch-clubs; to the Rotarians, the Kiwanis, or the Boosters; to the Oddfellows, Moose, Masons, Red Men, Woodmen, Owls, Eagles, Maccabees, Knights of

Pythias, Knights of Columbus, and other secret orders characterized by a high degree of heartiness, sound morals, and reverence for the Constitution."[2]

The organization man of the 1950s was a product of his times. He was successful enough to have leisure time, thus being able to distinguish himself through his participation in civic organizations from the working class, whose discretionary time was more limited. The joiners were more likely to be salesmen, owners of small businesses, middle managers, and professionals; less likely to be farmers, day laborers, carpenters, or construction workers. Belonging to an organization strengthened their very identity, and they took pride in organizations that were not only well run but linked to national or international structures that bestowed on them a kind of prestige which transcended the local community.[3]

Being an organization man was especially important during elections. Candidates (nearly always men) advertised the fact that they were lifelong residents of the community and members of the Elks Lodge, the American Legion, and a local church. Members also reveled in big projects, such as raising money to build hospitals or to launch national programs to help children, even though most of what their local chapters accomplished was quite meager, such as hosting an annual picnic or sponsoring a raffle. The middle class was increasingly recognizing the need for higher education or at least some kind of professional-technical expertise, and civic activities that were well orchestrated appealed to this orientation. In fact, belonging to a service organization was a way of demonstrating that one was a legitimate member of the aspiring white-collar class. As one Rotarian in the 1950s explained, "Service placed the business man on the level with the professional man, the scientist, or the artist—men whose avowed object was service—the business man was no longer a profit-maker or even a bread-winner, he was a public servant."[4]

But many of the activities in which service organizations engaged could be performed by men who learned the rudiments of organizing a picnic or constructing a horseshoe pit in the local park, rather than requiring the expertise of full-time specialists. In contrast to the image of high-powered managers that was to become prominent over the next quarter-century, the organization man was often a virtual amateur who could function well with good intentions, common sense, and a little help from his friends. Especially in civic organizations, being an organization man was as much play as it was work. Lions and Kiwanians shouldered such tasks as putting on pancake feeds, sponsoring fishing contests for local children, and hosting minstrel shows and tap dancing performances.[5]

The fact that organization men were indeed men, and that their civic participation took place in male-only organizations, is partly attributable to the continuing exclusion of women from the labor market. The bond that formed at lodge meetings and Rotary lunches was often based on men's roles in business. But organization men also shared a gendered understanding of how to utilize their leisure time. Some were characterized in contemporary literature as henpecked husbands escaping from miserable evenings at home with their wives. Others were happily married but understood manly responsibilities more in terms of influencing the wider community than of simply being a devoted husband. Getting together with other men was an important perquisite of civic involvement. The organization man enjoyed the camaraderie of good jokes, good business tips, good fishing stories, and good cigars.[6]

Above all, organization men were *members*, who participated in their service clubs and lodges over long enough periods of time that they became known to their fellows. They were thus constrained to live by an implicit code of respectability.[7] Conformity could tolerate minor deviations, but an organization man was expected to behave honestly, to be faithful in marriage and a good provider for his children, and to have a quiet commitment to his faith and a somewhat more boisterous (if not openly jovial), good-natured interest in politics. He thrived on competition, encouraging it in his sons and using it in his civic activities, just as he did in business, but he was expected to refrain from cutting the throats of his fellows. He was supposed to be strong, more in his stoic approach to emotions than in muscular prowess, and with strength came an independent resolve to look out for his own.

It was taken for granted that service organizations would promote the good of the wider community whenever they could. But the operative meaning of service for the organization man was *loyalty*. Members understood, just as they did at work, that they should "Be loyal to the company and the company will be loyal to you." Loyalty meant paying their dues, showing up at meetings, taking on whatever committee assignments they were given, and treating fellow members with special respect. It was thus less a matter of impulse, let alone deep inner commitment to a cause, than an implicit sense of obligation to fellow members that provided the basis for civic involvement.[8]

The natural complement to the organization man was the club woman, a form of civic involvement that reached its apex in the 1950s and early 1960s. Although there had been literary circles, reading clubs, and ladies' church guilds in the eighteenth and early nineteenth centuries, what were known as "woman's clubs" began to appear after the Civil War, one of the first being the Sorosis Club, which formed in New York City in 1868 and was instrumental in the formation of the General Federation of Woman's Clubs in 1889. From the sixty-three delegates who met in 1890, the movement grew to include more than a million members by 1912, and by the 1920s clubs were well established throughout the country.[9]

From the beginning, members were often compelled to legitimate the time they spent away from hearth and home; for example, in a 1905 article in the *Ladies' Home Journal*, Grover Cleveland advised women not to join clubs at all, except for ones dedicated to "charity, religious enterprise, or intellectual improvement."[10] Many leaders also sought to distance themselves from the zealots, reformers, activist suffragettes, and prohibitionists who gave up everything for their cause. In contrast to these, club women were expected to lead ordinary lives as mothers, wives, and homemakers. Service to the wider community came to be emphasized in response to the need for public definition. As the club woman Mary Wood explained in 1912, "The one motive, behind and beneath the multiple and multifarious activities of the woman's club, is set forth in the one word, *Service*."[11]

The service ethic was distinctly identified as a middle-class virtue, providing a language that was increasingly used in business and that largely replaced the earlier concept of benevolence. It took account of the fact that growing numbers of women did not have to participate in the labor force and had more free time as a result of labor-saving devices, but it shunned the extravagant self-interest of the wealthy, arguing that women of moderate means had a responsibility to play a more active role in their communities. The service ethic also reflected the gendered understandings of the period, defining a role for women that was complementary to that of men and legitimating this role in terms of a new idea of the humanitarian contribution of women. After the Civil War, arguments about the need for women to be of service to their country as men had done on the battlefield began to appear, and these arguments gained in importance after each world war in the twentieth century. Being of service meant caring for the sick and playing ameliorative roles in times of war or natural disaster; it meant doing the jobs in local neighborhoods that men did not have time for; it also included a kind of continuing education that would make women better companions for their husbands—"culture surrogates," as one writer put it—and better sources of inspiration for their children.[12]

During the first half of the twentieth century, as women's clubs proliferated, the ideal of service came to mean service to one another within the club itself. Loyalty was as important as kindness. The organization of the club was thus an important mark of understanding service. Participation in an organized activity was a way to demonstrate that women could work together in a spirit of goodwill for the benefit of themselves and the community. Club women were thus practical. It was the "starry-eyed idealist" they especially disliked.

In the 1950s a club woman might still belong to the Women's Christian Temperance Union (WCTU), whose struggles against the "liquor industry" had already been lost in most states and whose members were now bringing home literature to their children in an effort to combat comic books. She might also belong to the Legion auxiliary, where she could help put on a Mother's Day tea, or to an organization like War Mothers that made neckties and ashtrays to distribute to hospitalized veterans. Some women were joining new clubs that deliberately aimed to complement the service organizations to which their husbands belonged. Jaycee-Ettes and Lioness clubs became popular. Women's sororities and female versions of masonic lodges, such as Deborah and Rebekah lodges, remained popular. A typical evening at one of these organizations might include piano solos followed by tap dance numbers and a reading on the benefits of lodge membership. Other women belonged to such organizations as the Wide Awake Housewives Club and the Rangerettes. In all, there were estimated to be at least 100,000 women's clubs in the 1950s, and including small local clubs the number may have ranged much higher.[13]

At the grassroots level, leaders of women's clubs worked hard to promote interest in their organizations. Getting members, keeping them, and making sure they participated actively in meetings were primary considerations. Competitions within and between clubs became a popular way to heighten involvement. Women competed to see which club could produce the best scrapbook, the best holiday decoration, the best musical performance, or the best home health or safety tip. For the athletically inclined, bowling and tennis leagues nurtured the same competitive spirit. The clubs also encouraged participation by providing numerous committees on which to serve and minor offices to hold. Being appointed or elected to a committee or office was the surest way to get one's name in the local newspaper. Election as a delegate to a regional conference or to a national office became a badge of higher honor. For the majority of club women in the 1950s who were mothers, the clubs served too as a way of linking family and community. Mother-daughter banquets preserved the gendered division of labor in the home, and clubs provided opportunities for mothers to showcase the singing and dancing talents of their offspring.

Women's clubs reflected many of the same views that characterized the organization man. They may have devoted much of their time to informal socializing, but they were highly organized. Most had a board of elected officers, held business meetings, and had bylaws. Many had committees charged with carrying out specific functions (sometimes there were more than a dozen committees in a local club), and many printed formal programs announcing their activities for the year. The members often prided themselves on how well organized they were. One of the women William Whyte interviewed in the 1950s remarked, "I was such a stupid little thing. I didn't think about anything except shopping and the babies and things like that. Now that I'm in the League of Women Voters and the school board I feel so much more worth while. When Joe comes home at night I have so many interesting things to talk to him about."[14] Another woman looking back at that era said, "It challenged my abilities, my intelligence, my organizational skills and my managerial skills. That was wonderful. It was just a nice feeling to know that you're doing something that's valid."

Like the men's organizations, women's clubs reinforced an ideal of civic involvement that emphasized community "progress" long after the Progressive era was over. In the 1950s women's clubs were fascinated by the labor-saving devices that were giving their members more time to participate and by the need for greater technical skill. Home improvement was a popular topic, as were scientific methods of cooking and gardening. Being a responsible citizen meant being informed about community issues. Outside speakers who talked about sanitation or Communism shared time with local members who showed slides of vacation trips or talked about home decoration. The clubs sought to "conserve and preserve" values, as their slogans sometimes said, by cultivating the gentler arts, but they also sought to broaden their members' horizons, making them more interesting conversationalists for their husbands and giving them opportunities to work on projects such as libraries, museums, and art displays.

The civic ideal that was modeled by the club woman of the 1950s was thus a diffuse role that included practical knowledge, sociability, and service. Contributing to the common good was defined more broadly than it had been by the literary circles and the reformers earlier in the century; it nevertheless was a responsibility that had been reinforced by religious teachings and by an understanding of the obligations of women privileged enough to have husbands with good jobs.[15] Fulfilling these responsibilities required working on specific tasks, such as planting trees, visiting shut-ins, or providing orange juice for school children. Yet many of these activities were regarded as almost incidental compared with the broader virtues of meeting with other women, encouraging them, and engaging in self-improvement. Club women were expected to respect one another's freedom and diversity of interests, religious backgrounds, and stations in life. Service included personal improvement that resulted merely from associating with one another. In a larger evolutionary scheme of things, it was sufficient for women to learn from one another, to gain experience in public speaking, to acquire greater personal confidence, and to come to understand how organizations worked.

The third model of civic involvement in the 1950s was the good neighbor. Being a good neighbor extended the idea of service to include everyone, not just the elite whose names appeared in the newspaper because of the offices they held in clubs and organizations. Good neighbors did not have to be friends or confidants; they were valued for their familiarity, their predictability, perhaps even more than their dependability. They were affable members of the community who respected boundaries, kept their homes in respectable condition, and did not pry into the intimate details of neighbors' lives. But they also abided by well-established norms of civil behavior that included routine acts of kindness and hospitality.[16] People who remember the 1950s recall neighbors who brought casseroles when someone was sick or who shared baked goods at Christmas. Some speak fondly about neighbors who invited children in for cookies or were there when emergency help was needed; one recalls that his wife ran to the neighbors for help when he fell off a ladder and gashed his head. Women are especially likely to remember that good neighbors came to visit when someone was sick or paid a call at the hospital or mortuary. Neighbors seldom went out of their way to help in times of crisis, but some expression of concern was expected because, as one woman recalls, "we always knew if a neighbor had a problem."

In retrospect, many people remember how homogeneous their neighborhoods were. A good neighbor was quite likely to be someone like oneself. Good neighbors were Catholics who went to the same church, or they were Irish, or Jewish. Most often they were white if one was white, black if one was black. They were mostly of the same social class, working in the same kinds of occupations and rearing their children similarly. Plumbers and carpenters were neighbors. Auto workers were neighbors. Because of these similarities, good neighbors frequently shared interests as well. People talk about good neighbors they saw at church or with whom they shopped or played bridge. A good neighbor was also someone who shared. Mothers really did run next door to borrow a cup of sugar, and families shared pruning shears and lawn mowers. When television first came to a neighborhood people who had a set were more or less expected to invite those who did not to spend an evening viewing popular shows.

In contrast, bad neighbors were the ones with whom there had been a falling out, perhaps over a piece of property or a business deal. Just as often, bad neighbors were the misfits and outcasts who did not play by the rules, or they were people who "kept to themselves." They might be people who fell into recognizable categories of deviance, like the widowed uncle who went crazy and wandered the streets naked, or the alcoholic father who smashed into the neighbor's fence and yelled at the police, or they might be simply neighbors who did not reciprocate when greeted casually on the street. A bad neighbor could also be someone who was "too neighborly," as one woman in the 1950s put it—someone who "knew more about your private life than you did yourself."[17]

A good neighbor was implicitly a point of reference, but one that was attainable. People poke fun at themselves for always comparing themselves with "the Joneses." In retrospect, some view these comparisons as an invidious aspect of living among neighbors. But neighbors were also often a source of positive comparisons. Keeping up with the Joneses meant that the lawn got mowed regularly and that one's children did not sneak away too often to smoke cigarettes. The sort of neighbor who was not appreciated lived too high above the standard of others or flaunted these differences. Good neighbors were the kind of people one could live among and not know if one's own family was rich or poor. "Everybody seemed to have about the same," one older person recalls.

Because they were simply there, good neighbors were not necessarily people with whom one interacted often or intimately, but as familiar features of the local geography they fostered a sense that community consisted of both people and place. Enough was known about them that they did not pose a threat to the security of the neighborhood. Their coming and going, how they sat on the porch, and what time they turned on their lights in the evening were part of the rhythm of daily life. Many years later, some people talked about missing a neighbor who had died or moved away, even though they had not been friends.[18]

Although being a good neighbor was a way to contribute to the community without joining an organization or club, belonging to something was an important aspect of being a good neighbor. It was so for two reasons: neighbors who belonged to something were considered more trustworthy than those who did not ("you knew they fit in somewhere, they weren't loners"); and their belonging gave them a reason not to be available at times ("they have their lodge" or "they're off with their friends"). The activities in which they participated could be informal as well as formal. Neighbors who spent some time drinking coffee at the café or helping at the firehouse became sources of local information. They were also living their own lives, so to speak, rather than expecting too much from their immediate neighbors.

During the 1960s much of what had characterized the service ethic of the 1950s remained intact, despite the unrest sparked by the civil rights movement and the Vietnam war. Those who headed the traditional civic organizations were generally older, established residents of their communities, while much of the social upheaval occurred in southern cities and on college campuses. Many of the women's clubs did not become racially integrated until well into the 1970s, and veterans' organizations, Masons, and Chambers of Commerce were openly critical of student protests. By the mid 1970s it was nevertheless evident that the organization man, the club woman, and the good neighbor were all being significantly redefined. There was growing awareness of the social problems faced by people different from oneself, and a budding understanding of the complexity of these problems. What had euphemistically been termed "case poverty" or "island poverty" was now transformed into "the other America," in Michael Harrington's memorable phrase.[19]

As more women sought gainful employment, the club woman was criticized by feminists and by women who worked outside the home as being unprofessional and perhaps exploited as well.[20] The organization man was criticized for spending too much time away from home engaged in arcane masculine rituals. In response, organization men and club women used their skills to start nonprofit organizations, expand municipal government, and create service agencies: a women's club might sponsor a study group to consider responding to a statewide initiative to found local community colleges; a men's service organization might hold a benefit to expand the local hospital. A clearer distinction developed between service and leisure. Service activities came to be more focused on serious problems, such as crime and urban redevelopment, while leisure was commercialized for mass consumption, so that people attended movies and professional sporting events rather than playing cards or going bowling with members of their civic clubs. Temporarily the activist role that had once been evident among suffragettes and union leaders reappeared and civic involvement shifted from service associations to political participation.

People who grew up during the 1960s and 1970s were less likely than those who remembered the 1950s to speak fondly of their neighbors or neighborhoods. The exodus from inner cities to suburbs and beyond may explain this. They spoke of particular friends or schoolmates, but seldom talked of the neighborhood having any particular meaning other than as a place to live. One man put it well: "I never had a neighborhood. I grew up in a suburb!" For many, neighbors were less important than colleagues who shared their commitment to social change. Increasingly, the public image of involvement was defined by such organizations as Students for a Democratic Society, the Women's Equity Action League, Friends of the Earth, and the Citizen's Action Program. Looking back on these changes, one feminist writer has asked, "What politically minded female . . . would join the bland and matronly League of Women Voters, when she could volunteer with Planned Parenthood or NOW or Concerned Women of America, and shape the debate instead of merely keeping it polite?"[21]

One of the more profound changes in the meaning of civic involvement resulted from the more inclusive sense of community that was being promoted by the civil rights movement. Some organizations established more inclusive membership standards, which resulted in growth but an alteration of purpose as well. Newer organizations were founded to promote egalitarianism or to represent those who had been excluded. The idea of a good neighbor necessarily changed, sometimes being broadened, as neighborhoods were criticized for being exclusive. The Vietnam war and the civil rights movement interrupted families' proud traditions of serving their communities by joining veterans' organizations, belonging to service clubs, and looking in on their neighbors. Young people found themselves unable to participate in these conventional ways. Other problems were more urgent and new avenues of involvement were suddenly available. People who cared about their communities took part in public demonstrations or worked in movements that aimed to transform political realities.

The meaning of civic involvement was also reshaped in communities that showed little sign of being influenced by the activism and unrest of the 1960s. Other forces were at work, such as professionalization and specialization. There was a growing sense that special expertise was required to accomplish the improvements that were desired or to address the problems that were being identified. Higher education, science, and technology were being emphasized, and more people were entering the professions. Greater concern was being voiced about population, the environment, aging, and race. Through federal, state, and local expenditures, communities were building senior citizens' centers, junior colleges, hospitals, and nursing homes. As national community service and volunteer agencies expanded, local organizations took on the role of supporting these specialized efforts rather than attempting to initiate amateur efforts of their own. The typical speaker at a women's club or Rotary function was no longer a private citizen showing slides of his or her trip to an exotic spot, but a representative of the March of Dimes or a Peace Corps volunteer.

In these years the idea of service expanded gradually to embrace a wider variety of activities. People with careers in the professions regarded these careers as legitimate ways in which to serve their communities without joining particular organizations. Young people talked of choosing jobs that would make a worthwhile contribution to the world rather than simply putting bread on the table. Some convinced themselves that high-paying positions would permit them free time in later years to make meaningful contributions to human needs. The conviction that established institutions such as universities and government agencies produced injustice or stifled human potential gave a rationale for pursuing nonconformist activities that may have contributed little to the community other than the opportunity for individuals to express themselves, such as street theater and mail-in petitions. The growing emphasis on personal fulfillment, new insights, and heightened levels of consciousness permitted young people to believe they were making a contribution to humanity by pursuing these self-realizing aims.

Some of the broadening of the definition of service was clearly inspired by the need to dress self-interest in socially acceptable garb, but the changes also reflected a new awareness of the scope and complexity of social problems. Poverty, racism, and environmental dangers were more pervasive than had been realized a decade earlier, and their sources were more complex. If it was possible to address these problems in straightforward ways, it was also conceivable that they were rooted in structures and attitudes that demanded a wide range of solutions, including political activism, the efforts of professionals, and personal efforts to rethink perceptions and to live differently.

As the idea of service became more encompassing it was nevertheless conditioned by a growing awareness of the need to address community problems in effective ways. Professional training was required to understand such problems as transportation and urban planning, sanitation, mental illness, therapy, social work, and race relations. In comparison, the efforts of established community organizations came to be regarded as amateurish and ineffective. Joining such organizations for the sake of belonging made less sense if they were deemed second-rate ways of serving the community. Some potential members opted for longer hours at work or more time with their families, where they felt they could truly make a difference. The same emphasis on effectiveness encouraged the thought that it was better to wait until something better came along than to participate in something that might be a waste of time.

The overall character of these changes can be illustrated by the history of the Larimer Woman's Club in Larimer, Colorado, an organization founded in 1913 that became affiliated with the national Federation of Woman's Clubs a year later and was still a prominent community institution in the 1970s.[22] From its inception, it was integrally connected to other local organizations; its founder was the wife of the founder of the Elks Lodge, it was commonly referred to as an "order," it grew out of an auxiliary unit of the City Improvement Association, and it was initially named the Ladies Improvement and Development Society. In 1916 it was responsible for opening the public library, which acquired its own building in 1922, and its main activities during the next two decades included raising money for the library, organizing an annual spring banquet at the country club, and hosting biweekly teas at members' homes followed by informational lectures, piano recitals, and book discussions.

During the 1950s the club's spring festival of musical selections grew to require meeting in the high school auditorium, it sponsored a cancer drive in addition to supporting the library, and its biweekly meetings focused on juvenile delinquency, ridding newsstands of objectionable comics, radio-free Europe, and anti-Communist activities. Its competitors in the 1950s were not dissimilar from the other clubs and interest groups with which it had competed in the 1920s and 1930s. They included several ladies' missionary societies, a home demonstration club, an auxiliary of the Lions Club, the Legion auxiliary, and several dessert bridge clubs. New competitors included a women's rifle club and a women's bowling league comprising ten teams. Men's organizations reflected parallel interests, including the Chamber of Commerce, the VFW and American Legion, a Lions Club, several masonic lodges, and two bowling leagues (comprising twelve teams).

By the early 1970s the Larimer Woman's Club was still meeting as it always had on alternate Wednesday afternoons. As a result of an aggressive membership drive in the late 1960s its numbers had climbed to more than 160. Although it had adopted a formal bureaucratic structure of elected officers and committees from the start, its committees had now become "departments," it had added several new positions, its annual reports made more of a point of listing the names of state and national officers, the library had been placed under a separate board, and it was devoting itself to more specific "projects." These included community improvement, sponsoring a refugee family, working with scouting organizations, a beautification project, and sponsoring Youth Leadership seminars.

The club's established place in the community continued to give it prominence, and yet it faced a variety of new competitors that collectively gave a different face to the idea of service. The PTA, Chamber of Commerce, home extension club, Mothers Club, bridge league, American Legion, VFW, Kiwanis, and Red Cross were still present, but there was now an active local chapter of the American Association of Retired Persons

(AARP), which hosted speakers and held teas much as the Woman's Club did but for a more inclusive membership, and a Senior Citizens' Center had been constructed with federal Title V funds. The library had started its own "lifelong learning series" of speakers and informational programs. There was a Business and Professional Women's Club and a Christian Women's Club. There was also a community forum series, a local chapter of the National Association of Federal Employees, and a program of dance and exercise classes offered by the Metropolitan Recreation District (a department of the municipal government). Several new service organizations had emerged, including a Newcomer's Club, Antiquarians, Eta Omega, and Zeta Beta Tau. The idea of volunteering was becoming formalized through such organizations as the Retired Senior Volunteer Program (RSVP) and Volunteers in Many Services (VIMS). The first Alcoholics Anonymous group had been organized and had quickly spun off an Al-Anon group. And there were more specialized civic activities as well, such as a task force on child abuse, an education association (representing the community's interests to the school board), and an ad hoc committee of concerned citizens to build a residence for handicapped children.

Only part of the reason for these changes was that the community's population had grown. Other reasons were that more residents were college educated and worked in the professions, that more of the women were in the labor force, and that both governmental agencies and non-profits were more active in the community. Unlike the Woman's Club, many of the newer service organizations were open to anyone interested in the problems they were addressing, and they devoted less time to socializing. The idea of service was becoming more complex and specialized, and it implied working in a more highly institutionalized environment. The Woman's Club would survive, but its role in the community would diminish in the coming years.

In the wider society, the changes in ideas of service began to crystallize during the 1980s. But doubts also were expressed about many of the programs that had brought these ideas into being. Activism faded, especially on the left, and political careers ceased to be as clear a way of engaging in service. Other professions, especially in the health industry, underwent a transformation that raised questions about the meaning of service to the community. Whereas the organization man, the club woman, and the good neighbor had been eclipsed by the activist and the politician, these now gave way to an emerging cluster of roles, including the nonprofit professional, the volunteer, and the close friend or soul mate.

The more recent history of the Larimer Woman's Club again illustrates the larger context in which these changes were taking place. By the early 1990s its membership was the same as it had been in 1969, despite an approximate doubling of the community's population. Its membership was also aging: only 23 percent of its members had been in the organization ten years or longer in 1969, but by 1990 this figure had risen to 55 percent. Its annual activities still included a spring banquet, supporting the library, and hosting teas, and its meetings were still on alternate Wednesday afternoons.

In the wider community, most of the other organizations that had been established during the previous quarter-century were still in existence, but several new forms of involvement had become prominent. Whereas AA and Al-Anon had been the only support groups available in the 1970s, there were now an Alzheimer's Support Group, a Multiple Sclerosis Support Group, an Arthritis Support Group, a Respiratory Support Group, a Cancer Support Group, a Family and Friends Support Group, a Co-Dependents Anonymous group, and an Overeaters Anonymous group. Reflecting the continuing differentiation of service from leisure, there were also a number of specialized hobby groups, such as a Rock Club, a Nature Association, a Writers' Group, a Genealogy Group, a Needlework Group, a Women's Horse Club, and a Tai Chi group. Volunteering could be done in more venues and more spontaneously, as organizations advertised in the local newspaper for help on Saturday projects or offered training classes for prospective volunteers.[23] More nonprofits and municipal agencies represented the community, meaning that interested citizens could spend their time attending talks at the local rehabilitation center or hearings of the Public Works Board, serve on the hospital board or the Senior Center advisory committee, participate in the Cultural Arts Council, or do volunteer work at the visitors' center. Ad hoc activities, such as a task force to combat inhalant abuse, were also evident.

In broader terms, many people had become politely critical of the work of service organizations and clubs. They acknowledged that some good was being done, for example, by an organization that kept a box in the Post Office where people could donate used eyeglasses and by another club that delivered food baskets to needy families on Thanksgiving. But they regarded such activities as "very minor," to use one man's words, and somehow more in tune with an earlier time when problems were simpler. People also regarded these organizations as being cliquish, with long-term members who knew one another well, jealously protected their traditions, and spent more time socializing and holding meetings than contributing to the good of the community. For people in the 1990s, civic involvement was defined less in terms of membership than in terms of effectiveness and accomplishments. In a 1997 survey of the U.S. population, only 16 percent said they would "admire a lot" "a person who belongs to a club or service organization," whereas 72 percent said this about "a person who tries to help the poor," as did 66 percent about "a person who knows how to get things organized."[24]

The meaning of involvement has changed as people have come to see the problems facing their communities or the larger society as extremely serious. To the organization man, the club woman, and the good neighbor, the challenges of community life generally seemed tractable. Often they required making improvements, such as building a library or a park, rather than confronting serious ills. Or they pertained to specialized populations, such as the handicapped, and they could often be conquered by national efforts. In contrast, the problems on which many people in the 1990s focus seem to pervade the entire society or have defied the best efforts of several generations.

Such problems strike people as being too serious to be dealt with by amateurs. Nonprofit professionals especially believe that community problems must be addressed by people with special skills who have ample resources at their disposal and who are sufficiently committed to devote themselves to full-time efforts. When problems are "overwhelming" or "phenomenal" and "intractable," part of being a professional is knowing how to avoid burnout and having the training required to avoid "letting it get to you."

These perceptions are linked to the ways people think about the alleged breakdown of their communities. A majority of Americans think their communities are somehow breaking down. But when asked what they mean, only a few refer to people no longer being good neighbors or participating in community organizations.[25] They are not focusing on problems that could easily be addressed by the kinds of community involvement that characterized the 1950s. Instead they talk about the schools not being able to teach effectively or the police being unable to stop crime and drug use. Often it is other groups that people become most agitated about, such as groups that don't respect the flag or that have lax attitudes about abortion. In other cases people point to the problems facing the poor or the handicapped. The problems are generally larger than ones facing their own community. They are problems that have been defined by the mass media or by government leaders or social movements. Thus they are problems that can be addressed most effectively by professionals and volunteers, and by nonprofit agencies and public officials.

The nonprofit professional has emerged as both the embodiment of civic involvement and a significant source of how it is now defined. Nonprofit professionals include the human service workers, technicians, and staff people who serve their communities in paid positions provided by nonprofit agencies. Many of these agencies are the products of federal, state, and local governmental programs initiated in the 1960s and 1970s. Their number has grown dramatically, from 309,000 in 1967 to 1.4 million in 1992, and they currently employ approximately 8 percent of the labor force (or 18 million people).[26] Many of these agencies receive donations and public funds or charge fees that are then used to pay the salaries of professional service providers. Although funds are also contributed by private donors, a substantial share of operating expenses are covered by a combination of government programs.[27]

For nonprofit professionals, community involvement is not simply getting people to interact more with their neighbors or even to show up in greater numbers at the polling booth. Nonprofits exist to fill a need. Their definition of involvement is working to solve particular problems. As one professional says, "I've got to prove that the community has a problem, so I go out and do research. Then I stick it in people's faces and say, 'What are you going to do about it? Damn it!'" The problems are typically enduring but capable of being alleviated, by activities such as feeding the homeless or tutoring needy children.

Nonprofit professionals are organization men (or women) in their own way. They represent continuity with some of the ideals of the 1950s, including the view that working together with others in an organization is the most effective way of being involved in one's community. The organization men of the 1950s probably felt ambivalence about this role, but it appears that nonprofit professionals of the 1990s are particularly susceptible to such feelings. They emphasize personal involvement with their clients and resent the time they have to spend on administration. They are thus vulnerable to the arguments of critics who suggest that nonprofit work is not community involvement at all. Their ambivalence may be heightened when they perceive problems in their communities getting worse despite their best efforts.

Whereas the success of a service club or organization depends on maintaining the loyalty of its members, that of a nonprofit organization depends more on its ability to provide a service that clients will pay for or the cost of which will be covered by a third party. Membership loyalty is encouraged by a hierarchical system of rewards for long-term and particularly active members. It depends on providing services to the community that can be performed with relatively little demand on the time or training of members, thus enlarging the pool of potential members and avoiding unintended internal distinctions among them. The services must have a ceremonial dimension, nevertheless, that dramatizes the distinction between members and nonmembers, and this distinction is often reinforced by internal rituals, such as festivals, parties, and commemorative events.

In contrast, nonprofit professionals must draw income sufficient to maintain their salaries. They are more likely to supply specialized services to targeted populations of clients. Nonprofit organizations may experiment with different services until they find one that is commercially viable, or they may diversify in order to ensure a more stable flow of revenue. For instance, a women's health clinic in one community has abandoned neonatal services because it was losing money on them, continues to provide abortions for the opposite reason, but is also seeking to develop its base as a primary care provider.

In keeping with the idea that special expertise is needed to address problems, community involvement comes to mean being concerned about particular issues and uninterested in others. What is sometimes viewed by outsiders as apathy or self-interest is seen by the professionals themselves as a way of focusing their attention on what they know best. A teacher, for example, may worry about how well children in her community are learning their lessons, and may try hard to create a good atmosphere for learning in her classroom; but knowing she cannot control what goes on in the school system at large, let alone in other organizations, she may deliberately limit her interest in those problems. To be involved is thus to do one's job to the best of one's ability, trusting that others will contribute to the community in their own ways.

An important part of how nonprofit professionals view the world, therefore, is that they can devote themselves fully to what they believe, rather than having to contribute only during their spare time. As a young man who works as a fundraiser for a nonprofit social service agency with a $20 million annual budget that supports twenty-two different programs explains, "It's one thing to have convictions and it's another thing to have that be the reason why you get up in the morning and do what you do." He elaborates, "If I didn't do this, I would say, 'Well, this is what I believe,' and talk and talk and make a few donations and maybe volunteer a few hours a month or something like that, but then I'd just go back to my regular job, doing something else."

At first glance, nonprofit professionals seem to run counter to the idea of loosening connections to civic organizations. They are involved in their communities in a full-time capacity, rather than as members of service clubs that may meet only a few hours a month. As part of the fluid workforce that increasingly characterizes the economy, they are nevertheless subject to many of its dislocations. Nonprofit employees are as likely to be temporary or part-time workers as are employees in other sectors. They switch jobs and move into whole new lines of employment. And they are especially susceptible to cutbacks in government funding or changes in the direction of social programs. It is perhaps for this reason that they differ so markedly from the earlier pattern. As a follow-up study of the organization men of the 1950s concluded, "[Their] children, utterly lacking their fathers' loyalty to a specific organization, [are] more inclined to join many ever-shifting networks than to seek a niche in one immortal hierarchy."[28]

There is a kind of psychological detachment from professional work that causes some observers to argue that this form of civic involvement is more limited than that of service and social club members. Professional workers are governed by contractual relationships with their communities. Their approach may thus be governed by norms of professional advancement that do not always coincide with the interests of the community. Loyalty to the profession may encourage people to uproot in order to gain a higher salary or greater job security. In addition, professional norms include specialization, meaning that nonprofit professionals may be dedicated to a particular task but exhibit relatively little interest in voting, helping their neighbors, or learning about other community issues. For some people, work is also compartmentalized from what they consider to be their "true self." It is a role that they play in public, whereas in private life they can pursue other interests. Their commitment may therefore be regarded by others in the community as somehow less genuine or intrinsically motivated than that of volunteers or association members who give of their personal time.

Many professionals, however, do engage in volunteer work and belong to community organizations.[29] More important, the idea of a career creates a psychological relationship between work role and the self that is often quite deep and enduring. Although particular tasks or places of employment may change, the career provides continuities that depend on specialized training and experience. But the career is also a feature of individuals more than it is an attachment to the community. The chief criticism leveled at nonprofit professionals is thus that they may adopt an individualistic or instrumental orientation that results in their being only loosely connected to any community.

In addition to the nonprofit professional, the volunteer has come to be a preferred way of defining the meaning of civic involvement. Volunteers are greatly admired, evoking favorable responses far more often than the members of clubs or service organizations do, and approximately half of all Americans engage in volunteer activities.[30] Indeed, the proportion of the American public who volunteer at least occasionally has risen significantly since the 1970s, even while organization memberships have been declining. The increase in volunteering has kept pace with the growth in nonprofit organizations, and the two have reinforced each other.

Moreover, the line that separates volunteers from nonprofit professionals is often thin. As in Grace Bishop's case, a professional who works for a human service agency is likely to learn about needs that are not being adequately addressed by the agency itself. Partners for Peace is a spin-off organization created largely by her own volunteer efforts. It succeeds because she has connections through her work and because she devotes lunch breaks and evenings to it. This pattern was fairly typical among nonprofit professionals we interviewed. Sometimes the volunteer work was simply a way to build up a resume or to earn a promotion. In other cases it developed mainly from personal friendships that had been established at work. For example, a professional might volunteer to help with a voter registration drive or to advise a church's planning committee, even though these were not part of the person's job description.

Although volunteering is quite different from working as a paid professional at a nonprofit organization, there is a symbiotic relationship between the two. Indeed, volunteerism has been reinforced by nonprofit professionals, not replaced by them. This is an important point because it reverses an idea that has long prevailed in popular discussions. According to that idea, tasks such as healing the sick and caring for the needy were performed by volunteers until sometime early in the twentieth century, but the gradual rise in professionalism has squeezed out these volunteers.[31] In some interpretations, this development has also resulted in huge, costly bureaucracies, leading some to believe the best way to approach social problems is now to cut bureaucracies and return to a simpler time when volunteers saved their communities.[32]

But the volunteer as we know it today is a relatively recent invention.[33] It is a specialized role that differs from being a good neighbor or a club member, and is contingent on there being nonprofit organizations in which to volunteer. The emphasis on volunteering has strengthened at the same time that employment in the helping professions has increased, and the one is not simply a substitute for the other but is made possible by the other. Most volunteers serve through agencies that are staffed by paid professionals, such as social workers, physical therapists, nurses, or clergy.[34] The volunteers perform auxiliary tasks that may range from answering telephones to serving coffee to clients, and people often learn about opportunities to volunteer from solicitations by nonprofit agencies. Because there are full-time employees to "mind the store," most volunteers are able to take part in relatively loose, ephemeral, or limited ways. For instance, the average volunteer devotes only two hours per week to volunteering, and this activity is unlikely to be devoted to a single organization over the course of a year.[35]

The symbiosis between volunteering and paid professionals is evident when volunteers describe their reasons for becoming involved. Many admit that they volunteer to discover whether or not they want to enter a profession or to gain experience that will help them find employment in a profession. Some say they became involved because they knew and admired someone who worked for a nonprofit agency and who asked them to help. Others say their careers prevent them from serving others full time or they do not have the personality for such work but they want to do a little to broaden themselves. These connections shape volunteers' understandings of what it means to serve, encouraging them to feel that training and experience are worthwhile or to quit if they are not able to be effective.

Volunteer work is sporadic enough that people also feel they can terminate it fairly easily. Geographic relocation is often a reason for stopping.

Other changes of status also give people a reason to quit. Sometimes it is a new job. People want to prove themselves and so they work longer hours than necessary instead of volunteering. A new baby makes it harder to get away. Or when a child graduates from high school, parents do not have as much incentive to do things in the community.

Volunteering has developed in ways that make it more amenable to people who are geographically mobile or who lead their lives in porous institutions. Volunteers' stories about how they became involved in community activities reveal the influence of living in a changing society. Some sign up as volunteers because they have just moved to a new community and are hoping to meet people. Some have been laid off when their company downsized and start volunteering to fill their time. Some have been forced into partial retirement, giving them an opportunity to volunteer. Some are hedging their bets by volunteering at organizations that might be potential employers.

The other traditional form of community involvement—the good neighbor—has diminished somewhat in importance. Its decline was not associated with any conscious decision that being a bad neighbor was acceptable or that neighboring was no longer significant. Indeed, most people still assert that they are civil to their neighbors, trying not to be a public nuisance and chatting if an occasion arises, and most people claim to be personally acquainted with at least a few of their neighbors.[36] But people are also troubled that they do not know more of their neighbors or interact with them more often—troubled enough to have developed rationales that reveal much about the way community life has come to be understood.

One of these rationales is that people should select who they interact with on the basis of shared interests; if they share no interests with their neighbors, then it is acceptable not to get to know them. Another rationale is that one's home is a *private* space in which one has the right to withdraw from public interaction, including interaction with people who live close enough to intrude. As one woman, a six-year resident who knows few of her neighbors, explains, "My private space has always been pretty important to me, so I've never gotten chummy with neighbors." Yet another rationale is that being a truly good neighbor is too costly in terms of time and emotional energy. Interaction has thus become more intentional, involving choices based on a calculation of costs and benefits, rather than simply being part of the geography in which one lives.

The idea of being a good neighbor has been partly replaced by home-owners' and neighborhood associations, which have grown to include an estimated 31 million Americans.[37] These are generally legal entities that regulate such matters as the kinds of roofing residents can put on their homes or the number of vehicles they can park overnight on neighbor-hood streets. They may collect funds to be used for street repairs and maintain clubhouses or pools. They are a form of self-rule that reduces the burden on township or municipal officials of overseeing the activities of large developments, such as townhouse or condominium complexes. They obviate the need for some neighborly interaction, such as settling disputes about improperly maintained lawns, and they sometimes encour-age interaction, say, at pool parties or annual meetings. They are also an important way to extend the civic pride that has long been associated with homeownership to encompass a somewhat wider area. But homeowners' associations often promote little community involvement, relying perhaps on one or two volunteers who negotiate with management companies, landscapers, and construction crews. With only a few exceptions, people who belong to neighborhood associations say it is hard to recruit volun-teers for committees or to get quorums for annual meetings. As one notes, "We've got a real apathy problem; out of 329 residents, you can have a meeting where only 4 show up!"

More than the neighborhood association, it is the close friend or "soul mate" who has taken the place of the good neighbor. Soul mates are those few intimate acquaintances with whom people feel free to share their deepest interests and their innermost feelings. The quest for soul mates arises from the desire to overcome the loose connections that characterize other relationships. Soul mates are the exceptions, the ones "to whom we feel profoundly connected," as one writer suggests.[38] The number of soul mates a person has is limited by the time and effort it takes to cultivate them and by the desire for substantially overlapping interests. A soul mate is more than a neighbor with whom one exchanges casual greetings. Soul mates are more special even than friends.

Soul mates are bound together not only by shared interests but by an implicit commitment of caring and affection. They are the few people to whom one has chosen to disclose oneself. They allow one to demonstrate that one is not a loner or callous but a caring person. They are often people who have become important during an earlier phase of one's life and who no longer live in the same community. A man in his eighties who has lived in eighteen different places as an adult provides an example. Although he and his wife have lived in the same village of three hundred people for the past twenty years, they know only one other couple in the village well enough to visit them regularly. Instead of making friends with his neighbors, the man keeps in contact by telephone with a man with whom he worked and a couple he knew through a church in another community. He explains these relationships in terms of caring and common interests: "You need some close friends. Not a whole lot, but a few dependable friends. You care about them and you have a joint interest in things."[39]

The desire for soul mates profoundly influences current understandings of community involvement. Relating to a soul mate is a way of working out one's own identity, of finding personal fulfillment, or of overcoming the sense of inauthenticity that comes from playing multiple roles in loosely connected settings. Relationships to the wider community may be less gratifying and thus take lower priority in one's allocation of time.

The idea of community itself has been colored by the imagery of soul mates. To be part of a community is to have warm, intimate relationships with soul mates. The community is "the people I like to be with," one woman explains. Churches are communities insofar as they cultivate openness, acceptance, smiles, and hugs. To be involved in such a community is to participate, to share. Laughter and conviviality (or just "hanging out") have become the essential features of community. Service means developing an emotional bond with the community. People assert that their communities are good places to live because they generate certain feelings of nostalgia or because they meet aesthetic criteria.

In place of simply being good neighbors, people join self-help groups and other special-interest groups, the numbers of which have grown enormously in the past two decades.[40] One reason is that transportation and telecommunications make it possible to recruit people who share interests but do not live in the same neighborhoods. As one man points out, another reason is that this is the only way to get people together. When neighbors no longer know one another, starting something has to be done by advertising or through a nonprofit organization, and the basis for gathering is usually a special interest, rather than sheer proximity.

Self-help groups combine the ideal of the soul mate with that of the volunteer. Participants look for emotionally gratifying relationships with a few other people who become their "community." Because they participate intentionally, they also understand their involvement as a kind of voluntary service, sometimes remarking that they "volunteer" to help other members or that the group's activities are a form of volunteer work. The widow of a policeman who was killed in the line of duty illustrates this understanding of self-help in talking about her Parents Without Partners group. She finds people in it with whom she can cry and share her deepest fears about being alone. She also sees it as a group that works better at some times than at others. "Like any other volunteer organization," she says, "it's only as good as its volunteers." Her group makes a deliberate effort to balance the two ways of being involved. Some meetings are purely for emotional support, where people "make connections" and sometimes become close friends. Other meetings are service oriented, including instructional presentations or field trips for children. She says of the group, "It's my way of serving people in my community."

Even self-help groups that focus mainly on emotional problems, such as therapy groups or certain kinds of twelve-step groups, are now widely viewed as ways of making a positive contribution to the community. To be sure, most people do not view them in the same way as an organization that is directly engaged in helping the poor or working to clean up the environment. The logic is rather that they are addressing problems that prevent people from getting involved in "good causes." Selfish or apathetic people are understood "to be hurting inside," as one man puts it. They are unable to focus on the needs of others because of some traumatic experience in their own life or because of being raised in a dysfunctional family. In this view, the problem is not that people are simply immoral or that they have been corrupted by advertising or big government or by wanting too many material things for themselves. It is an emotional problem, deep within their personality, that can be healed only by talking it out and by receiving support. Self-help groups are thus an acceptable solution for such problems. In the course of dealing with such problems, participants in self-help groups also develop informal ties with other participants, hear about opportunities to do volunteer work, and in many cases learn civic skills or become interested in activist causes.[41]

The old-fashioned virtue of helping neighbors who are in need has by no means died. When people are asked if they have ever received help from somebody in their neighborhood, virtually everyone can think of at least one such occasion. Some mention having their driveways plowed after snowstorms; some talk about medical emergencies; many speak of help with fixing flat tires or starting stalled cars. People also talk about helping their neighbors in small ways, such as looking for lost pets or taking home-grown vegetables to the people next door. Many Americans believe, too, that their neighbors would be there to help them if some serious crisis emerged.[42]

But these deeds of neighborliness pale in significance compared to people's memories or idealized images of how neighborhoods used to be. One man, talking about his suburban community's annual picnic, observes: "A once-a-year community picnic is different from a community where they had a dance every Saturday night and turned out to help each other with whatever needed helping with, childbirth, crops, or providing one person to teach the younger children in the community. I don't see that togetherness."

As people bemoan the problems in their communities, many lament the lack of good neighbors.[43] Some make a point of saying that people are no longer neighborly or that everybody has become too selfish to spend time helping neighbors. But their comments also betray an understanding of neighborliness that has changed since the 1950s. For many, being a good neighbor has become an abstraction that they see as a panacea for the problems of the wider society. Some speak of neighborliness as the solution to the decline in morality; others think it would reduce the number of abortions or teenage pregnancies. Yet it is not evident that they have a clear idea of how this would happen. Others point to real or hypothetical examples of people being good neighbors. These examples, however, often consist of voluntary behavior performed outside the neighborhood itself or for a nonprofit agency. The good neighbor is thus exemplified by someone who works for Habitat for Humanity or who founds a soup kitchen.

In the current understandings of civic involvement, the role of political participation is more often in the background than it was in earlier understandings. The ones that prevailed in the 1950s took for granted that people would vote, that organization men might run for minor elected positions, and that club women would invite representatives to speak at their social events. The activist models of the 1960s assumed that people would engage directly in attempts to bring about political reforms. Of the current images, the nonprofit professional is most likely to be aware of interacting with government agencies. In comparison, volunteers may shield themselves from thoughts about government, while soul mates operate on a more intimate level.

How relevant politics is perceived to be varies considerably from one type of community to another. But there is an implicit understanding that civic involvement and politics are quite different. Despite continuing statistical relationships between participating in community organizations and voting, people insist on a sharp conceptual distinction between the two. It is possible for people who do little in their communities to believe that politicians can be trusted to do the work for them. And it is equally possible for people who are intensely involved to say that politics is a nasty business that leaves them cold. This capacity to separate the two is partly attributable to Americans' long-standing tendency to be skeptical of government compared to efforts by citizens to help themselves. It seems to reflect some tacit awareness that we are living in a time of inordinate complexity. Setting government to the side of one's thinking may have become the condition for believing that civic involvement matters at all.

The changes in meanings of civic involvement over the past half-century should not be exaggerated. Millions of Americans still play out the scripts they have learned about being good organization men, club women, or neighbors. Yet it is also clear that civic participation is no longer defined exclusively in terms of these models. Newer meanings of civic involvement that focus on nonprofit professionals, volunteers, and soul mates reflect the fact that American society is now far more densely populated with nonprofit organizations, volunteer centers, and self-help groups than it was in the 1950s. These newer ways of thinking about civic involvement help people make sense of what they are doing and regard it as a legitimate form of community service, even if it differs from the way their parents or grandparents thought about service in their communities.

3

Porous Institutions

NEW WAYS OF THINKING about and getting involved in the larger community have emerged because of changes in our social institutions. Were it not for these changes, Americans might well feel comfortable participating in their neighborhoods, towns, and cities through the men's and women's clubs of the past, through fraternal orders, and as good neighbors. The belief that one can contribute more effectively to the community as a nonprofit professional, volunteer, or member of a self-help group has come to make sense because our lives are molded by social conditions that make looser connections seem more appropriate. In opting for these newer forms of civic involvement (or in many cases choosing to remain on the sidelines entirely), Americans are adapting to large-scale changes in the society.

Social institutions are the vehicles through which people pursue the activities that are important to them. Institutions represent the accretion of individual decisions and of personal relationships, but they are more than this; they are patterned social arrangements that depend on implicit norms, such as driving on one side of the road instead of the other, and on the resources to enforce these norms, such as police departments and highway commissioners. To say that travel is institutionalized means not only that many individuals take trips but that an entire industry (airlines, travel agents, hotels) has emerged to promote travel.

The integrity of social institutions depends on being able to draw distinctions among them and thus to prevent the resources they have accumulated from being dissipated. The family is an institution because Americans value such activities as expressions of love and intimacy, the sharing of living quarters, reproduction, and the training of children—and because these activities can be distinguished from, say, running a business or playing tennis.[1] Norms that encourage people to marry and have children, to spend time with them, and to pass personal assets to them help maintain the family. Some of the distinctions that set institutions apart are embedded in tradition or law; others in taken-for-granted ways of behaving (working in a location separate from the family helps to demarcate the two). These distinctions signify boundaries which can be rigid or flexible depending upon the nature of the institution and its exclusivity.

Porous institutions have social boundaries that permit people, goods, information, and other resources to flow across them with relative ease. A permeable boundary between family and workplace may exist, for example, when both activities occur in the same space or when the rules governing their separation are unclear. A parent who works from an office at home may find that the line between job and family is easily transgressed.[2] People who work on a flexible schedule may often need to resolve which role they are playing at a given moment and, therefore, which rules pertain to their behavior.

Differences of this kind can be found at almost any level of social organization, not just between whole institutions. A child may grow up with a strict sense of who is a family member and who is not (we are the Hatfields and they are the McCoys); while another child may be somewhat unsure whether the kid down the street is just a friend or a cousin, or whether the woman who drives him to school is really an aunt or just someone he calls his aunt. One person may be employed by a corporation that demands a certain mode of dress and that has a clear job ladder that employees are expected to climb, while another person may contract with one employer to do a specific task and then contract with a different employer a day or two later.

Social boundaries can be porous in two ways. One is that the distinctions are not very clear or important and thus permit flows to occur by default. This may be the case when it simply is not important whether an "aunt" is a blood relative or only a neighbor. The other is that boundaries are clearly defined but permeable. The employer who hires short-term, project-specific workers has a clear sense of who is an employee and who is not, but is content to have people enter and exit this category with relative frequency.

The increasing porousness of American institutions is especially evident in the family. Enormous change—what the sociologist Arlene Skolnick has described as a "cultural earthquake"—has overtaken families in recent decades.[3] These developments may or may not signal the breakdown of the traditional family, but they show that once-rigid definitions of the family as a mother, a father, and children are less clear than in the past and that some kinds of familial relationships are not permanent while others have become more distant or sporadic. Many people relate to their families by visiting on holidays or by making long-distance telephone calls, rather than by living nearby.

In national surveys, almost everyone says that the family is one of their most important values, that their own family is a major source of satisfaction, and that having a family is an essential feature of their self-worth. Not surprisingly, the vast majority of Americans (more than 90 percent) put these values into practice by getting married, and a large majority of married couples have children. Yet the divorce rate has risen from approximately one divorce for every four marriages in 1950 to one for every two marriages in the 1990s, and even with this trend leveling out in the past few years, the cumulative impact is that the proportion of divorced Americans is now about four times as high as it was in 1960.[4]

The most notable consequence of porous marital relations is the rise in numbers of children raised by a single parent. The proportion of all U.S. family groups with children under 18 who were "one-parent family groups" rose from 13 percent in 1970 to 31 percent in 1994. By the latter date, one-quarter of all white family groups were single-parent, as were 36 percent of Hispanic family groups and 65 percent of African American family groups. The loosening of ties between marriage and childrearing is also evident in the fact that births occurring out of wedlock rose from 5 percent of all births in 1960 to 31 percent in 1993.[5]

Another change in family life is the number of people who live together as unmarried couples. Between 1970 and 1994 this number increased from 523,000 to 3.6 million; among persons under age 25 there was a fifteenfold increase, and among people between the ages of 25 and 44, a twentyfold increase. Although these arrangements are not necessarily short-term, they do indicate a growth in the perception that individuals can establish relationships without invoking the legal structures that helped define the family as a social institution in the past.[6]

Families have become more malleable in a number of other ways as well. Children of divorced parents move into and out of relationships with biological and step-parents, sometimes living temporarily with one and then another, and often visiting for short periods of time. Although divorce is a legally distinct social category, the grounds on which it may be granted have become increasingly blurred, especially with the preponderance of cases filed on grounds of "incompatibility." Blended families (the name is suggestive) mean it is harder to draw clear distinctions between family members and nonmembers. In interviews people sometimes mention step-parents and half-siblings and sometimes do not; who counts as family is a matter of subjective definition. The statistic that most clearly demonstrates the rising prominence of blended families is the proportion of marriages in which neither bride nor groom has been married before. In 1970 more than two-thirds of all marriages were of this kind; by 1990 only half were. Thus, approximately half of all currently married couples have some other person with whom there is a potential for continuing psychological or financial ties or some sharing of parental obligations.[7]

Porousness is also evident in other relationships between parents and children. In few cases are biological relationships contested, but the social boundaries that define children as being close to or distant from their parents have become more subjective and easily transgressed. Adult children are less likely than in the past to live nearby, work in the family business, or pursue the same line of work as their father or mother. For example, a study in 1957 showed that only 15 percent of parents aged 65 and older lived more than thirty minutes away from at least one of their children, whereas by 1986 this figure had tripled to 45 percent.[8] Closeness is thus less likely to be defined in terms of geographic propinquity or financial dependence; it is more likely to mean an emotional bond. Long-distance telephone calls make it easier to move into and out of these moments of closeness.

Part of what people are reacting to when they complain about the "breakdown" or "fragmentation" of the family is that the relationships by which people know they are or are not part of a family have become harder to define. On average, young adults wait three to four years longer to marry than in the past, extending the transitional period in which it is less clear whether they are still members of their families of origin or "on their own." In these years, it is more acceptable to cohabit and to engage in sexual relationships, but also more difficult for friends and parents to know what to say about these relationships. Parents with children from both current and former marriages often express anxiety about how best to meet their obligations to them. With fewer children following in their parents' footsteps, it is harder to know whether or not values are being properly transmitted from one generation to the next. And with children maturing over a longer period of time, participating casually in the labor force, attending college, moving away from parents, returning temporarily, and having a harder time figuring out their career preferences, the very definition of adulthood becomes, as one writer observes, "as difficult as pinning Jell-O to a wall."[9]

Contemporary families are no longer insulated in the home. They are permeated by influences from the outside world. A century ago these intrusions were limited to an occasional mail-order catalog or visit from a neighbor; now the typical family is subjected to a constant barrage of direct-mail solicitations, telephone calls, and television advertisements. As recently as half a century ago, relatively few women worked outside the home and many Americans lived in single-car or carless families; now the majority of women are full- or part-time members of the labor force and many families have an automobile for each of their members. The family space is no longer clearly demarcated.

Similarly, places of employment have become porous, perhaps even more so than families. The most visible sign of flexible boundaries is the frequency with which workers change careers. Rather than being able to count on staying in the same job for a lifetime (such as being a farmer, an automobile assembly-line worker, or a dentist), most young people now realize that they may be training for a career that will disappear by the time they have been in it for five to seven years. According to a survey conducted for the U.S. Bureau of Labor Statistics, the average length of time employed Americans have spent in their current occupations is only 6.5 years, and the average time with each employer is only 4.5 years. The median number of different careers listed by people aged 45 or over in the U.S. labor force is now three; the traditional pattern of working in only one career now typifies only 21 percent of all workers aged 45 or over.[10]

For business firms the most significant indications of porousness are downsizing and outsourcing, both of which result in more ephemeral relationships with workers. During the early 1990s the number of corporate downsizings doubled, to approximately 600,000 layoffs annually, and many of these layoffs occurred in the largest corporations, such as AT&T, IBM, and RJR Nabisco. Counting layoffs of all kinds, the social impact of downsizing was considerable. According to a poll conducted by the *New*

York Times in 1996, 20 percent of the public had been laid off sometime in the past fifteen years, 14 percent said someone in their household had been laid off, and 35 percent said someone they knew well had been laid off, bringing the total who said they or someone close to them had been "affected" by a layoff to 72 percent of the public. Although downsizing itself does not imply porousness (smaller companies can have rigid boundaries), it has largely meant reducing layers of middle management whose main function was to keep tight control over subordinates. In a survey conducted by the American Management Association, more than half of all firms studied indicated that they were undergoing "flattening."[11]

According to management consultants, the reason for downsizing has partly been that more of the control function can be exercised by computers but also because a less rigid structure is desirable when information, markets, and product lines change rapidly. Outsourcing has been the correlate of downsizing. More tasks are performed by independent consultants and external suppliers than by divisions within large corporations. In addition, temporary workers, adjunct professionals, and adjusted-time employees have been used to a greater extent, often to avoid paying benefits that would accrue to regular employees. In some realms this so-called contingent labor force has increased dramatically; for example, in American higher education the proportion of faculty who were in part-time positions rose from 32 percent in 1980 to 47 percent in 1996.[12]

The extent of downsizing should not be exaggerated, especially when it has occurred over a relatively short period and can be understood partly as a response to economic cycles. Nevertheless, the fact that many large corporations have been able to reduce their workforce by as much as 30 percent without any apparent reduction in output or profits leads observers to believe that downsizing is a fundamental characteristic of the contemporary corporate environment. If so, its sources can be traced to a number of related conditions, including more efficient technologies of communication and control, a preference for outsourcing, and a reduction in benefits paid to provisional workers. The consequences include many of the marks of porousness: more temporary relationships between corporations and suppliers, more information and services flowing across organizational boundaries, more frequent employment changes among workers, and more workers who move into and out of the labor force. Although the contingent labor force is still relatively small as a proportion of all workers, its significance is evident in one study of 521 companies in which 78 percent used independent contractors and 97 percent drew help from temporary agencies.[13]

The permeability of corporate boundaries is evident in exchanges of capital. The trading of stock, where new mechanisms of exchange make it possible for resources to be transferred more easily from one firm to another, is an example. With electronic and computer-generated trading, quicker information, and more brokerage firms, many more shares are traded each day than in the recent past. On the New York Stock Exchange, 74 billion shares were traded in 1994, up from only 11 billion in 1980. Porousness is also evident in the number of new firms that are initiated each year and established firms that die. New incorporations rose by 152 percent between 1970 and 1992, and business failures multiplied nearly tenfold during the same period. In addition, mergers and acquisitions climbed from 1,700 in 1985 to 3,500 in 1992. Overall, the number of incorporated businesses in the United States rose from 2.8 million to 9.0 million in the last decade alone.[14]

The economy itself is more porous in terms of the number of new products of which it is composed. Between 1980 and 1995 the number of patents issued annually grew by about 50 percent. During the same period the number of new consumer products introduced annually in the food industry increased from 1,100 to 4,000; in the beverage industry, from 250 to 800; and in the health and beauty industry, from 800 to more than 2,600. Studies suggest that this growth, moreover, was facilitated largely by market mechanisms and advertising, as evidenced by the fact that nearly two-thirds of the innovations were described as new formulations or new packaging, while less than one percent were attributed to technological innovations.[15]

Apart from specific innovations, the economy has also become more organized around information and services and less devoted to agriculture and manufacturing, leading many observers to argue that organizational boundaries are adapting in a way that permits information to flow more easily and that takes better account of the complex individual needs that must be met by effective services. The growth in information is readily evident in statistics on telecommunications and computing. And major corporations are deeply implicated in this growth. IBM and AT&T have huge stakes in developing new information technologies. Television stays in business because people watch it, but also because companies like

Procter & Gamble, Philip Morris, and General Motors each spend more than a billion dollars annually on advertising. Overall, the advertising budget in the United States climbed from $75 billion in 1983 to $138 billion in 1993. "Each day of our lives," writes one media analyst, "twelve billion display ads, two and one-half million radio commercials, and over three hundred thousand television commercials are dumped into the collective consciousness." The walls that surround the typical family or individual are easily breached by this kind of information.[16]

These changes in the economy do not automatically result in different kinds of civic involvement. But they do affect the ways in which many Americans carry out their civic responsibilities. Temporary workers often move from community to community in search of new jobs and for this reason fail to establish long-term memberships in civic organizations. The information technologies that make it possible for businesses to interact with employees scattered around the world have a similar effect on civic activities: they make it easier for people to take part in special-interest groups outside their own communities.

The increasing importance of "service" occupations in the U.S. economy affects the ways in which community needs are being met. To speak in general of "services" is misleading: the term covers occupations as different as cleaning services and medicine and sometimes includes the fast-food industry. Even when it is restricted to professional and semiprofessional occupations, the growth in services is readily apparent. Between 1983 and 1994, for example, the number of psychotherapists increased from 247,000 to 430,000; the number of psychologists from 135,000 to 280,000; and the number of social workers from 407,000 to 667,000.[17]

Increases like these mean that some of the social needs that used to be filled by family members or by volunteers are now being dealt with by paid professionals. For example, the U.S. labor force currently includes approximately 308,000 special education teachers (up more than 300 percent in a decade), and 305,000 correctional officers (double the number a decade ago). Some of the volunteer assistance that used to serve a support function in service organizations is also being replaced by paid semiprofessionals, technicians, and clerical workers: for example, the number of teachers' aides is now nearly 600,000, almost double what it was in the early 1980s. And the growth in helping professions is likely to continue. According to U.S. Labor Department projections for the year 2005, fourteen of the twenty "fastest-growing" occupations will be in the helping professions: human services workers, physical therapists, paralegals, special education teachers, correction officers, and child care workers, among others. Manufacturing employment is expected to decrease 3.1 percent, while service employment is expected to grow 34.7 percent.

The relevance of this growth in services to the question of porousness is that people in the helping professions generally work in small organizations and depend heavily on networks connecting them to other kinds of professionals, thereby promoting permeable boundaries between organizations. By most standards, the United States has remained a nation of small organizations: 87 percent of all organizations employ fewer than twenty people. The prevalence of small organizations nevertheless is partly a function of the shift away from a manufacturing economy toward a service economy. Among all service organizations (which now account for more than a third of all businesses), 90 percent employ fewer than twenty people; the comparable figure for manufacturing establishments is 67 percent.[18]

Whereas the production of goods can often be standardized to meet a fixed schedule of input and output, organizations that specialize in human services often face issues that cannot be dealt with so neatly. Management consultants have pointed out that a service economy needs to be organized to provide for flexibility in bringing the right combinations of skills to bear on particular problems. "Professional service firms have long been organized in a different manner," observes Tom Peters; they are organized to deal with a "more fickle environment of shifting, temporary assignments." Peters notes that many kinds of firms are responding to this fickle environment by focusing less on owning resources and more on securing them through networks that include other professionals, clients, consultants, suppliers, distributors, and franchisees. The preferred management strategy, Peters argues, "boils down to (1) flattening the organization; (2) inducing fluidity; (3) projectizing; (4) joining in temporary networks with all sorts of partners to accomplish a limited goal in the marketplace; (5) getting very independent, modest-size business units to 'own' a market by serving it better; and (6) getting 'beyond' close to the customer—that is, achieving symbiosis with the customer."[19]

Along with the family and the economy, the community itself is characterized by increasingly porous boundaries. Compared to the geographic stability of many traditional societies, the ease of movement of the American population has long been a remarkable feature. Americans have not become more geographically mobile in recent years: the same proportion changed residences from one year to the next in the early 1990s as in the early 1980s. But this overall measurement masks the high mobility of certain segments of the population. Whereas the growing number of older Americans are less likely than average to change residences, younger Americans are considerably more likely than average to do so. Among people in their twenties, more than a third change residences every year.[20]

The boundaries of local communities are permeated in many ways in addition to residential mobility. Few neighborhoods serve as enclaves in which people can work and worship as well as live. Virtually all communities are penetrated by the mass media, chain stores, and government regulations. One indication of the movement across community boundaries is the fact that the average commute from home to work is eleven miles each way (about two miles more than in 1970). Shopping may be an even more important escape from the neighborhood. While the number of vehicle trips from home to work has held steady, the number of trips for shopping has increased 62 percent since 1970, and the average distance has also edged up slightly. Even more dramatic is an 111 percent increase in vehicle trips for family and personal business.[21]

Local communities are particularly subject to penetration by the images of distant places that are introduced by television and motion pictures. The effect is not simply to evoke comparisons between "here" and "there" but to blur the very distinction between here and there. One puzzling development that has received comment in recent years is American teenagers' lack of familiarity with national and world geography. But this can be understood in terms of the media age in which we live. A knowledge of geography was important when people actually needed maps to get somewhere, but with television (and airlines) remote places are brought into the immediate present almost instantaneously. They are simply part of one's everyday reality.

The impact of communication technology can be overemphasized, but it may also erode the distinctiveness of community boundaries by changing the ways in which we classify ourselves and others. Anthropologists point to the spatial and linguistic categories that surround us as providing the most basic cues to who we are. In the past, people often identified themselves in terms of geographic neighborhoods and on the basis of skin color or patterns of speech; increasingly, people identify themselves in terms of personal achievements, beliefs, and varied experiences that are more difficult to classify. Visual images themselves add to the fluidity of these identifications. As the political scientist Richard Merelman has argued, visual images break down the stable categories that are more common in written and printed forms of communication. Written language requires a linear ordering of time and often includes lists, charts, and an ordered hierarchy of arguments. Visual communication, Merelman claims, "becomes a continuous flow of more or less unbounded images."[22]

Whatever the sources, the public's *perception* that communities are changing is indisputable. In one study, three-quarters of the public said the "breakdown of communities" is a serious national problem. In another, 90 percent said it was important to participate in community organizations, yet only 21 percent said they did so. The same survey showed that 82 percent of the public thinks "people don't seem to care about each other as much as they used to." Other studies suggest that a declining number of Americans think people can be trusted, and that a majority think their fellow citizens are most interested in looking out for themselves.[23]

Compounding the problem is the fact that "community" itself has become an ambiguous term to many Americans. Although it is much discussed by everyone from therapists to clergy, community is no longer easy to define in terms of neighborhoods, and the larger contexts in which people live, work, shop, and vote convey mixed signals about what it may mean to be a part of any community.[24] This problem is especially acute in the suburbs of metropolitan areas that are made up of scattered and overlapping political jurisdictions. The problem was expressed well by one suburban resident who complained, "There's no central community and no feeling of 'us' and 'we do things this way.' I'm jealous of people who live in manageable-sized towns. People here aren't concerned about issues of the community because their loyalty is everywhere. They don't feel at home in any one community."

Yet it is not as if most Americans are simply lamenting the erosion of strong community loyalties. The individualism we regret is so deeply ingrained in our traditions that we also take pride in it. Individualism guarantees us our freedom to achieve, and we cherish it because it helps us distinguish ourselves from the crowd, to set ourselves apart, and to stake out a small corner of the world for ourselves. It is an appealing ideology in a society that encourages individuals to break ties so readily with their families, workplaces, and communities.[25]

National boundaries provide a final example of porousness as a fact of contemporary life. Although the United States is a nation of immigrants, the assertion that more people have been displaced from their countries of origin during the twentieth century than ever before is undoubtedly true.[26] Certainly the United States has experienced a new wave of immigration in recent decades. During the 1950s and 1960s, 5.8 million immigrants came to the United States; during the 1970s and 1980s, 11.8 million came. The latter figure rivaled that during the period between 1900 and 1920. In addition, the number of temporary visitors increased from 8.4 million in 1985 to 19.9 million in 1993. And an estimated 4 million undocumented immigrants came to the United States during this period. Thus by the early 1990s approximately 8 percent of the population and more than 9 percent of the labor force was foreign born.[27]

The lure of tourist dollars is another factor promoting porous national boundaries. Between 1970 and 1995 the number of foreign visitors to the United States increased 95 percent, while the number of U.S. citizens visiting foreign countries rose 111 percent. The growth in communication across national boundaries has been much more dramatic. In 1980 Americans made 200 million overseas telephone calls; by 1993 this figure had mushroomed to more than 3 billion.[28]

The perception that American society is now more "fluid," "open," or even "chaotic" than it was a generation or two ago thus has a strong basis in reality. Changes in business conditions, in law, in the economic circumstances of families, and in attitudes are all involved. Seeing how these changes reinforce one another requires viewing them from a broader perspective, and to gain this perspective it is instructive to consider the social conditions that work *against* the formation of porous institutions.

When a society or organization is faced with a serious external threat, it is unlikely to permit people or goods or ideas to flow easily across its borders. To do so is to invite enemies into its camp; being unable to count on outsiders to provide trustworthy and useful resources, leaders cultivate their own autonomous resources and try to protect them. Fears of government conspiracies provoke survivalists and cult leaders to draw tight boundaries between themselves and the external world.

Impermeable social boundaries are also more likely when circumstances permit human resources to be closely supervised. Organizations that exemplify such boundaries include armies, prisons, company towns, plantations and mines that utilize slave labor, and even sweatshops and assembly lines. Although the specific mechanisms of control vary, the common feature is that someone is in charge and has the capacity to monitor what subordinates do. Subordinates cannot move freely into and out of the organization; rather, their lives are regimented according to the organization's rules.

Another condition that encourages impermeable social boundaries is a lack of alternative opportunities. Company towns can dictate how residents behave because these residents have no hope of gaining employment elsewhere. The variations in porousness of families can partly be understood in these terms as well. Some marriages may stay intact because abused wives lack the economic resources to raise their children on their own, whereas a wife who has an independent career may be able to choose divorce. Similarly, extended family ties may be reinforced when people have fewer economic resources enabling them to survive on their own.

Impermeable social boundaries are sometimes a function of stable competition. For example, strong in-group loyalties are associated with long-standing feuds between families, such as that between the Hatfields and the McCoys, or between rival corporations, such as Coca Cola and Pepsi. The strength of these loyalties is likely to increase at times when the rival party constitutes a genuine threat. Even under less threatening conditions, however, the very stability of the relationship often encourages impermeable boundaries because each party's identity is clarified by its competition with the other. People are more likely to know who they are by virtue of knowing who they are not. The competition also may narrow the range of possible behaviors so that the norms governing the two parties begin to resemble each other (a cola drink becomes the norm, whether it is Coke or Pepsi).

These considerations bear on the conditions that have contributed to the increasing porousness of American social institutions in recent years. The lack of a significant external threat to the nation from a rival military power is one of these conditions. During World War II and the Cold War, concerns about national security led to tighter policing of borders and of the information that could flow across them; the same concerns helped legitimate a large standing army, a strong system of federal bureaus, and tighter controls over some commercial organizations whose products were considered vital to the national interest. With these specific threats giving way to a more generalized atmosphere of uncertainty, minor skirmishes, and economic competition, resources have been permitted to flow more easily across national boundaries.

As the nation has moved from an economy based on the production of manufactured goods to one grounded in information technology and services, the level of supervisory capacity has also diminished. At one extreme, a coal mine or a textile mill encourages high levels of supervision because most of the raw materials needed are located in a single place. At the other extreme, information-intensive work is harder to supervise, partly because the information is invisible or portable, but also because it is likely to be more complex and distributed among a wider range of people. Professional associations and computerized surveillance make it possible to control technical information, but organizations often have fewer incentives to do so because their best innovations come from unexpected sources and from informal networks of people and organizations with whom information has been shared.[29]

Porousness is also attributable to the relatively abundant alternatives that the society provides for most people and for most organizations. Although the life situation of many Americans has deteriorated in recent decades, there are still many more options available than in most parts of the world or in previous centuries. These options are a function of America's relative affluence; they are heightened by information technologies, mass communication, and transportation. People who are disgruntled with one product can readily shop for others, and such shopping can pertain to their places of employment and houses of worship as well. Changing levels of education have also had a profound impact on the society. As recently as 1960, only 41 percent of U.S. adults had finished high school and less than 8 percent had completed four years of college. By the middle 1990s, 81 percent had finished high school and 22 percent had completed college. More education makes individuals better equipped to work at information-intensive jobs or in professional and managerial occupations.[30]

The porousness of contemporary life is reinforced as well by the unstable and complex competition that characterizes the American economy. Markets are in flux as a result of innovation and shifts in fashion. Organizations expand and contract to meet changing demands and opportunities, and they are forced to keep in touch with many suppliers and clients in order to anticipate new sources of competition. More and more American products compete in international markets that are subject to unpredictable economic and political conditions. The small size of firms and the number of new firms and new products that appear each year also increase uncertainty.

It should be evident that tightly bounded systems remain viable under certain circumstances; the recent increase in porousness is not an irreversible trend or one that is rooted only in the expansion of information technologies. Nevertheless, porousness is highly compatible with market capitalism and with its attendant ideologies. Downsizing and outsourcing are consistent with corporations' quest to reduce costs and to maximize profits.[31] In market capitalism, a firm makes profits by occupying a position in an exchange relationship. The more that goods, ideas, and people are encouraged to flow through these relationships, the more opportunities there are for profiting from them.

The same economic system that generates a relatively high standard of living for most Americans is thus a factor in the increasing porousness of institutions. Market relationships encourage people to move to new communities in search of better jobs and draw people into the labor market in ways that make it possible or desirable, when new circumstances arise, to leave parents and partners behind. The complexity of the market also reinforces an ideology of individual freedom, of consumption, and of faith in markets themselves as the only conceivable way of addressing such complexity.

The heightened porousness of America's major institutions has significant consequences for the character of civic involvement. The most important is that more and more needy people are falling through the cracks. Civic involvement, whether in the form of voluntary assistance or of working for social programs to alleviate the suffering of these people, is more badly needed than in the past. Needy children, the unemployed, and the marginalized are among the most visible casualties of institutional porousness.

Studies consistently demonstrate the adverse effects of family upheaval on children. For instance, the combination of being raised by a single parent and living in a family without an adequate income or support for daycare and health care increases the likelihood of children being abused and neglected. Some evidence also points to lower self-esteem, more involvement in juvenile crime, and greater anxieties about growing up to be adequate spouses and parents among children of divorced parents. Since children pick up emotional cues from their parents, children growing up in single-parent households may also be affected by the higher rates of depression among divorced and separated adults.[32]

Corporate downsizing is also expected to intensify the need for social services. In one study men who had been laid off by large corporations and who had taken jobs with independent consulting firms were earning about half their previous salaries; some were forced to declare personal bankruptcy. Downsizing results in more people on unemployment rolls or temporarily between jobs. Forced retirements increase the number of elderly people without secure sources of income. The problems associated with job loss are compounded because relatively little public spending is devoted to job training and placement. According to one study, expenditures for such purposes amounted to 0.24 percent of Gross Domestic Product in the United States, a lower rate than those of Belgium, Canada, Finland, France, Germany, Italy, the Netherlands, Norway, Spain, Sweden, and the United Kingdom. Most important, large segments of the population do not have health benefits or pension plans to fall back on when needs arise.[33]

This last development is ironic. The twentieth century has witnessed more legal and governmental guarantees than ever before to protect people from the ill effects of personal and institutional catastrophes. Old-age and disability insurance are the most notable examples. Private pension plans, life insurance, and health insurance also provide such protections. But communities, workplaces, and families that bind people less securely to themselves make it realistic for large numbers of ordinary citizens to fear that they may have no protection when they need it.[34]

Another category of people whose lives are affected by the tenuousness of contemporary institutions is the homeless, whose numbers are estimated at approximately 600,000 on any given night and as many as 7 million over a five-year period. Critics point out that homelessness is partly "created" by an industry of government officials and social agencies in whose interest it is to provide services to the needy. To the extent that the homeless include families who are temporarily without shelter because of unemployment and who in the past would have been helped by extended families, employers, or welfare programs, however, homelessness must be understood as one of the by-products of porous institutions.[35]

A significant correlate of the growing porousness of social life is that more people are isolated and thus cut off from the informal ties that give them personal support, motivate them to care about others, and mobilize them to take an active part in their communities. Much has been made of the fact that growing number of Americans are "bowling alone," for example, and similar observations could be made about the number of people who eat or watch television alone. Probably the most arresting statistic is the rising number of Americans who *live* alone: between 1970 and 1994 it increased from 10.9 million to 23.6 million. By the early 1990s, therefore, approximately one of every four households in the United States was a household of one.[36]

When people live alone or in other ways feel poorly integrated into their communities, they worry more about crime. Often their fears are justified: criminals can prey more easily on people who are isolated; it is also harder to prevent crime in a transient community with few service organizations. Crime is one of the problems Americans worry about most, and not without reason: one person in five has been a victim of violent crime, and one in two has suffered theft or burglary. In absolute terms, crime has risen moderately in recent years, with the highest increases in rates of aggravated assault and auto theft. Homicide and suicide rates have edged up slightly since the 1960s, accounting for approximately 25,000 and 31,000 deaths respectively each year. Young people especially appear increasingly to be at risk.[37] A young man who lives in a low-income section of Chicago speaks of the people in his neighborhood as so afraid that they venture out as little as possible: "There's no people on the streets because they are hiding, basically. The young people stay inside unless they're in gangs because they don't want to be part of the madness out there."

While the sheer numbers of people who fall through the cracks in one way or another have increased, it is also worth noting that a more porous society changes the *nature* of the needs that pose the greatest challenges to community life. In tightly bounded communities, one of the most serious challenges is to promote the rights of those who are categorically excluded from fair treatment. Thus, the kind of civic action that has characterized the nation through much of its history has been the creation of orphanages and poorhouses, the construction of mental hospitals, the maintenance of segregated schools and colleges, and more recently the furtherance of laws to break down segregation and to protect the rights of minorities and the formation of organizations to combat the power of employers, as well as laws to guarantee the livelihood of the disabled and the elderly.

Under such circumstances, many of the remaining problems were readily handled by families and neighbors or through tightly knit organizations such as neighborhood churches or ethnic and nationality associations. Under today's more porous conditions, those who have traditionally been disadvantaged, such as minorities, the poor, new immigrants, and the elderly, are still likely to suffer most, but they are more likely to slip through the cracks as individuals rather than as entire classes of people, and it is thus more important to find ways of dealing compassionately with them as individuals, rather than simply responding to discrimination against entire classes of people.

Besides allowing more people to slip through the cracks, porousness makes it harder for their needs to be met through the established sources of voluntary assistance. Community organizations sometimes find it more difficult to recruit members or to enlist them in programs that require regular commitment over long periods of time. Daily schedules become more complicated as people keep up with blended families, as they juggle the demands of family and work, and as they struggle to stay ahead of an uncertain labor market. Moving in and out of marriages, jobs, and communities takes an emotional toll that requires people to spend more time on themselves, perhaps leaving less time or energy to devote to their communities. In a *New York Times* study of layoffs, those who actually were laid off increased their volunteering and civic participation (they had more time), but those who said they were worried about the possibility of a layoff were significantly more likely than other people to reduce their volunteering and civic participation.[38]

The amount of time that Americans devote to personal activities, including civic involvement, has been changing. There is some dispute about how much time is available for such activities, but substantial evidence suggests that it has been declining in recent decades—and that people perceive it to be declining. One study concludes that the average American works a full month longer than was the case two decades ago. Another study took into account child care and other household management tasks and found that the average mother of two children worked 113 hours longer per year in 1987 than in 1969 and that the typical father of two worked 132 hours longer. Other research shows that most working Americans believe they are working harder than they did five years ago and a majority say they have too little time for their families and wish they could work fewer hours. Besides working, Americans spend more time than in the past commuting, shopping, and driving to appointments.[39]

The impact of these changes has been particularly acute among the growing number of working women, many of whom also take responsibility for household chores and the care of children. In 1960 only 28 percent of married women with children worked in the paid labor force; by the middle 1990s 69 percent did so. Thus larger numbers of American families have to juggle their time around complex schedules. In a survey of the U.S. labor force, 71 percent of working women with children at home complained about not having enough time for their families and 56 percent said they wished they could work fewer hours. In the same survey, 77 percent said getting the housework done was a difficult issue and 48 percent said this about arranging child care. Not surprisingly, 44 percent said they experienced conflict between their work and their families.[40]

Women who work part time are more active in civic organizations than those who work full time.[41] But this difference is not simply a function of the hours women spend working. In fact, women who work at least sixty hours a week are more likely to donate time to voluntary organizations than those who work less.[42] The reason women who work full time are less likely to give time to voluntary organizations has much more to do with their off-work responsibilities than with the sheer number of hours they spend on the job. Those who have children at home are significantly less likely to volunteer than those who do not. In addition, women who feel they have control over their daily schedule at work are almost twice as likely to volunteer as those who do not control their schedules, while those who come home or little or no energy are significantly less likely to volunteer.[43]

Working men appear to be subject to some of the same pressures as women who work full time. For instance, men who say they have a lot of energy left after work are significantly more likely to donate time to voluntary organizations than men who have hardly any energy left. And men who control their daily schedules at work are much more likely to volunteer than men who do not.

Civic activities themselves appear to be changing in ways that reflect the scheduling pressures caused by the more fluid conditions in which many Americans now live. Older membership organizations such as Kiwanis or the League of Women Voters show declining vitality. Among service clubs, the Federation of Women's Clubs has experienced a loss of 59 percent since 1964; membership in Lions Clubs is down by nearly 70,000 members (12 percent) since 1986; membership in Jaycees, down 44 percent since 1979; and the Red Cross has 61 percent fewer volunteers than in 1970.[44]

Other organizations have also declined. Membership in the NAACP dropped from approximately 450,000 in 1976 to 356,000 in 1994. Over a shorter period, the Sierra Club has lost nearly 80,000 members since 1990 and the Wilderness Society more than 100,000 since 1980. Similarly, membership in Girl Scouts has dropped 12 percent since 1970, and in Boy Scouts by 15 percent. From 1974 to 1994, according to national surveys, the proportions holding memberships in fraternal groups dropped from 14 percent to 10 percent; in hobby or garden clubs, from 10 to 8 percent; and in labor unions, from 16 to 12 percent.[45]

In contrast to these membership declines, individual volunteering for charity and service activities has increased during the past three decades. The sociologist Christopher Jencks has calculated that the proportion of adult Americans who did any volunteer work during the past year rose from 18 percent in 1965 to 24 percent in 1974 to 47 percent in 1981. Jencks also estimates that the average number of hours volunteered per week increased from approximately 0.28 in 1965 to 0.58 in 1974 to 0.77 in 1981.[46]

Other evidence points to a decline in organizational memberships and an increase in individual volunteering. Between 1974 and 1991 the proportion of Americans who held membership in at least one organization declined from 74 percent to 56 percent.[47] Individual volunteering appears to be a more attractive way of being connected to one's community. Between 1977 and 1991 the proportion of Americans in Gallup surveys who said they had engaged in some kind of "charity or social service activity" in the past year increased from 26 to 46 percent.[48]

Volunteering can be a more transient, short-term activity than belonging to fraternal orders, service clubs, and other membership organizations that reward loyalty and long-term commitment. A volunteer can spend an evening a week on an activity for a few months as time permits, rather than having to make a long-term commitment to support an organization. Although volunteers speak of making friends with fellow volunteers, evidence also suggests that volunteering is less likely to be a source of the deep, enduring relationships on which people can depend for assistance than is participation in churches, neighborhood gatherings, or bowling leagues.[49]

Prior to 1950, voluntary associations were more likely to be large, national organizations with a central bureaucratic structure that governed and coordinated the activities of local chapters. In contrast, national civic associations founded since the 1950s have tended to be smaller in membership, and more of these organizations have been localized or specialized entities that do not emphasize membership or that focus on creating networks with other organizations. Examples of the earlier kinds of associations include the NAACP, founded in 1909, Kiwanis (1915), the 4-H (1900), and Camp Fire Boys and Girls (1910). Examples of the more recent organizations include the City Kids Foundation, founded in 1985 to work with inner city youth in New York, and the National Network of Youth Advisory Boards, founded in 1975 to promote youth involvement in juvenile justice programs and human service agencies. Although some of the associations founded since 1950 have grown large, the average size tends to be much smaller than among those founded in the earlier period.[50] This means that organizations have to depend on loose ties with other organizations and individuals, rather than expecting as many activities to be orchestrated by a single administrative structure.

One of the most revealing indications of how civic involvement is changing comes from responses to questions asking about people's likelihood of joining civic organizations with various characteristics. When asked about "a group that is part of a large national bureaucracy," only 15 percent said they would be very or somewhat likely to join. An equally small proportion (17 percent) said they would be likely to join "a group that expects you to be a member for life." When asked about "a group that is run by a small circle of long-time members," this figure rose to 40 percent. A group that "accepts only men or only women" was attractive to only 20 percent. Even fewer (6 percent) said they were likely to join a group that "has secret rituals." And only 2 percent said they would join a group that "has a history of racial discrimination."[51] Bureaucracy, lifetime membership, secret rituals, and gender or racial restrictions are characteristics of well-bounded organizations, such as the fraternal orders and clubs that were popular earlier in the century. These characteristics no longer appeal to many contemporary Americans.[52]

A majority of Americans still belong to some kind of civic organization (especially if all professional societies, interest groups, and school activities are included), but such organizations are by no means the only ways in which people connect with one another. In one study only 20 percent of the public said they "regularly attend or participate in a civic organization or service club, such as the Chamber of Commerce, the Kiwanis Club, or the P.T.A." In comparison, 40 percent of the public regularly participate in a small support group of some kind and as many as 50 percent regularly engage in some kind of volunteer work. In another study, which asked about various loosely connected social activities (such as sports teams, community centers, and issue groups), only 9 percent of the public were *not* included in some sort of social activity. Among the others, 30 percent belonged to a professional group, 21 percent to a social or card-playing group, 18 percent to a neighborhood improvement association, and 15 percent to a community center. Such studies do not provide comparisons with the past, but they do suggest that Americans are involved in a wide range of social and civic activities, many of which require relatively little commitment.[53]

The changing character of civic involvement, however, cannot be understood only in terms of the changing interests or opportunities of individual Americans. Civic involvement is also being reshaped at the institutional level, as organizations imitate one another and as they attempt to adapt to the porousness of institutional life. Community organizations are responding to changing social conditions by altering their own programs and appeals. The wider array of social needs means that community organizations continue to have legitimacy and to attract funds and volunteers. But the uncertainty of volunteers' schedules means that community organizations try to divide tasks into smaller units, and they face more competition from other organizations for volunteers' time. Community organizations are having to respond to changes in what has been termed their interorganizational environment. With growing numbers of human service organizations and people in the helping professions, community organizations are entering more often into loose alliances with these organizations and professionals.

An one indication of these loose alliances, we asked people who had done volunteer work in the past year whether or not they had come into contact with various types of people or organizations through the primary organization for which they had volunteered: 41 percent had come into contact with other nonprofit organizations, 29 percent with health professionals, 24 percent with social workers, 22 percent with government officials, and 19 percent with service clubs. Volunteers who dabbled in a number of different activities were the most likely to develop diverse contacts (see Methods, Tables 2–3). In short, volunteering links people into complex networks, and it does so because volunteer organizations function as parts of loose alliances.

The effectiveness of volunteer organizations thus depends increasingly on their ability to cultivate connections with the other organizations in their environment. Many of these organizations are nonprofit entities that specialize in professional services. They utilize short-term volunteers but also draw on the help of paid professionals and depend on wider connections for information and advice. They are less often membership organizations to which people belong over long periods of time than projects devoted to specific tasks. They range from urban development projects costing millions of dollars to babysitting co-ops costing nothing, from participation on region-wide planning commissions to sponsoring a co-worker in Alcoholics Anonymous, from a carefully orchestrated effort to feed the homeless or sponsor a community parade to a spontaneous task force to combat violence in the schools.

Some of these loosely connected organizations bring people together temporarily to address specific issues that arise in their communities: for example, a citizens' action committee that flourished briefly in a suburb of Buffalo, New York, to advocate a referendum for restructuring the local police department, or a committee in a Texas suburb consisting of disgruntled homeowners who joined forces against their insurance companies. Sometimes they develop skeleton staffs that maintain rudimentary activities over a period of years, like Denver's Concerned Citizens Action Committee, which monitors gasoline prices, or the New Jersey–based Childhood Cancer Cluster, which formed as a watchdog against the state's pharmaceutical companies.[54]

The concept of networking often fits these initiatives better than the idea of organizations. Using existing organizations and relying on telephones, fax machines, and electronic mail to keep in touch, volunteers can serve the wider community without having to set up new administrative units. For example, a network of volunteer attorneys in New Jersey processes more than 12,000 of the state's juvenile delinquency cases each year, and the American Bankers Association's network of 5,000 volunteers makes educational presentations at more than 32,000 schools and civic organizations annually. In other instances, independent organizations have been started to maintain networks of volunteers who become involved for short periods of time. Examples include Interlink, a nonprofit that coordinates a volunteer network in northern Kentucky that assists more than 1,000 elderly people who live alone; Master Gardeners, a volunteer network in Maine that provides advice to low-income residents who qualify for free garden space provided by the community; and Pittsburgh's Adopt-A-Nonprofit Organization, a lawyers' volunteer network that provides legal assistance to qualified nonprofit agencies.

The transient character of these connections is illustrated by city-wide networks, such as the Albany Indicators Group and Sustainable Seattle, that temporarily bring together volunteers from government agencies, universities, neighborhood associations, and other nonprofits to assess community needs and publicize their findings. It is also evident among organizations that attempt to promote awareness of community issues through concerts, parades, festivals, workshops, and other occasional events. Examples are Detroit's African World Festival, which draws an annual attendance of 1.5 million; Atlanta's Partners in Education network, which brings businesses and schools together to work on special projects; and the Mau Mau Rhythm Collective, an Oakland, California, group that uses hip-hop concerts to teach African American youth about jobs and the value of education.

There are exceptions, too. Examples of more tightly bounded groups that have grown in recent years include militias, of which 15,000 Americans are members, many of them long-term members with strong in-group loyalties. An even larger number of Americans—an estimated 625,000—belong to street gangs, also noted for intense levels of commitment.[55] Other organizations may have an enduring structure, but participants stay briefly because of changing needs and interests, like the MOMS babysitting co-op, which includes eighteen families in a Milwaukee suburb, or WEATOC (We're Educators, a Touch of Class), a Boston-based organization that trains young people to teach workshops, conduct rap sessions, and speak out on self-esteem issues in their communities.

On balance, the increasing porousness of American society makes it harder for many established civic organizations to function effectively, but new groups, networks, and innovative forms of volunteering are filling up the space. These newer ways of becoming involved in civic activities fit the complicated schedules of busy family members; they also fit a social environment that is rich in nonprofit organizations. Despite these innovations, the problems in many communities remain acute, and there is enough uncertainty about how well the newer models may work that many Americans long for a return to more tightly bounded organizations and neighborhoods. But such thinking may reflect a yearning for a world that no longer exists. As corporate leaders are finding, even large-scale organizations are unable to control events the way people may have hoped to do in the past. The challenge is to recognize that people do need to band together, but in more strategic ways, more loosely, and in a wider variety of networks.

4

Saving the Suburbs

SUBURBIA IS WHERE the porousness of contemporary life is most strikingly evident. The majority of middle-class Americans who live in suburbs are two-career couples whose work takes them out of the community during most of their waking hours. Many have chosen their communities carefully in order to send their children to good schools, to ensure that the resale value of their homes will remain high, to escape crime in the inner cities, and to avoid having to commute any farther than they already do. Many have lived in the same community for a decade or more. Yet their choices also position them to take flight if necessary: when employment opportunities arise elsewhere or when their children finish school, they are ready to move.

Civic involvement in America's suburbs is an array of apparent contradictions. Even though life is relatively comfortable for most suburban residents, they are often troubled by the feeling that people do not care very much for one another. Many suburbs generate an extraordinary level of volunteerism, many suburban residents work in the helping professions, and many participate in self-help groups. Yet they are convinced that civic involvement is not what it once was (or what it should be). Although they believe firmly in the virtues of democracy, they are also aware that special-interest groups sometimes achieve inordinate influence in their communities. They think it is important for everyone to do his or her part, but they are aware that a few people do far more than their share to keep civic organizations running smoothly while many others do little to help. Although they sense that more should be done to promote involvement in their own neighborhoods, they worry that their communities are becoming too isolated and insular. Making sense of these apparent contradictions requires a closer examination of the ways in which the porousness of suburban life is shaping the character of its civic activities.

From the late 1930s to the early 1970s, suburban housing developments replicated the ethnic neighborhoods and small towns from which their residents had come. With small children, families supported the construction of neighborhood parks and elementary schools, and the PTA became a focal point of the community. Protestant denominations and Catholics constructed new church buildings in record numbers, and Jews built new synagogues and neighborhood centers. Legion halls found space in many of the suburbs, and new chapters of Lions, Rotary, and Jaycees held luncheon meetings in local hotels and restaurants or in church fellowship halls. Township and borough halls provided meeting space for civic organizations and in many communities became the place where zoning and bond issues were debated.[1]

The face of suburban America has changed in several significant ways from its appearance as recently as three decades ago. Many of the suburbs that were settled by young families during the 1950s and 1960s now have declining social infrastructures and aging or demographically changing populations. Whereas expansion once made it possible to pay for new services, a stable population size makes it harder to supply social services and to maintain sewers and streets through tax revenues alone. In other suburbs, older residents have fled to retirement communities, leaving housing units to be purchased by younger families with lower incomes. Another significant change to suburban life is that fewer married women spend time at home with their families and in their neighborhoods, choosing instead to commute to jobs in other communities.[2] Suburbs have become more diverse racially and ethnically, as well as being composed of long-time residents and newcomers, leaving people feeling that they do not live among neighbors with whom they share interests or can interact comfortably.[3]

The suburban middle class has maintained itself economically through the income provided by a second wage earner, but has failed to achieve the real increases in income that many families enjoyed during the 1950s and 1960s. Although geographic mobility has leveled off, it continues to be a pattern of life for people in their twenties and thirties.[4] Many younger suburbanites find it difficult to develop strong attachments to their neighborhoods or to feel they have time to spend on civic activities. For those who are more civic-minded, the suburbs accentuate many of the conditions that promote looser ties to civic organizations: information technology makes it possible to maintain casual ties with a wider variety of people outside the community, and commuting makes it necessary to do so.

Consequently, complaints about the lack of community are endemic among suburban residents. The comments of a forty-year-old mother of two who runs her own word-processing business from her home in an ethnically diverse middle-class suburb are typical. When asked if she knows many of her neighbors, she says, "Not really. It was such a shock to move here [eight years ago] and find out that everybody stays to themselves and you never see the neighbors. Where I grew up [a small town], people were always outside in the afternoons, watering the grass and talking to each other while the kids played." She sighs. "I'm reconciled now to this neighborhood, but I'm not completely happy with it. You practically need a written invitation to go in someone's yard." Asked what the problem is, she responds, "Heck if I know. I'm a friendly person. You just never see any of the neighbors."

This woman, like most suburbanites, is basically satisfied with her community, despite the fact that she finds it lacking in the very kind of sociability that would make it more truly a place that she could call home. Indeed, 88 percent of suburban residents nationally say they are satisfied with their communities, and 45 percent say they are "very satisfied."[5] The reason they like their communities is that they can pursue their own interests and do so in relative comfort and safety.[6] As one comments, "It's very rich in opportunities. I think there are enormous resources here. In terms of human resources and cultural resources, I think that this could be a model area because there is a good cultural mix. There are well-grounded educational institutions here. Very diverse." Another says simply, "It's such a trouble free, nice place to live." Nationally, 89 percent of suburban residents say the word "comfortable" describes their community, and 85 percent consider their community "quiet."

The comfortable security of the suburbs ("We have a lot of nice things here," as one woman puts it) is nevertheless a source of worry for many of their inhabitants. They talk about complacency, boredom, stagnation, even snobbery. "We're all pretty much into our own little worlds here," one observes. It is a self-absorption rooted in the hectic pace required to maintain the comforts to which they have grown accustomed. Another resident says that people in his community are so "stressed out" that they can think about little else. He describes the typical family: "Two parents who are both working 45 hours a week and then they come home to the kids and they're so tired they hardly know what the hell to do." He adds, "How can they possibly get involved with the community when all they can do is barely keep their heads above water?" Other people talk about being caught in consumerism, trying to keep up with the Joneses, spending too much to maintain their fancy houses, gardens, and cars, and therefore not having time to do anything but work.

The perception that something is wrong in suburbia thus stems less from overt dissatisfaction with the community as a place to live than from the sense that there is no community in the place where people live. It is not an indication that people are uncaring; their concerns suggest that they do care about their communities. But they perceive, rightly it appears, that institutional life is changing in a way that makes it harder to connect meaningfully with their neighbors. One man puts it well: "The worries of de Tocqueville are alive and well [here] in terms of people becoming isolated from one another. People close themselves in their little enclaves and don't care about what's happening outside. They're afraid or not exposed or not sufficiently committed to the wider community."

Although the suburbs are generally perceived as secure enclaves, many of their residents feel besieged by forces they cannot control. Developers who bring in new people, new problems, congestion, and pollution are a frequent target of suburbanites' invective.[7] So are politicians who raise taxes and employers who demand too much or provide too little security against layoffs or transfers. The mass media are among the most frequently mentioned sources of outside interference. Despite their dependence on the media for news and entertainment, people recognize that the media shape public opinion in ways over which they can exercise little influence. Parents express fears that the media are corrupting their children by bringing them ideas about crime, alternative lifestyles, sexuality, and consumer products. If nothing else, the perception that they are besieged gives suburban residents an explanation of why life is not as neighborly as they would like.

The busy lives of most suburban residents can conjure up images of vitality, but people often use images of death and decay to describe their communities. Living in comfort seems to have a deadening effect on their senses, and if that does not take its toll, the exhaustion that comes from rushing around usually does. Some people say they can't feel the sunshine's warmth on their skin as vividly as they used to or appreciate the smell of roses. Somehow, their own existence doesn't seem real or authentic. They talk about being restless or dead and needing to find themselves or wanting to relate more intimately to others or to experience love and beauty in a deeper way. One woman contrasts the sheltered life of the suburbs with that of a neighbor who drives into the inner city to do volunteer work. "It's like the rest of us have all sat by the fire all winter, while she's been to the North Pole."[8]

One reason for these images of decline is that many residents long for a time—perhaps one that never existed—when the neighborhood was alive with people greeting one another, working together on community projects, and taking satisfaction in helping one another. Instead, their present neighborhoods seem to be filled with apathetic people, from whom they do not exclude themselves. A middle-aged woman observes that people in her community "want what's best for them and business and their family and their tax situation." Speaking for herself, she admits, "It's very hard to want equality and a good life for everybody. You have to take care of yourself." An older man who is a lifelong resident of his community comments similarly: "During the 1980s selfishness became respectable." He elaborates: "You just think about yourself. You say, 'Each person is responsible for his or her life, and if they're poor, it's time they get their act together and improve their lives.'"

In some places people still have a sense that civic participation is strong, although perhaps not as strong as it once was. They point to people attending school board meetings and participating in church activities. But some also say candidly that they have doubts about the spirit of this participation. As one explains, "An 'us versus them' mentality has developed. Civic participation too often centers around protecting me, mine, and ours, as opposed to building a better community as a whole. It becomes too segmentized, too separated."

There is an awkward awareness that the community is an enclave that focuses its attention inward rather than generating concern capable of transcending its protected borders. An upper-middle-class woman remarks, "We have mostly the same income. We have mostly the same race. Mostly the same educational level. And while I've grown up that way, and I'm really secure and feel safe like that, I'm also disappointed that I haven't challenged myself more to find something different." However, as homogeneous as the community may be, it is itself fragmented to the point of being difficult to define. This problem is interesting because suburban residents in the 1950s and 1960s proudly reproduced the sense of spatial attachment that their parents had known in rural villages or in urban neighborhoods, doing so by naming their communities, remodeling their homes, doing yard work, building churches, shopping locally, and voting in local elections.

Part of the reason community is now harder to define is that unified school districts often create jurisdictions that do not correspond with suburban boundaries and that commuting to work broadens the horizons of everyday life.[9] In addition, residents are more likely to shop at a megamall along an interstate highway than at a smaller mall or town center. Local television news encourages people to identify with a broadcast region more than with specific suburbs. Large churches and synagogues are more likely to draw from several suburbs than from one.[10] Long-distance telephone calls and travel create yet another horizon of involvement.[11]

Under such conditions it is hard for people to feel attached to their community, let alone become involved in it. Some people are transient residents, like a woman on the East Coast who flies to Michigan every weekend to be with her husband, or a man in Buffalo who carries on a commuter marriage with his wife in Chicago. Others talk about their "shopping area" as a way of defining community, even though this may include a large area in which they have no other personal contacts. Many others identify their community in terms of fellow professionals, like an artist who keeps in touch with other artists in a five-state region or an architect who is deeply involved in a national architects' association.

Most suburban residents use the word "community" rather casually, as if they have a clear idea of where their community is located. When pressed to say what they mean, they often mention the political jurisdiction in which they live, such as the suburb of Greenville or the suburban township of Millvale. But as they talk further it becomes apparent that their conception of community also means their immediate neighborhood or housing development. At other times it means the wider metropolitan area around their suburb, and at others it refers to a nongeographic entity, such as people who share their faith or the middle class at large.[12] One woman illustrates this scatteredness vividly as she says that her children's unified school district spans three suburbs, that she attends a church whose members are mostly from two other suburbs, and that she works in yet another suburb. When asked what she considers her community, she answers, "The people I know are my community."

Suburbanites often complain about the lack of connection to others in their communities. Even those who do become involved in civic activities explain their actions in terms other than community interest. Instead, they use a language of self-interest or regard their involvement as a kind of accident. One man says there is really no reason for his getting involved, other than somebody having asked him. A woman who organized a self-help group says she did so to deal with her own problems; she finds it hard to motivate others, so she just tries to be upbeat and enthusiastic. Others say they have time on their hands (implying that busier neighbors should not be expected to participate).

Such statements notwithstanding, some of the civic involvement in suburbs is motivated by an awareness of community needs that suggests more than an ephemeral connection with other people. People are very aware that families are homeless in their community or that crime is increasing, but they are generally aroused by individual cases rather than broader social conditions. They want to help a needy family or comfort a victim of crime, but they are less motivated to do something about poverty or crime in general. Similarly, those who volunteer stress how good it feels to be helpful. They feel more worthwhile about themselves. They've made friends. Their volunteer work has given them a way to fill their mornings. Such understandings make volunteering personally meaningful but reinforce the sense that loose connections may not be the same thing as deep loyalty to the community.

Suburbanites explain their lack of civic participation primarily in terms of time pressures at work and at home. Says one woman, "I'm just excessively busy. I treasure the moments I can be by myself." A man with two young children offers a similar explanation: "It's time problems. Most organizations meet in the evenings or on weekends, during the time that I spend with my family and kids." But the trouble is not just that residents are otherwise occupied. Their lack of involvement is deeply influenced by the pattern of suburban life itself. Because of steady employment, places to shop, and paid public officials, residents can get by without cultivating deep and lasting connections with their neighbors.

Community organizations compete for the scarce time and energy of suburban residents because each organization represents a different set of interests with which residents identify. One reason for loose connections to these organizations is that people do in fact have divided loyalties and are thus unwilling to devote very much time to an organization that represents only one kind of community for them.[13] Much of the energy that goes into these organizations is concerned with giving participants a sense of belonging, a feeling that there really is some community of which they are a part. Unfortunately, this is often at the expense of making a substantial contribution to solving the community's problems. Two people who are involved in civic activities in the suburbs provide examples of why it is difficult to achieve a strong sense of connection to the community.

Mara Wertheimer is a forty-four-year-old businesswoman who lives in a suburb of a large city on the West Coast. Mara is more extensively involved in the civic life of her community than many of her neighbors. She was temporarily one of the few women members of Rotary in her state. She is nominally a board member of the nonprofit daycare center her children used to attend and currently volunteers once in a while as a homeroom mother at their elementary school. She has also given a few hours over the past year to a group of women who want to create a home for abused women and children. As a single parent, she juggles her sons' needs with her own and with the demands of the consulting firm she runs, but she feels a responsibility to serve the community as well.

Jake O'Neill chairs the Hillsdale Memorial Day Parade Committee. It is responsible for organizing the main event that brings the local citizens together each year.[14] About 25,000 people live in Hillsdale, a middle-class community on the East Coast that grew from a small nineteenth-century outpost of inns and taverns to a bedroom suburb feeding commuters into one of the nation's largest cities. Approximately 10,000 of Hillsdale's residents turn out each Memorial Day for the parade. This is Jake O'Neill's tenth year on the parade committee. He runs one of the stores on the street down which the parade passes. At sixty-nine he should be thinking seriously about retiring, but he has too much energy to sit on the sidelines. He keeps the business running, takes an active role in the Hillsdale Business Association, goes to Mass every Sunday and Wednesday at the local Catholic church, attends veterans' functions at the American Legion, and makes sure the parade comes off smoothly.

Mara Wertheimer's connections to civic organizations are relatively loose. She found it easy to drop out of Rotary because she saw the long years she would have to devote to it in order to feel she really belonged. Her volunteering takes small amounts of time, and she will probably be doing something else in a year or two. Her most predictable commitment is spending time at her sons' school, but there are days when she has to cancel, just as there are evenings when she has to prepare her own reports instead of reading her sons' homework. On the whole, her civic involvement reflects her scattered commitments, including the facts that she does not work in the same town in which she lives, that her sons attend school in yet another neighborhood, that she cares deeply about her work, and that she identifies more with a women's group she has joined than with her immediate neighbors.

Jake O'Neill's interests are all concentrated in one community. His business in Hillsdale makes it more meaningful for him to head the parade committee than to participate in activities outside of Hillsdale. He sees the same people at the business association as on the parade committee. Several are members of his church and several belong to the American Legion.

Despite his attachment to Hillsdale, Jake O'Neill senses that the centrifugal forces evident in Mara Wertheimer's activities are beginning to have an impact on his community as well. His friends are traveling more than they used to, often to visit children and grandchildren who live in different parts of the country. Some are less willing to make commitments to civic organizations that might curtail their freedom to travel. Jake notices that newer residents shop and work elsewhere. He fears that the Memorial Day Parade gives them a temporary feeling of community but does not generate longer-term engagement.[15]

Jake O'Neill and Mara Wertheimer sense that part of the problem in their communities is that residents have little meaningful contact with public officials. Residents feel estranged from the larger political entities in which their communities are embedded. These entities seem so distant that it is easy to treat them as objects of scorn. For some residents, the personal scandals in which politicians and their aides become involved provide proof of their incompetence. Others seem almost gleeful about the inefficiencies of public officials: the bridge that falls down, the subway that caves in, the airport that opens late, the sports arena that costs twice as much as it should, the government contractors who take long coffee breaks in the shadows of their tractors. All occasion complacent smirks. If people are truly to make a difference in their communities, the grimaces say, it will have to be in small ways, through their jobs, with their families, in churches, and by volunteering; certainly not by getting involved in politics.[16]

But because many suburban residents demean political practices and institutions, the few who aspire to political influence can sometimes exercise an inordinate share of power—a possibility that raises concerns about how well democracy can be sustained when civic ties are too loose. This possibility is greater when voter turnout is low, as it often is in local elections. A man in Pennsylvania who has been active in Republican politics explains that approximately 60,000 people live in his district, 30,000 of whom are registered to vote, and as few as 10 percent turn out for primaries and special elections. Anyone who can get at least 1,500 votes for a particular candidate or issue is sure to win. In his view, three or four well-connected people can control local politics with little difficulty. A woman in another state says she was elected to the local planning board on a Democratic ticket shortly after graduating from high school. All she had done was show her loyalty to the party bosses by volunteering as a precinct worker during several campaigns.

Apart from controlling local party offices, a small number of suburbanites with political ambitions can organize powerful grassroots movements if they understand how to secure resources from the outside. Working around the lack of interest that characterizes many communities, they can pursue their political goals unimpeded by local opposition. Conservative religious movements, such as the Christian Coalition, have succeeded by combining local church networks with expertise from national offices to reach individuals in the community on political issues.[17] One local Coalition leader explains: "All I have to do is send out faxes through my phone tree and I can get a thousand people writing to Washington about some bill." National activists interested in protecting or extending citizens' rights to bear arms have been similarly effective at the local level.

An inside look at one such organization is available through the eyes of Peter Jackson, a twenty-seven-year-old computer specialist who is the founder of an effort to promote the carrying of handguns.[18] Peter became worried about crime a few years ago when a mother of a small child was abducted in the parking lot of a suburban mall by a man who forced her into her car at knifepoint and took her to a secluded place where he raped and killed her. The abduction took place in the same suburb where Peter's wife made home health visits as a community nurse. Peter was convinced that the only way to prevent such crimes was for people like his wife to carry handguns.

With a college buddy, Peter formed what he called the Coalition for Self-Defense and wrote a letter to the Association of Rifle and Pistol Clubs.

They were eager to help, sending an organizing kit and offering to pay minor costs of mounting a petition drive. Peter printed up 30,000 petitions to be sent to state officials whom he identified by calling the number in the telephone book for the state's Office of Legislative Services. He and his friend assembled the packets and distributed them to local gun stores. He recalls that they were "snapped up faster than you can imagine."

Soon after, Peter was invited to a meeting of a statewide organization called the Coalition of Sportsmen. Its leaders offered to help him distribute more petitions and invited him to participate in board meetings. From those meetings he learned that the government was threatening citizens' rights in other ways. For example, he learned that it was difficult to obtain licenses for high-caliber rifles even if they were to be used only for target practice. He also learned that there were at least 600,000 people in the state who could be mobilized to vote one way or the other and that elections for state and local office often hinged on only a few thousand votes.

Over the past two years Peter has been networking in every way he can to expand the influence of his coalition. He doesn't know his neighbors and worries that they may not agree with him, so he has not gone door to door and is careful about what he says at parties. He is also careful at work because he doesn't want to be labeled an extremist. He has posted a copy of the U.S. Constitution on his door and put a target with some bullet holes in it on his bulletin board. If someone's curiosity is piqued, he says he is a sportsman and has concerns about self-defense. Most of his networking involves contacting other organizations that may be able to put him in touch with people who share his views. He has found allies in the Libertarian Party and in some local organizations interested in jury reform, Civil War history, and religious freedom.

By coordinating with people in these other organizations, Peter has been able to maximize his efforts. They take turns writing op-ed pieces for the newspapers, generally masking the fact that they are in contact with one another. Sometimes they present a consolidated front, for example in inviting public officials to join them at "shootouts," or in organizing classes for women at gun clubs. At other times they divide up tasks to be more effective. Peter may scout out sources for public service announcements while someone from another organization prints fliers.

A computer specialist, Peter has also availed himself of the Internet to contact other people. He recently organized an electronic mailing list and now has over a hundred subscribers who share ideas about their right to bear arms. Peter maintains the list and posts announcements of events and pending legislation as well as copies of some of his editorials. Other subscribers post messages they have received from national organizations or simply air grievances and reactions to what they see on television. They also send e-mail messages to state legislators encouraging them to vote for or against particular bills.

In this respect Peter and his friends are different from many suburban residents. Many people either do not have access to the Internet or dislike using it because it is impersonal.[19] In contrast, Peter finds it an effective way of sharing information. He is less interested in developing soul mates and more intent on sharing practical information about guns and legislation.[20] For him, the Internet exemplifies how people can coordinate their civic efforts, despite the porousness of contemporary social life.

Peter's organization has not yet achieved its goals, and its members' views are still in a small minority according to national polls. But it has experienced some success, such as persuading one of the state legislators to introduce a bill that will make it easier for people to carry handguns. Because of his involvement, Peter feels he has a clearer sense of the dangers of government and a stronger conviction about his responsibilities as a citizen.

People like Peter Jackson who lead quiet lives in the suburbs are able to exercise civic influence by networking with a few other like-minded individuals. Their civic involvement is expressed primarily through special-interest groups. These groups connect their members with organizations that have similar agendas, often in other geographic areas, rather than bringing them into contact with a wide range of local organizations. Peter Jackson's gun organization is in regular contact with gun stores throughout the region, the National Rifle Association, a state organization concerned with property rights, and several other gun lobbies. Peter says he has little contact with other local organizations (in fact, cannot name any).

Special-interest groups like his are one of the ways suburban residents are adapting to current social conditions. Feeling a lack of ties to their immediate neighbors, many seek out like-minded people wherever they may be. One man talks about his activity in a local gay rights organization. It interacts mostly with Parents, Families, and Friends of Lesbians and Gays (PFFLAG), a gay and lesbian business organization, and similar organizations in neighboring cities. A woman who heads a sobriety self-help group has little contact with any local organizations other than the hospital. This is also true of a Parents Without Partners founder, whose group is part of an international network but has no contacts with local churches, government agencies, or service organizations. In short, the success of special-interest groups often does not require them to develop strong ties to their host communities. Proximity is no longer imperative to their sense of community.

In contrast to these special-interest groups, certain highly visible institutions in suburbs claim the interest of virtually everyone. The one institution that most suburban residents claim they care about is their school system. They may have little awareness of what the town council does or be oblivious to the presence of public welfare agencies or even the police, but their satisfaction or dissatisfaction with their community varies in proportion to how they feel about the schools.[21] Indeed, many people think that the schools are in a better position to solve community problems than almost any other organization, with the possible exception of churches and families. Residents mention deteriorating morals, broken homes, petty crime, and juvenile delinquency as threats to their neighborhoods, and then suggest that the schools could do the most to teach the kinds of values that would alleviate these problems. In similar fashion, national studies show that participation in school events is a significant contributor to more general feelings of attachment to one's community. For example, a study of parents of twelfth-graders found that 88 percent of those who often went with their son or daughter to school events felt involved in their neighborhood, whereas this figure dropped to 63 percent among those who did not attend school activities. It is likely that school involvement reinforces community attachment and vice versa.[22]

But public schools are perceived to be in crisis, and serious involvement in parent-teacher organizations and on school boards has been declining in recent decades. Participation falls far short of what many administrators would like. In a study of high school principals, only one in five reported that a quarter of parents were members of the PTA, and only one in six reported that a quarter of parents actually participated in PTA meetings. Only 7 percent of the principals said that a quarter of parents did volunteer work at the school.[23] The problems that schools are experiencing are clearly part of the malaise that troubles many people in the suburbs.

One of the reasons for the decline of sustained involvement in school organizations is the unpredictability of family schedules; working parents (mothers usually) may be able to make a commitment to attend a meeting now and then, but long-term involvement on a committee that meets regularly is too much for their schedule. Some people are burned out after taking on heavy responsibilities in the past and others are discouraged because fewer volunteers means being able to accomplish less. A more pressing problem is that the business of schools has become so complicated that few people feel they have the time to understand it fully. As a result, another style of civic involvement has emerged: serving almost full time in a highly specialized capacity, but for a relatively short period. Retired persons often serve in this way. Doing so is a way of becoming involved in one's community. But it is also an example of a loose connection: a short-term commitment that can be undertaken when one's job or family responsibilities have diminished.

This kind of involvement is one of the reasons organizations in the suburbs have been able to survive as well as they have. It can be illustrated through the activities of Ralph King, age sixty-four, who took early retirement from his job as an engineer for a public utility company and is now devoting himself to civic activities. He lives in a suburb of a major city. Nearly all the population are white and most earn incomes well above the national average. They take the commuter train into the city to work in high-rise office towers or drive a few miles in the other direction to an office park that houses companies specializing in insurance and satellite communications.

Compared to people in suburbs farther away from the city, the Kings live in a fairly stable neighborhood. Many of the families there settled two or three decades ago, raised their children, and are now looking ahead to retirement. As a result of its age, the suburb's infrastructure is beginning to show signs of decay. Despite the population's relative affluence, streets are sometimes in poor repair, shopping has mostly moved to megamalls in another township, and the public schools have deteriorated just enough to encourage an increase in the proportion of residents who send their children to private academies.

Over the past five years Ralph has become more actively involved in the community. At present he is serving as school board president. The school board oversees the education of approximately 2,800 children and is ultimately responsible to the community for the $34 million of tax money that it devotes each year to public education. It holds regular meetings twice a month and many other meetings and hearings on an ad hoc basis. One of its major tasks is developing and approving the annual budget. Hearings begin each fall and continue, including not only local citizens but also meetings with state officials, until the final vote is taken on June 30. The board also approves the curriculum, hires the superintendent and the principals, approves each decision involving the hiring or firing of a teacher, hears grievances from parents, and negotiates salaries and benefits with the teachers' union.

As president of the board, Ralph meets with the superintendent each Friday to go over the agenda of upcoming meetings and to talk about any other concerns that need to be communicated to the administrators or that the board needs to consider. He also meets regularly with the district's business manager, curriculum director, and personnel director. These meetings consist of reviewing their work, receiving proposals from them that need to be taken to the full board, and generally staying in touch. Ralph also meets periodically with subcommittees of the board, and he is often the point of contact for meetings with teachers, groups of concerned parents, representatives of the PTA, state officials, labor negotiators, and lawyers.

All these activities take about twenty hours a week. Ralph considers the school board a half-time job, and he recognizes that many people would not have the time to serve in this capacity. When his own children were in school, most of the school board members were women whose husbands earned incomes sufficient to support them. Now it is much harder to find women to serve who are not employed. Those who have the time are generally rich or retired, and many of the latter are unable to put in the long hours and attend the late-night meetings that the board requires.

Much of Ralph King's time on the board is spent in gathering, processing, and exchanging information. In an earlier era (say, when Tocqueville visited), communities could make decisions about their schools with much less communication. As recently as a half-century ago, a county with a population the size of Ralph's suburb might have had as many as a hundred separate school districts, each with its own one-room school within walking distance of nearby families, and most decisions could be made by those families, with some coordination by the county superintendent. Ralph's board has to deal with many more governmental entities and with the many different professionals on whom education now depends—from curriculum experts to auditors and roofing contractors. Much of the information needed to coordinate these activities is technical, and the school board is a place for receiving reports and studying technical documents. But it also involves a small core group who know each other well enough to understand their different points of view and to communicate informally. "It's a matter of communication and understanding each other and listening," Ralph summarizes.

It is critical for Ralph's school board to be in regular communication with civic organizations and agencies at the state and regional levels. However, most of the small, ad hoc civic organizations that have sprung up in suburban communities in recent years provide few of these kinds of connections. Instead, they bring people together for an hour or two a week to work on specific projects and then disband. Someone like Ralph King who gives so much time and energy is virtually a nonprofit professional, even though he serves as a volunteer. It takes professional expertise to run an organization as complicated as the school board. Even though the PTA in his district still functions, it cannot often supply anyone who can sustain attendance at many meetings and occasional hearings. Once in a while, a group of parents may become incensed enough about a problem that they temporarily form a special-interest group, and there have been a few philanthropic organizations established for such specific tasks as raising money for a new scoreboard. But most of the work of the schools is done by the staff and by the few volunteers like Ralph King who have the time and skills to serve effectively.

The service requirements of the school board typify what has been happening in many of the other voluntary associations that are still prominent in suburban communities. They function less often than in the past by recruiting a broad membership base within the community and elevating some of the more committed of those members to positions of authority. Instead, they resemble a system of nodes connected by strategic exchanges of information and personnel, with a floating pool of volunteers and casual participants who move on and off the stage as dictated by local events. The nodes are likely to be staffed by paid professionals or by a few heavily involved volunteers who bring special expertise to their jobs. They network with people in business or in other civic organizations, hold public hearings, solicit volunteers, and spend much of their time staying abreast of regulations, funding opportunities, and budgets.

A strength of these arrangements is that they take on the complex tasks of running large-scale community organizations, such as schools, hospitals, and human service agencies, more effectively than can civic associations that are self-contained and composed largely of well-meaning amateurs. An additional strength is that citizens' participation in these efforts can expand and contract as needs arise, rather than having to be maintained at constant levels through social events and special projects. The weakness is that many residents are able to ride on the efforts of others without becoming involved at all. As a result, the few who function as nonprofit professionals complain of red tape, financial uncertainties, and burnout, while others perceive (correctly) that their communities are run by the short-term, strategic activities of specialists rather than the long-term commitment of people who care about one another.

It is nevertheless important to understand what the newer arrangements accomplish. In one suburb, where the Kiwanis club had recently expired after its membership fell from 75 in the early 1970s to fewer than 30 in the early 1990s, the YWCA had grown to a membership of 5,000 served by a staff of 100 and by several hundred volunteers, ranging from many who helped a few hours a week to a former Kiwanian who spent at least ten hours each week keeping the organization's finances straight. Critics might dismiss the YWCA, calling it a business providing swimming lessons and fitness classes. Yet the YWCA brought about a significant reduction in juvenile delinquency by starting an afterschool basketball league in the winter and a T-ball program in the spring.

In the same community, church attendance has been declining modestly in recent years. But the churches have pooled their resources and opened a food distribution center, and are doing more to help the needy than they were a decade ago. The hospital is no longer the community-operated clinic it was in the 1950s, having added several new wings and a large ambulatory care facility, but its coordinator of community services spends more time making sure public health issues are addressed and enlisting more occasional volunteers than would have been conceivable a generation ago. There is a new nonprofit organization that serves the developmental needs of handicapped children through a combination of paid and volunteer help. Several of the banks in town have made interest-free loans to these organizations, and one of the law firms provides voluntary legal advice. Rotary remains active, mostly by working with nonprofit organizations instead of initiating projects of its own. For all these reasons, life functions pretty well for the people who live in this suburb, even though many of them sense that their community is not quite as cohesive as they imagine it was in the past.

Although volunteering in suburbs is often sporadic or limited to short-term projects, large membership organizations still play an important role in civic affairs, just as they do in the economy. Elks and Kiwanis may have downsized, but they are still massive compared to many of the newer networks that have sprung up in recent years, and some of these organizations—such as Rotary and Hadassah—have retained large memberships.

The members of these larger and more established organizations are more committed to being involved over the long haul, and therefore are more readily available when new issues arise. They tend to feel more connected to the larger community and to hang around after the meeting to exchange gossip about politics and community affairs. Yet both established organizations and loose networks play important and complementary roles in communities. Indeed, established organizations increasingly generate loose connections. Their members help facilitate temporary alliances and draw other people from the community into short-term civic commitments, be they opportunities to volunteer a few hours a year to help the needy or chances to participate in a self-help group. The resources these organizations can provide are like ballast that gives stability to a ship sailing through turbulent waters.

Those who worry about the instability of loose connections can sleep better at night knowing that many of these activities are tethered to established civic organizations. The new forms have a symbiotic relationship with the older ones, and as in all symbiosis, the benefits flow in both directions. Established organizations are able to accomplish more in their communities by cultivating loose ties than they could if they permitted only members to participate. In so doing, however, established organizations also limit themselves, using some of their energies to promote new coalitions rather than for their own development. This may help to explain the recent decline in traditional memberships.

How an established civic organization can do more by cultivating a wider variety of activities, including short-term projects and innovative coalitions, is well illustrated in the work of Hadassah. The largest women's volunteer organization in the world (with activities in thirty countries), Hadassah includes 380,000 members in the United States alone. It was founded in 1912 by Henrietta Szold for the purpose of setting up a maternity center in Palestine. During World War II Hadassah was instrumental in helping thousands of children flee extermination in Europe, and over the years it has retained its interest in health care issues. Hadassah University Medical Center in Jerusalem houses clinics, research, maternity centers, a medical school, a school of nursing, and other institutes of technology and education which support the hospital. In the United States Hadassah raises money for programs in Israel and promotes local efforts to improve awareness of health and reproductive issues, to attract young people, and to lobby on a wide range of national policy issues.[24]

Sara Mermel is the president of a Hadassah chapter on the West Coast that has approximately 600 members, about 10 percent fewer than a decade ago.[25] She is a speech pathologist who shifted from full-time to half-time employment three years ago at the age of sixty. Her inspiration to join Hadassah came twenty-five years ago when she and her husband visited the Medical Center in Jerusalem, but the idea "lay fallow" for several years. Then, after moving to their present community, she decided to join some Jewish organizations, including Hadassah. She was working full time and her two sons were in high school, so she attended few meetings, making time only for those which genuinely interested her. Fifteen years passed, and eventually someone asked her to serve on the program committee. Still working full time, she accepted reluctantly, and what she saw did not immediately impress her. There was conflict within the leadership and a lack of vision. But when she retired from her full-time job, she took on the presidency of the organization as a way of keeping active.

The chapter that Sara Mermel heads devotes about half its energies to raising money for Hadassah projects in Israel. The remaining half of its efforts focus on the United States. At the local level, it works closely with the six synagogues in its area to draw women into its projects. It prints a monthly newsletter filled with announcements of upcoming events, stories about recent successes, and information culled from the national media and from other organizations' newsletters. Recent events have included a luncheon lecture by a member of Hadassah's national board, a fashion show, a book discussion series, an all-day institute for women interested in exploring the relationships between Hadassah and their "religious lifestyle," a Chanukah fundraiser, and a lecture about Jewish women's issues by a local college professor. Sara speaks glowingly of the organization, saying that its activities are "mushrooming" and that its potential is limited only by the time and energy she has to devote to it.

From comments like these one might not guess that Hadassah has been struggling with questions about its identity. Several years ago its national office commissioned a survey and a series of focus groups to determine more precisely why it was having difficulty attracting new members. "We learned that the majority of women believe Jewish organizations in general do not welcome 'newcomers'; are overly preoccupied with fundraising with not enough focus on community building, spirituality, social action activities, and social interaction," said Shulamit Reinharz, who headed the research effort. As a result, many Jewish women have become disenfranchised from the Jewish world. These problems, compounded by growing numbers of interfaith marriages and qualms among younger women about Zionist activities, have forced Hadassah to rethink its mission and how best to carry out its civic activities.[26]

Sara's chapter has responded by aggressively seeking alliances with non-Jewish (as well as other Jewish) organizations. The most vivid example is an interfaith alliance to combat right-wing religious groups that have been working to shut down abortion clinics and pregnancy counseling centers. This alliance is little more than a paper organization at the moment, but it has its own chair, its own board of directors, and its own newsletter. Hadassah is listed simply as one of a number of sponsoring organizations, even though it has supplied most of the leadership. Other members include mainline Protestant churches, Seventh-Day Adventists, Muslim organizations, Sikh and Buddhist temples, and civil liberties groups. In addition to lobbying state and local officials to protect reproductive rights, the alliance has waged a campaign against a conservative Christian effort to promote prayer in the public schools and has sponsored a lecture series on freedom of religion.

The other kind of activity that has proven successful is short-term, task-specific projects. These depend on temporary coalitions and short-term volunteers.[27] Were it not for Hadassah, many of these connections would not be made. Its role in the community, despite a continuing struggle for membership, has been to provide ballast against the tides that have been making it harder to solicit long-term civic participation. Despite her enormous enthusiasm, Sara says that taking on the leadership has been like "being pulled into a maelstrom." She says it looked like an interesting position at first but quickly became a "huge complex" of things that demanded more time, skill, and energy than she had ever imagined. Finding herself lying awake at night worrying, she decided it was time to pull back from the maelstrom for her own protection. It was also time to scale back her expectations of what the organization could do by itself. This is one of the main reasons she is focusing on building coalitions.

The stories told by members of Lions clubs, Kiwanis, Rotary, and Junior League are much the same. Membership is either declining or barely holding steady, often with retirees doing most of the volunteering, and often with new programs receiving emphasis. Members speak eloquently of national and international programs, as if to ward off criticism of focusing only on local needs, but their activities demonstrate the great extent to which these organizations depend on strong local attachments. Typically, volunteer time is devoted chiefly to attending meetings, serving on committees, and working on local projects, such as pancake breakfasts or recycling programs, that raise money which is then allocated in small amounts to agencies that actually do the work of helping others. The participants are thus able to experience camaraderie with other members, to feel involved in their communities, and to reinforce their sense that people in their community are pulling together. At the same time, much of what they are actually supporting consists of newer, more loosely structured agencies and programs, such as a Parents Anonymous group, a violence-prevention program in the schools, or a shelter for abused women. To survive, they are having to develop their own form of loose connections. Traditional civic organizations are still important in most suburbs, but their effectiveness depends increasingly on strategic alliances.

Insularity remains a problem for suburban communities even though many organizations reach out to the wider world and even though travel and communication bring suburban residents into closer contact with that world. Indeed, some research suggests that insularity may be increasing as a result of economic shifts that have brought more stores and corporate headquarters into suburban areas, while other studies suggest that political campaigns have increasingly been catering to this insularity.[28] Many suburban residents are tacitly aware that their quiet neighborhoods are part of larger regions to which they need to be attentive. As one woman remarks, "The world's too small for you to isolate yourself; you need to be involved in the region. You can't just ignore other communities." But in many cases, such comments seem to express an intellectual conviction that people find difficult to put into practice. The wider region includes places they have never been and would not want to go. In their bones, they feel little attachment to it, except perhaps to its professional baseball or football team or some part of it that is relevant to their own profession.

This insularity is especially evident in attitudes toward the inner city. Many suburbanites say they never venture into the inner city at all. They talk about "shopping downtown" as an anachronism, noting that the downtown area has been in a long-term decline as a result of department stores closing and new shopping malls having been built in the suburbs twenty or thirty years ago. Their impressions are shaped by local television stories about shootings and fires. Downtown is a source of crime, a place where victims live who sometimes evoke sympathy, but more often a place that is "just not safe to go through." Downtown is also perceived to be racially different from the suburbs—"a euphemism for 'the black community,'" one man observes—and is regarded as a place of racial tensions. As one woman admits, "I like to ignore all that stuff. It doesn't affect me personally."

Some people who live in the suburbs participate occasionally in activities that benefit people in the inner city: volunteering for an hour a week at a clinic or a housing project, or helping at a local church that sends food or clothing outside the neighborhood. Nationally, 20 percent of suburban residents say they have done volunteer work in a poor inner-city area; yet only 8 percent have done so within the past year. The suburban citizen who becomes deeply engaged in problems outside his or her own community is thus the rare exception.

Despite their efforts to help others, suburban service clubs and churches are not immune from such insularity. As their budgets have shrunk, they have focused more on local needs and have devoted fewer resources to national and international programs. Some members have been concerned about the disjuncture between local and nonlocal activities, arguing that there should be more integration between the two. These arguments become more compelling as suburban residents find themselves in the midst of conflicts brought about by the changing composition of metropolitan areas. Overcoming insularity then takes on such practical connotations as thinking about conflicts in racially integrated school systems or addressing the interests of new immigrants.

The struggle to overcome suburban insularity is illustrated by the efforts of Anna Murray, age fifty-three, a mother and wife who lives in a relatively isolated suburb on the edge of a medium-sized city. She and her husband have graduate degrees, hers in education and his in engineering, and both have been the victims of downsizing. His job at a manufacturing establishment was phased out ten years ago when heavy industry in the region began relocating overseas. Her teaching job disappeared several years earlier as local schools anticipated the decline of the regional economy. He has been a self-employed engineering consultant since then, working from a basement office at home, but he has seldom been able to secure an equivalent of full-time work. She has worked part time teaching English as a second language and has tried to supplement her salary through part-time jobs at nonprofit organizations.

Anna Murray's interest in issues that transcend the local community dates back twelve years to a time when she was teaching English as a second language through a program run by a Catholic social agency. The priest in charge of the agency was attempting to relocate refugee families from Southeast Asia and encouraged Anna and her husband to provide housing for one of the families. They did so, and through the experience became interested in promoting peace and intercultural dialogue.

The peace organization they joined focused on promoting cultural exchange between citizens of the United States and the Soviet Union. After the collapse of the Soviet Union Anna decided to work on issues closer to home, especially racial and ethnic conflicts. Her conviction that this was an important issue was reinforced by an intensive training program on such conflicts. At the end of the program the participants attended a film about racial violence that had just appeared in the theaters. After the film Anna was standing in the parking lot talking with some of the others when a shot was fired. "I rushed over and a woman was screaming and holding her husband's head in her lap, rocking back and forth on the pavement, and a figure was running away. They had been driving out of the parking lot and a young man had sashayed back and forth in front of the car and wouldn't move, and the man had gotten out to have words and was shot in the head."

The difficulty was to get anybody in her own community to support a program aimed at healing racial tensions. At the time Anna was working part time for the peace organization she had joined earlier. It was faltering, its board members feeling burned out and sensing that it needed a new focus. Anna persuaded them to rename the organization and shift its attention toward intercultural dialogue and conflict resolution. There were some early successes. She recalls an Anglo-Latino dialogue that brought residents from two sides of the city together to discuss their perceptions of each other. Each group was able to express some of its fears about the other. On another occasion 900 students gathered in the high school gymnasium to talk about tensions between blacks and whites; it was all Anna and another woman could do to keep the assembly from turning violent, but they succeeded and the students were able to express feelings that had long been smoldering. But these events were the exceptions.

The problem was typified for Anna a few months after the high school assembly when she was invited to set up a display of curricular materials on race relations and diversity during a faculty workshop at the same school; only three teachers stopped to talk, and none of them took materials. On another occasion she mailed information packets to all forty-five school districts in the city offering to provide training in race relations and diversity, and she received no replies. The donor base for her organization began to shrink dramatically.

Over the past three years the organization has found itself drawn toward teaching a new method of conflict resolution in schools called peer mediation. A typical case involves a shoving match between two students or tension between a student and a teacher. Anna will be called in for a few weeks to get the parties involved to talk about their anger, confront each other in a nonviolent way, discuss deeper issues contributing to their conflict, and find ways to get along better. The school districts have money to pay for this kind of activity.

The trajectory evident in Anna Murray's story is not unique. What started as an effort to promote interaction and understanding across cultures has shifted to a kind of therapeutic enterprise. Rather than attempting to bring Anglo and Latino neighborhoods together, Anna spends most of her time helping students in her own community talk out their anger toward one another. This is what she is able to get financial support to do, and it does help people on an individual basis.

Stories like this are not atypical. Although suburban residents give lip service to the idea of helping others, they are capable of insulating themselves from serious social problems, and they are reluctant to favor social programs that might benefit others at expense to themselves. A mid-1990s national study of attitudes toward specific programs is revealing: 64 percent of white suburbanites favored major spending cuts in public assistance and welfare programs, 53 percent favored cuts in food stamp programs, 52 percent in federal aid for cities, 48 percent in legal aid for poor people, and 42 percent wanted to reduce tax credits for low-income families.[29]

As the foregoing examples suggest, civic involvement in suburban America is enormously diverse, and it is by no means dead despite the decline of some traditional membership organizations. Yet this involvement also registers the influences of residential mobility, the commuter lifestyle, two-career marriages, divorce, corporate downsizing, and the prevalence of information technologies. Suburban residents generally enjoy being well-off enough to be the givers of services rather than the recipients. Although it troubles them that neighbors are seldom their friends, they define community as much in terms of ambience as in terms of social relationships. The fact that a neighbor's lawn is neatly trimmed is often more important than whether they ever speak to that neighbor. Crime, drug use, problems in the schools, maintaining the streets, traffic, mistrust of government, and the influences of neighboring cities are all of concern to suburban residents; yet many of them are affected so infrequently or indirectly by these problems that they rarely mobilize community movements entirely for the preservation of their own way of life. More often they speak of wanting to help others, even though these may be their own children, and their interest in service is still reinforced by civic-minded individuals who do the lion's share of the work needed to provide such opportunities.

The porousness of suburban life is evident in the ways in which people volunteer for community activities. Although many suburbanites still hold memberships in service organizations, churches and synagogues, clubs, and fraternal orders, the most common way of doing volunteer work is to through an activity that requires relatively little time commitment over a predefined or brief period. Thus a man like Jake O'Neill can get a few people to help organize the Memorial Day parade by promising that they will not have to spend more than a few hours a year, and a woman like Mara Wertheimer can help at her sons' school for a few years and choose a few other activities that dovetail easily with her career.

The civic involvement that characterizes suburban life is conducted almost entirely in the private sphere. Volunteers participate in service organizations or through churches and synagogues; those who commute outside their communities volunteer at nonprofit organizations, as do those who work as nonprofit professionals. Self-help groups are mostly run by private organizations as well. This pattern means that few suburbanites come into direct contact with government agencies or have reason to think about how these agencies function except during election campaigns or when they receive tax notices. Unless they become involved in "causes," as Peter Jackson did because of his interest in gun ownership, they are likely to perceive state and national politics as distant issues toward which they can choose to be indifferent.

The suburban residents who do become involved in volunteer efforts make an obvious and important difference. Without them, many of the nonprofit organizations that serve the needy would not be able to function. Their activities are nevertheless structured in a way that limits their effectiveness. Jake O'Neill keeps a spirit of community alive by organizing the Memorial Day parade, but this event is mostly symbolic, giving Hillsdale residents feeling of being part of their community without their having to devote any time to it. Mara Wertheimer's scattered volunteer activities give her a sense of being part of the larger metropolitan area in which she lives, but she feels frustrated that she has so little time or energy to devote to them. Peter Jackson's work on behalf of gun ownership has put him in touch with kindred spirits and given him a script with which to express his fears about random violence, but it has also convinced him that politicians cannot be trusted and caused him to doubt that American democracy is a workable system.

Ralph King is carrying the school system on his back, functioning more like a nonprofit professional than a volunteer. His experience with the school board reveals why many residents feel they have neither the time nor the expertise to volunteer in such capacities. Sara Mermel is animated by her involvement in Hadassah, and her efforts show the important role that traditional service organizations play in anchoring other volunteer activities. She also illustrates how these organizations are having to adapt to suburban tastes by forming self-help groups and providing easier ways in which volunteers can become involved. Anna Murray's story is equally instructive, showing how community activities are sparked by good-hearted people whose careers in the helping professions have been detoured by an uncertain job market and how much the success of these activities depends on the availability of public funding. Although her efforts to promote peace and interethnic understanding are sorely needed, they also illustrate how a culture that emphasizes good feelings and warm relationships can direct such efforts into unanticipated channels.

Despite residents' perceptions that their communities are falling apart, most suburbs continue to function fairly well. The reason is that most middle-class suburbanites can fend for themselves or rely on friends and relatives when they need help. In addition, established civic organizations still play a vital role in most communities, and this role is augmented by many short-term forms of civic involvement. Both the perceptions and the civic activities are shaped by the porousness of suburban life. This same porousness permits many suburban residents to focus on their own interests, without having to confront the serious problems that are prevalent in many other communities.

5

Against the Odds
in the Inner City

OF THE MANY AMERICANS who have not fared well as a result of the increasing porousness of the nation's institutions, the most substantial proportion is concentrated in inner-city areas. Because of AIDS, poverty, crime, joblessness, and despair, these neighborhoods are dying. A generation ago many of these problems were less acute, even though they were serious, and in recent years the number of services available for dealing with them has declined significantly.[1] Fiscal problems are partly to blame, judging from a recent study of municipal officials, but evidence also suggests that economic growth in larger metropolitan areas often does not provide added revenue for inner-city programs; youth violence has thus been rising at the same time that public schools, family services, and even garbage collection and police protection have been deteriorating.[2] The decline has also been notable in the number of community service organizations in inner-city neighborhoods. Churches remain, but often with severely limited resources, and the kinds of civic associations that are still relatively common in the suburbs, such as service clubs and fraternal organizations, have disappeared almost entirely. Inner-city residents are far less likely than suburbanites to be satisfied with their neighborhoods as places in which to live.[3] Whereas loose connections generate perceptions of malaise but function fairly effectively in suburbs, they are much less effective in dealing with the problems in inner cities.

The nation's cities include many wealthy and middle-class residents as well as poor ones, and these more affluent inhabitants play an important role in urban charities and service organizations. Yet poverty is increasingly concentrated in cities. As recently as the late 1950s, fully two-thirds of Americans in poverty lived outside of cities; in the early 1990s, approximately half of the nation's poor lived inside central cities. This means that the number of inner-city neighborhoods with large proportions of poor people has been growing. Specifically, the number of census tracts in which at least 40 percent of the population is below the poverty line increased by 579 during the 1970s and by an additional 624 during the 1980s. By the early 1990s many inner-city areas were being overwhelmed by high concentrations of poverty.[4]

One reason for this increase in inner-city poverty is that many white and black middle-class families have fled to the suburbs, leaving behind those who are worse off economically and providing opportunities for new immigrants with low incomes to find inexpensive dwellings. In addition, manufacturing establishments that once provided jobs paying moderate wages in inner cities have closed, while newer businesses have located in suburbs and rural areas, leaving inner-city workers unemployed or having to seek low-paying service jobs. Evidence also points to the continuing effect of segregated housing markets on inner-city poverty.[5]

Inner-city residents are keenly aware of the problems in their neighborhoods. In the Civic Involvement Survey, 65 percent of those living in central cities said drug abuse was a serious problem in their communities; 54 percent said this about crime, 47 percent about a lack of jobs, and 44 percent about problems in the schools. The perceptions of these problems are significantly higher among inner-city residents who live in low-income neighborhoods and who are African American or Hispanic.[6]

The pastor of an inner-city church summarizes the problems this way: "There's a downward spiral of decay and poverty within the city. Folks who are newly arrived, folks who don't have as much knowledge of how to operate within our society, people that have more marginal skills and less marketable skills are forced, basically, to purchase homes or to rent homes in areas that are continually disintegrating. So a lot of folks with a lot of problems are concentrated in one area. The schools are overwhelmed, and those who live out a ways from the city have no stake in making that better."

Other community leaders draw a strong connection between inner-city problems and changing economic and cultural factors. The economic factor is a widening disparity between the incomes of people at the top and those of people at the bottom, a disparity that is often evident within a few city blocks. The cultural factor is an accompanying sense among the rich that they are somehow absolved of responsibility for the poor, or that the poor should be able to fend for themselves. One leader puts it this way: "We used to have programs based on the idea that 'this is something we're doing so that children don't go hungry because we're not the kind of people that let our children go hungry,' but now we say, 'this is a hand-out to somebody who should take responsibility for their own lives and get themselves off the dole and make enough money to feed their kid, and if they can't do that, well, we should take their kid away from them.'"

In many communities the decline of inner-city neighborhoods is also attributable to state and local tax policies that encourage developers to build in suburban areas, where taxpayers are asked to subsidize the cost of roads and sewers, rather than rebuilding urban areas, where such incentives are absent. One person, noting that inner-city areas are becoming "donut holes of poverty surrounded by donuts of affluence," emphasizes that zoning and insular political jurisdictions have long allowed suburban residents to escape paying taxes to deal with region-wide problems. Another person, who works in the inner city and lives in the suburbs, admits that he spends a third of his life in the former but pays no taxes to support the services he uses while he is there.

What the sociologist William Julius Wilson has termed "the new urban poverty" has had a particularly profound impact on African Americans living in inner-city areas. In the fifteen predominantly black, high-poverty neighborhoods Wilson and his team studied in Chicago, only 37 percent of adults were employed during a typical week in 1990, compared with 54 percent in other black communities and 57 percent in the city at large.[7] Besides the loss of employment and income, residents of these neighborhoods have suffered from cutbacks in welfare programs and declining availability of low-income housing. These conditions make it more difficult for residents to mobilize their energies and act collectively.

Because the new urban poverty is defined increasingly in terms of its geographic concentration, the character of civic involvement must be understood in terms of the social ecology of entire neighborhoods, rather than as an attribute of individuals or families alone.[8] Lower incomes and sporadic employment or permanent unemployment have made it harder for voluntary associations to maintain stable memberships in low-income neighborhoods. Many of these neighborhoods have lost population, leaving fewer people to participate in organizations, and those who have moved to other neighborhoods are more likely to have been community leaders in the first place. Labor union membership has declined in propor-

tion to the closing of manufacturing establishments. Those who are unemployed are less likely to hear about organizations through networks that
other people develop at work. Some evidence suggests that residents who
are better off may also isolate themselves from their neighbors for fear of
becoming involved in crime and drugs. Other evidence shows that political participation has declined significantly in inner cities, compared with
relatively modest declines in suburbs.[9]

In the Civic Involvement Survey, the effect of these factors is clearly in
evidence. Residents of low-income, central-city areas are significantly less
likely than other respondents to say they can count on their neighbors for
help, even though many claim to be acquainted with their neighbors. In
addition, membership in civic and other voluntary organizations is significantly lower in low-income, central-city areas than elsewhere, and this
difference persists when most characteristics of individual respondents are
taken into account (see Methods, Tables 4–5).

Other national surveys show that membership in voluntary organizations has declined most significantly among people with the characteristics of those who live in such neighborhoods. Between 1974 and 1991
the proportion of adults who belonged to at least one voluntary organization fell by 12 percentage points among people in low education categories, and by only 3 points among people in high education categories;
similarly disproportionate declines were evident among respondents
whose fathers had less than a high school education, those from lower-in-
come backgrounds, African Americans, and those with larger numbers of
children.[10]

Residents of inner-city neighborhoods are often aware of these declining memberships, attributing them to the fact that voluntary organizations
no longer exist in their communities or to factors impeding participation,
such as a lack of child care or transportation.[11] The director of a housing
project in a midwestern city observes: "Transportation is always difficult.
Child care is always difficult. Just getting a meeting together can be an
incredible hassle for many of the families that you really want to have
there. You've got to find ways of making sure that those kids are taken care
of, that the people can get to and from a place, and that there be food."

More subtle factors are also involved. A woman from a low-income
neighborhood in the Northeast explains: "I think poor people don't feel
they have as much to offer. I think people who are more financially sound
feel as though they have more to offer." When she volunteers she notices

that other people in her neighborhood "apologize a lot for themselves" and "worry that they won't be able to be a volunteer because maybe they don't have transportation." Many of the people in her neighborhood cannot easily be reached because they have no telephones. A woman in another low-income neighborhood thinks it is harder for people to get involved because of declining support from their extended families: "When I was a new mother, my mother-in-law would come up very willingly and babysit for me when there was something I needed to do. But now that doesn't happen." The reason, she says, is that young mothers are more likely to live farther away from their extended families.

The virtual absence of traditional voluntary organizations in inner cities is evident in a 1994 study of African Americans living in inner-city areas and in suburbs. Only 15 percent of the former claimed to be members of any kind of voluntary organization (other than a church), whereas 37 percent of the suburban residents were members of at least one such organization. Moreover, virtually all of the inner-city memberships were in neighborhood centers, professional societies, or trade unions; only 1 percent of the inner-city residents belonged to service clubs, 1 percent to fraternal orders, and 2 percent to volunteer organizations.[12]

An important reason for low levels of civic participation in inner cities is fear. People stay at home because they are afraid to venture out. In one national study, 30 percent of parents of high school students said they had attended no meetings at their children's school, but among those who said their neighborhood was less safe than most neighborhoods, this figure rose to 43 percent. Only 17 percent of parents in unsafe neighborhoods had done school volunteer work, compared with 29 percent overall. In a national survey of parents of twelfth-graders, 83 percent of those who felt their neighborhood was "very safe" also felt that they were very involved in it; this proportion was only 43 percent among those who felt their neighborhood was "very unsafe." Of those who perceived their neighborhood as safe, only 14 percent had never attended school activities with their son or daughter; among those who thought the neighborhood was unsafe, this figure was 26 percent.[13]

At the same time that membership in voluntary organizations has declined, the role of nonprofit organizations that depend on public funding and that provide specific social services has expanded. One indication of their importance is that 37 percent of African American women with lower levels of education in central cities were employed in social services in the early 1990s. Many of these jobs were in hospitals, nursing care facilities, child care centers, and human service organizations.[14] This suggests that civic involvement in low-income neighborhoods may be increasingly centered around nonprofit organizations rather than voluntary membership associations.

The character of civic involvement in inner-city neighborhoods is thus quite different from that in suburban areas. Suburban residents can become involved in their communities by developing loose ties with any number of civic associations, and these organizations are still able to address some of the problems of the community, especially if a somewhat insular definition of the community is accepted. Other than the schools, public institutions such as police departments, city councils, hospitals, prisons, parole boards, and human service agencies figure little in the civic consciousness of suburban residents. This situation is reversed in inner-city neighborhoods, with civic involvement seldom connected with voluntary community organizations and more often linked with public institutions. Thus for suburban residents politics is more likely to be a remote abstraction, but for inner-city residents it is an inescapable reality.

The reasons people give for getting involved in their communities are often quite different in inner-city areas than in the suburbs. Rather than speaking about self-fulfillment, they talk of necessity and obligation. Necessity means that things have gotten so bad that it becomes impossible to stay uninvolved. Whatever the problems (crime, drugs, racism, police brutality), people say they can no longer ignore them. Obligation means feeling a strong responsibility to one's children or neighbors, especially if one has experience, connections, time, or other resources that neighbors may not have. Volunteers are thus more likely than in suburbs to say they are acting on behalf of their communities and doing so to address an intolerable situation.

This is not to say that people in low-income neighborhoods are particularly altruistic, but there is often a stronger sense of community when people do get involved. One woman reports that her attitude for a long time was, "I don't want to be bothered." But her neighbors kept after her, saying, "Come on, you can speak for us, you can do it." Some also have a feeling of gratitude that motivates them to pay back by helping in the community. For instance, one woman says that she made a vow after being on welfare to work whenever she could and also to try to improve the neighborhood. Once, when she was very sick, she promised God that she would help needy people in the community if God would let her live.

But mistrust of government flourishes in inner cities, and it takes a different cast than it does in suburbs. Suburbanites often laugh at government ineptitude, but inner-city residents cannot take lightly issues that affect their very survival, such as health, welfare, and shelter. They talk about the power of public officials to get things done—and about their unresponsiveness to inner-city needs. Public policy is disturbingly effective, in their view, but it is dictated by interests other than their own. The sports stadium that displaces their neighborhoods is evidence that city officials can get things done; its private boxes for the wealthy are evidence that the stadium's reason for existing is to serve the elite. The flight of industrial jobs from their neighborhoods and their replacement by low-paying fast-food and social service jobs are proof that politicians are selling out their communities for the benefit of outsiders. Government is perceived as "them" and as very distinct from "us."

Civic involvement in inner-city neighborhoods, therefore, not only has to address serious social problems but also has to enlist scarce resources from public agencies in a climate that breeds mistrust. Local efforts are often hampered by the unavailability of these resources, and people who cultivate them successfully become part of a public system that may provide few opportunities for employment elsewhere. The absence of private community organizations, other than churches, is one of the principal reasons why well-intentioned volunteers are unable to be more effective. According to some leaders, one remedy to this problem is to enlist the support of community organizations from the suburbs—but this remedy is often limited by the insularity of those organizations.

The changes in civic involvement in inner-cities are apparent in the experiences of Matilda Martin, a woman in her seventies who has been involved in civic organizations for almost forty years. She is an African American who grew up in one of the poorest sections of East Harlem. As a young woman she faced discrimination because of her race and because of her weight. After being denied admission to a nursing school and then losing a job with the telephone company, she married and settled down to raise a family that eventually included five children. Shortly after the last child was born her husband deserted her, leaving her penniless and living in a tenement building. That winter the utility company turned off her heat because she was unable to pay the bill, and soon afterward her baby died of pneumonia.

The organization Matilda Martin is involved in is called Union House. It was founded more than a century ago as part of the settlement house movement initiated by Jane Addams. Matilda had known of its existence as a child, but her first direct contact was when she went to beg for assistance after her baby died. In addition to lending her money, Union House was able to give her work from time to time doing secretarial or clerical jobs. After her children were grown, she was able to pay back some of this kindness by doing volunteer work for the organization.

One activity for which she has volunteered over the years is voter regis- tration. With other volunteers, she canvasses tenement buildings to make sure everyone is registered to vote. She works with tenants' associations in some of the buildings to distribute forms and in other cases goes door to door. Sometimes the volunteers set up a table in front of the grocery store, and sometimes they hand out literature at bus stops. Before each major election Union House advertises an information session for people who want to come and see a voting booth for the first time and learn how to use a voting machine. On election day itself they provide child care while mothers go to the polls.

In recent years Matilda Martin has also become involved in a "kinship program" through Union House. It is for people her own age who are raising their grandchildren because the children's parents cannot do so. In a growing number of cases, one or both parents are dying of AIDS. She says the program gives "support, encouragement, strength, revitalization" to people who at the age of sixty or seventy are raising a second family because "their son or daughter has died or the grandchild is messed up." An important part of the work is to provide emotional support. "When you find out you have AIDS," she says, "you're sort of in a stupor. You're in denial, then you're in anger."

Although many of Matilda's volunteer activities have focused on the needs of particular individuals, she is a firm believer that it takes political muscle to get things done, and she credits Union House with bringing the right mix of people together, putting them in touch with those in power, and providing ways to share the inevitable disappointments that come from working through political channels. Some people tell her she must be crazy, she says, because anyone who lobbies for better schools or hous- ing or bus service is going to "get hurt." She has been able to "keep going" because she has people at Union House to share her thoughts with and she knows whom to contact, rather than feeling she has to do everything herself.

Citing the relationships Union House has established with some city council members, she explains: "You have to learn how to share the burden around and be able to use their contacts at another higher level to bring about pressure, because it's not always helpful to organize and struggle at the lower level. There are people in higher levels of government, higher levels of politics. For instance, if you feel that things aren't moving in your neighborhood, sometimes you can talk to someone in the other district and they have contacts. You have to have networks."

The civic skills Matilda Martin has learned at Union House are fundamentally different from the ones people in the suburbs, such as Sara Melmer of Hadassah, have used in their service organizations. Both women are adept at using social networks; they know the value of taking initiative and of being well organized. But Matilda Martin runs into political issues at almost every turn, whereas someone like Sara Mermel functions in a private space that usually does not require any direct political action. A service organization like Hadassah teaches the value of cooperation, grassroots democracy, and interpersonal trust. Union House cultivates these same virtues, but at a different level and requiring different skills. For example, a federal health official recently asked Union House to hold a meeting so people in the community could express their concerns and have them relayed directly to Washington. Matilda worked behind the scenes, asking people privately to tell her their concerns, and many of them did because they knew her and trusted her.

Matilda Martin has developed the ability to interact comfortably with people who are wealthier and more powerful than she. But she observes that clients worry that they will be looked down on by the volunteers who come from middle-class neighborhoods. Many of her neighbors feel uncomfortable speaking in public or in groups of any size. Some do not come to meetings at Union House because they feel they do not have the right kind of clothing, others because they have nobody to care for their children. Matilda is glad she has overcome some of these intimidating factors, but she wishes there were ways to make more people feel accepted.

As federal funds have been reduced for low-income neighborhoods, more of the burden of providing social services has shifted to agencies of state and local governments. In the absence of many voluntary community organizations, these agencies have to depend on the few individuals who are willing to participate in civic activities voluntarily or at minimal pay. The connections that are established resemble those in which Matilda Martin has been involved. They are relatively tenuous because of unpredictable public funding and because of the shifting responsibilities and interests of volunteers.

The dependence of civic participation on funding from public agencies is evident in the experience of Darryn Walters, age nineteen, a high school senior in a large city in the South. He lives with his mother (who is unemployed) and a younger brother in a low-income housing development subsidized by the city. Besides going to school and pursuing his hobbies, Darryn is involved in the Neighborhood Youth Board (NYB), a civic organization run by volunteers and supported financially by the mayor's office, the department of community services, and the department of youth services.

The NYB develops projects that help teenagers and the wider community. Darryn recently worked on a senior lunch that brought in senior citizens from nursing homes and retirement centers, fed them, and tried to overcome the image that all young people are engaged in dangerous, selfish, or criminal activities. Many of the NYB's projects involve teens helping younger inner-city children. Events include swimming parties, going to movies, and taking field trips. For teens themselves, the NYB sponsors dances and puts on workshops (for instance, about teen pregnancy or being a parent or getting a job).

As the name implies, many of NYB's activities focus on the immediate neighborhoods of the NYB chapters. Darryn's neighborhood consists of approximately fifty apartment buildings, collectively known as "the project," that house more than a thousand families, nearly all African American. Other chapters are scattered throughout the city, some in white neighborhoods and some in Hispanic or Asian American neighborhoods. Through a central coordinating committee the various local NYBs get together, work on joint projects, and in this way promote better understanding among racial and ethnic groups.

The NYB is concerned with promoting in young people a stronger sense of ownership and therefore a greater feeling of responsibility for their communities. Darryn describes it as "a teen empowerment program that was designed to find ways to give the teens a voice in the community once again, to enable them to change things within their community as well as with themselves and to make it better." Adult sponsors from various municipal offices provide information and guidance, but teenagers make all the important program decisions themselves. "Basically, anything that we decide to do is what we do," Darryn explains. "It's planned totally amongst all my peers, all the youth and my peers." He thinks this is important because it gives young people "a chance to feel responsibility, like they're really needed, and that they did something without having to worry about everyone else taking the credit."

People like Darryn often find it difficult to feel they have a stake in the community. Many teenagers sense that they are marginal to the world in which adults live, and this sense is magnified by being poor and black. Even at his high school Darryn feels like an outsider, because he is bussed to a school in the suburbs where most students are white and middle class. NYB is thus crucial to his identity as a young person who is involved in something important—and he follows through on that identity by devoting approximately forty hours to it every week.

His most memorable experience was an event a few months ago for NYB participants from all neighborhoods in the city. They gathered for a weekend retreat at one of the major downtown hotels, a skyscraper overlooking the river with a revolving restaurant at the top. The physical location was important because it symbolized wealth, power, and inclusion for young people who were excluded from most of the well-established civic clubs. It was even more important for Darryn because it showed the possibility of people from all over the city coming together, overcoming racism, and learning to understand one another: "It was like a learning thing where we got there to learn about how to be good peer leaders and how to work together and trust each other. When we did that, that was the first time I really seen all the sites come together and really work together and have a good time and get to meet a lot of people they didn't know. It was just great."

Being a responsible citizen follows naturally from Darryn's conviction about the importance of being involved with others in the community. He recognizes that government officials need to exercise leadership, but he believes too many Americans sit back and do nothing, waiting for solutions to come from Washington: "We're too reliant upon the government and everyone else up in politics to solve our problems. Like when everyone elected Clinton to the presidency because of all his good ideas, they figured well, he's going to come in to solve all our problems. They don't realize he's only one man, he only has so much power. Some things he might be able to solve, but it's up to us to help make those things work. And that's the problem to me; people sit back and rely on everyone else to do everything else for them. As individual citizens, it's up to us to get out there as well and do our part to make that work."

Darryn Walters is fairly optimistic about his community, but he is atypical in this respect. The municipal activities in which he is involved are limited to a few young people, at least if they aspire to leadership positions, and they work better for someone like Darryn than for the many young people who drop out of school. The NYB has given Darryn a greater sense of his role in the city, but in general its activities thus far have done more to keep young people off the street than to help them find jobs or to put pressure on the municipal government to pay more attention to the concerns of its inner-city residents.

Although some inner-city areas are devoid of community agencies, more often there are a few well-established nonprofit organizations as well as the usual round of government-funded human service agencies. The most obvious way to encourage civic involvement is to expand the activities of existing organizations. In addition, new organizations are springing up in some inner-city communities. They are often smaller, less well funded, less formal, and more focused on specific activities such as violence prevention or AIDS. Some of them flounder or are absorbed by larger agencies.

These new organizations generally arise to fill a niche that is not being filled by established agencies. A smaller, informal effort may be able to fill this niche by drawing on the energies of people who are concerned about a particular issue, such as a neighborhood garden or a block security patrol, enlisting them while they are passionate about a specific grievance or at a stage in their lives when they have the time and the freedom to become involved. In addition, established organizations sometimes create separate new groups; typically, the new effort has a distinct identity but retains some connection with one or more established organizations.

Carmen Carlata, a twenty-five-year-old of Puerto Rican ancestry who lives in the heart of one of the nation's largest cities, helped start such an innovative organization in her neighborhood. Carmen's mother was a schizophrenic who had escaped from a mental hospital. After her mother tried to throw her in the river, Carmen was placed in the custody of her father, a drug addict who physically abused her. When she was a child, her father rented her to foster parents for the money. As an eighth-grader she escaped the drug users and prostitutes who frequented her father's apartment by moving in with a man who for the next six years abused her, raped her, and forced her to get several abortions. Whenever she sought help at the Bureau of Child Welfare, she was told they could do nothing unless she brought her father along. She couldn't because by that time she had no idea where he was.

The one positive thing Carmen learned from her father was that she would have to fight back if she was going to survive. Some of the girls at her school who were selling drugs and working as prostitutes started to intimidate her, and her father told her, "If you don't fight back, I'll kill you myself." Carmen did, often by yelling at the teachers who told her she'd never amount to anything, and then by missing as much school as she could. After dropping out of school entirely, she eventually earned her Graduate Equivalent Degree.

As an adolescent Carmen fantasized that she would become a doctor (so she could help her mother) or a lawyer (so she could put her father behind bars). As she grew older she realized these ambitions were beyond her, but she was angry enough at the way she had been raised to want to change things. Earning a meager living cleaning houses gave her little opportunity to do this. But she had met some other young people at a program called Jobs for Youth after she dropped out of high school, and they sometimes sat around in the evenings talking about how they could remake "the system."

When she was twenty-one Carmen and three of these friends formed an organization they called Action X. Its purpose is to inform young people about their civil rights. Carmen explains: "We do that in two ways. One is direct training and providing resources; the other is to encourage young people to get involved directly in advocacy and political issues that affect young people's lives."

Action X is an example of an advocacy group, the number of which has grown dramatically since the late 1960s. Advocacy groups now make up as many as a quarter of all nonprofit organizations. Like many innovative community organizations, advocacy groups often have loose connections to a variety of other groups. They concentrate their efforts on legislative and political campaign activities, demonstrations, boycotts, and litigation.[15] Carmen Carlata explains that advocacy consists of "organizing or participating in rallies, marches, demonstrations, and lobbying politicians." Action X tries "to get young people into government by helping them run for office, whether it be the community board or the board of education, and getting them onto youth councils that are part of government agencies around the city."

The reason Action X came into existence was that Carmen and her three friends had participated in a rally sponsored by a youth organization in their community. The rally was an annual event, run like a one-day conference, with about a thousand young people from all over the city being invited to listen to guest speakers. Its aim was to provide information about municipal government and to encourage young people to take a more active interest. One of the key issues at this particular rally was relationships between the police and the community. Some of the participants decided to conduct a survey; they did so over the next several months, and then they drew up a list of demands and presented it to the police commissioner.

At this point, their activity started to embarrass the organization that had sponsored the rally. It was attempting to secure funding from the police department, and its board was uncomfortable with the confrontation that was emerging between the young people and the police. Several of the young people held paid staff positions in the organization, and they were afraid of losing their jobs. The best solution was to form a new organization.

In the four years since its founding Action X has remained small, nearly all its work being done by six volunteers, but it has survived because of its leaders' aggressiveness in cultivating relationships with other groups. The established youth organization from which it sprang allows Action X to organize events to train young people to be more politically active. It provides space in which to meet, makes its photocopy machine and telephones available, and recommends the training sessions to its clients; in return, it is able to steer clear of any legal entanglements that might arise from Action X's direct involvement in politics. Two other youth organizations in the city have developed similar arrangements with Action X.

One of its most significant relationships was with the Community Resources Council, a citywide organization supported by tax dollars and private contributions. Action X received a grant from the Council that provided free technical assistance for a year. This assistance consisted of meetings that the four leaders of Action X could attend in order to learn how to keep records, deal with clients, identify relevant community agencies, and know enough about government to be effective in their own training sessions. Carmen formed relationships with several mentors and besieged them with questions.

Action X is effective because of its links to local young people. Carmen says that many of the larger, citywide organizations take young people outside their communities to conferences or to rallies or to meetings at the state capital; but, she complains: "They never really put it in context for them as to, 'Okay, this is how you as an individual living in this very, very small community in this one building, in this one apartment can affect this policy that's coming from the state or from Washington.' And so it just seems like this grand, unbelievable thing that could never happen!" By working with young people in the neighborhood before and after the large rallies, Action X is able to make the possibility of participation and change more believable.

The most significant traditional voluntary organizations left in many urban communities are the churches. When politics falters it is the churches that are expected to take up the additional burden of combating the problems of urban decay. Only 15 percent of inner-city African Americans in one study reported belonging to any kind of nonreligious civic organization, meaning that even fewer may attend meetings at those organizations regularly; but 37 percent said they attend religious services every week, and another 18 percent said they attend at least once or twice a month. The total—55 percent—is actually somewhat higher than among African Americans living in the suburbs. In the Civic Involvement Survey, the pattern for church membership was quite different from that for other voluntary organizations: although church membership was below average for young, unemployed men, it was not dampened merely by the fact that people lived in low-income, inner-city neighborhoods, and (taking other factors into account) it was more common among African Americans than among whites (see Methods, Table 6).[16]

Some inner-city churches are large, established congregations that can draw people from the suburbs to help with their programs, but storefront churches are a better example of the struggles of inner-city residents as they try to engage in community reform. Many such churches are small enough to give members a strong sense of belonging, compared with larger or less democratically organized groups. They provide opportunities to learn civic skills, such as how to speak in public, how to knock on doors, or how to keep a budget or put together a newsletter.[17]

Inner-city residents who do not go to church themselves often mention the churches when asked about the organizations that are trying to combat the problems in their communities. Most often they note church programs to keep teenagers off the streets, such as youth centers and sports nights. Occasionally they talk about parochial schools as alternatives to deteriorating or unsafe public schools. One man says that his nephew begged to be sent to a Catholic school because he was being physically attacked at the public high school. It is also common to hear about church-sponsored shelters and soup kitchens.

Storefront churches encourage deep and enduring relationships among their members, but their limited resources sometimes compel them to keep many of the people in their neighborhoods at arm's length. The story of Rafael Joaquin, age forty-five, who grew up in the Dominican Republic and moved to a city in Pennsylvania in his twenties, shows how storefront churches help—but also strategically limit their involvement in—the wider community. Rafael supports his wife and four children by driving a truck twelve hours a day for an express mail service, earning only slightly more than the minimum wage. The Joaquins live in a neat row house in a Spanish-speaking neighborhood. Drugs, violence, and tensions among ethnic groups afflict the community, but Rafael feels it is safer than many places.

He spends his Sundays attending morning and evening services at a neighborhood church that combines charismatic fellowship with aggressive obedience to the Bible. He also spends his Saturdays doing odd jobs at the church, and devotes several evenings a week to visiting families from the church with his pastor. Rafael is one of the lay leaders of the church. He serves as its treasurer, counting the money and paying the bills, and he helps the pastor print a monthly newsletter (in Spanish) that contains Bible verses, devotional thoughts, and reprints of items from other periodicals. When Rafael and the pastor visit families, they go as counselors, seeking to help them through emotional crises or marital problems by telling them about the Bible and giving them examples that show how the Bible works. Usually they pray with the families, and sometimes they give them money to help them through a difficult time.

For Rafael, helping people is a way of paying back the church for what it did for him. Shortly after coming to America, he separated from his first wife and also lost his job: "I was alone. I was hungry. I was practically destitute." He had no family or friends in the community to help him: "I was one of those victims." Without a place to live, Rafael was sitting on the curb one day when two men approached him and struck up a conversation. When they learned his plight they found him a temporary place to stay and got him enrolled in a job-training program. Rafael remembers: "They came and they fed me, and they brought the Word of God to me. Because of that, I became a new person. My life changed forever, and I wanted to share that with other people."

The church Rafael Joaquin attends was founded more than thirty years ago by the man who still serves as its head preacher. It is part of a pentecostal denomination made up of Anglos and a growing number of Hispanics. The denomination operates a seminary and provides some supervision of local churches but otherwise leaves matters to each congregation. About a hundred people attend Rafael's church each Sunday, but there are as many as two hundred members, and visitors are always welcome. The church's location in a low-income neighborhood near a declining industrial district puts it in daily contact with homeless, jobless, and needy families.

Although the church emphasizes loyalty among its members (what Rafael calls "bonding"), its evangelistic and service orientation permits its members to interact easily with a wide range of local people. Recipients of food or clothing do not have to be long-standing members of the congregation. The community is also transient enough that people who attend the church do not form a tightly knit body; rather, they bond with one of the pastors or with one or two other families who share common interests. Active as he is, Rafael says there are a number of people in the congregation whom he does not know. He admits there are boundaries separating younger and older people and those with better incomes from those earning low wages or not working at all. In his mind, keeping a certain distance from other people in the church is legitimate because God is really in charge and "God elects what I do or don't do."

What keeps the church from spreading itself too thin in response to community needs is its distinctive sense of mission. It emphasizes telling people about God and encouraging them to read the Bible. But it also imposes practical limits on how it pursues its mission. For example, it restricts its charitable services to those who come in person to the church or who can be visited directly by the pastors or lay leaders. As Rafael says, giving a person a meal may be necessary in order to tell that person about the Bible; implicitly, money is not given to other organizations or to individuals outside the community because they cannot be told directly about the Bible. Another limit is a strong conviction that people must take responsibility for their own lives. Rafael recites the saying that it is better to teach people to grow rice than to give them rice. This means that handouts are short-term, and those who do not make an effort to get a job (or to start studying the Bible) quickly lose favor.

The other way the church limits its activities is by carefully avoiding what its leaders regard as "bureaucratic entanglements." Its leaders recognize a need for a homeless shelter, for example, but they have taken no steps toward starting one because of worries about lawsuits and complications that might arise from working with other organizations. "There is a lot of technicality involved," Rafael observes. "There's the state licensing and the state requirements, the financial amount of money involved. They have professionally trained people to deal with those problems." He also believes the church should avoid doing counseling: "You can get sued and before you know, you lose your building. You lost all your assets and you have nothing."

Faith might suggest taking the risk, but wisdom says otherwise. "God is there," Rafael adds. "We believe in God and we know that God will protect us, but also, as human beings, we have a part to play, and the Bible tells us not to tempt God. I'm not going to go up on top of my house and jump from the roof because God is going to catch me. That's tempting God. But if I'm on the roof and I accidentally slip off my roof, I believe that God can do something to protect me from having a broken neck or a broken bone. I believe that, but I'm not going to go on the roof and jump."

Churches like Rafael's are common in the inner city. They are one of the few institutions left in some areas. They provide pastoral leadership, a place to worship and to congregate, and a way of meeting temporary needs of selected individuals and families. By restricting their involvement in the wider community, they protect the resources needed for their own operations. Yet there is often a sense at these churches that conditions are deteriorating despite their best efforts.[18] Some members complain that younger people are getting involved in drugs and are not learning what they should in the schools. Some complain that their communities are being overrun with new immigrants and that families with better-paying jobs are becoming "materialistic" and moving away. Rafael is typical. He is firm in his religious convictions, but he also wonders if more couldn't be done—by the schools, community leaders, even the federal government—to "instill moral values in people."

With limited resources of their own, community organizations in the inner city have turned increasingly to another form of loose connection: the metropolitan or regional community development effort that brings together short-term, strategic alliances that include volunteers and philanthropists from the suburbs as well as government agencies.[19] Some of what makes such alliances effective is illustrated in the experiences of Jacob Merrick, a financially successful white man in his late thirties who earned a bachelor's degree in economics from a prestigious university in the South and after college worked in his dad's business, a construction company specializing in large commercial and institutional buildings. After his dad's retirement Jacob became president of the firm. He is married, the father of four young children, and an active member of a Presbyterian church that attracts people from similar economic strata.

Several years ago Jacob Merrick was asked to serve on the board of elders at his church. He said he would consider doing so only if he was allowed to serve on the Outreach Council, the committee that oversees the congregation's benevolences to the wider community. Jacob was interested because it sounded different from his everyday business and family activities, and because of his love for the city. It was where his grandparents and parents had always lived and where he had grown up. It symbolized both "home" and "community," providing warm, nostalgic feelings associated with close-knit ethnic neighborhoods but also a vibrant sense of diversity. Unlike many of his suburban neighbors, Jacob was thus oriented toward the wider metropolis. He also knew that major sections of the inner city were being eaten away by poverty.

Soon after Jacob joined the Outreach Council, the pastor asked him to look into something called UIA, which stood for Urban Interfaith Action. It was a coalition of inner-city clergy, including several Baptists, some Lutherans, a few Presbyterians and Episcopalians, and two rabbis, who were trying to initiate an effort to help the poor. Rather than simply provide meals or temporary assistance, they wanted to do something on a larger scale, and the time seemed to be ripe. The mayor had recently visited a successful project in another city, and he wanted to invest some public monies in a similar effort. He had approached the UIA about a joint public and private initiative. Jacob was immediately drawn to the idea:

"The concept of public-private partnerships was really attractive to me. This is probably trite to say, but I think that the approach to urban problems of just writing checks to people, basically giving people a handout, is demeaning and not solution-oriented. It's a Band-Aid, not a cure. I think that situations can be set up where people can really be allowed to help themselves so that they develop pride and a sense of accomplishment and a sense of ownership. Public and private partnerships are about that."

The project turned out to be well suited to Jacob's knowledge of the construction industry: a plan to develop low-income housing for inner-city residents. Its goal was to provide affordable single-family townhouses or row houses that families with incomes near the poverty line could buy, and thus to generate a renewed sense of pride, ownership, and participation in the community.

"It's probably the best type of public-private collaboration," Jacob asserts. "The financial deal goes this way. The city has provided land for this community and is providing the infrastructure. There are a number of lenders who are from the private sector, in fact, who are from churches. Episcopalians are in for a million bucks. Presbyterians are in for a million bucks. And then there is a group known as the Community Reinvestment Fund. They're in for a million bucks. So these three parties put three million dollars into a fund and agreed to give that money to the development project for five years, interest free. So essentially they have the working capital to be able to build homes with no construction-period interest. Then the organizer for UIA put together a nonprofit construction team to design and to construct these homes."

The project has been under way for only a couple of years, but it is already proving successful: "As we sit here today, I think there have been thirteen families that have moved into these homes, and there are another fifty units that are under construction. I expect another ten units to close this month and probably a dozen or so to close every month thereafter. The vision is that this first community, when completed, will be home to 205 families. Then UIA will go to a second site and produce another 500 homes. So there's public money, in terms of the land and the infrastructure; there's private money that's put in without any expectation of interest; and these houses are made available to families who, depending on the number of children, have income levels that range anywhere from $17,000 to $25,000, and they are first-time homebuyers."

The UIA project spans the entire city, bringing together resources from various neighborhoods and channeling them toward a specific project. It depends on the fact that the clergy who initiated it had a power base within their own communities and were able to make themselves visible to the mayor. It also depends on their having had human and economic resources available within their congregations and through wider religious networks. For example, the "million bucks" put in by the Presbyterians consisted of $200,000 raised by the wealthy congregation that Jacob Merrick attends in cooperation with three other Presbyterian churches in the same suburb, plus a grant of $800,000 from the national office of the Presbyterian denomination, given on condition that the local share be raised first.

As an example of the human resources that facilitated the UIA project, Jacob remembers what happened when his pastor asked him to "snoop around" and see what the Outreach Council could do. When Jacob asked the council members if anyone had information about the successful project that the mayor had visited, one man replied, "Guess what? I've been involved since the git-go!" He turned out to be a former business partner of the man whose construction firm had built that project. He arranged for a group from the church to pay a visit. They toured the development and asked detailed questions about how it had been organized and how much it had cost. By the time Jacob Merrick presented his proposal to the full congregation, there were few questions he couldn't answer.

The ways UIA volunteers spend their time are quite different from the activities of people who work one-on-one with the needy. They do not get to know the victims of poverty in the same intimate way, and thus they do not establish trust at the same level. They contribute mainly by providing the kind of structure that enables religious organizations and city government to have confidence that monies are not being misused. Jacob Merrick volunteers about two hours every other week to participate in meetings of the Lenders' Consortium, an oversight committee that represents the various organizations that supplied money and hears status reports from the construction companies and other professionals involved in the project.

The main lesson that Jacob Merrick has learned from working with UIA is that democracy means more than politics. Were he to use a single word to describe it, he would say *partnership*, especially between government agencies and the private sector but also among a variety of groups in the latter. When pressed for the technical details of the housing project, he acknowledges that UIA is only a part of the larger story. UIA has provided leadership, oversight, and approximately $3 million in interest-free loans. The CEO of a construction firm has donated his time and is building the development on a nonprofit, cost-only basis. A nonprofit firm handles the finances and has supplied additional venture capital. This firm is a subsidiary of a corporation that attracts funds for municipal projects by issuing tax-free bonds. One agency of the city government provided the land for the project, another put in sewers and repaved the streets, another is responsible for inspections, and still another carries a second mortgage on the entire project so that families themselves are required to put in only 5 percent of the cost as principal. The funds to cover this second mortgage are provided by a block grant from Washington. Overall, the project involves dozens of organizations and approximately $65 million in investments. Jacob Merrick admits that the process is cumbersome, but he regards it as a way of doing everything "decently and in order" (an idea that appeals to his Presbyterian training).

Besides the benefit that UIA hopes will come to low-income families themselves, its members have also established new links that may serve as social capital for other projects, and that have opened their eyes to the growing diversity of American society. Through its various projects, UIA has now brought together some thirty congregations from all faiths and from all parts of the city. Jacob Merrick says their meetings remind him of Jesse Jackson's Rainbow Coalition: "You walk in and there are people from all over the city and all these different churches and a couple synagogues. So here's Temple Shalom as one of the synagogues, and so all the parishioners from that synagogue are sitting together. And here's First Presbyterian and then here's the Church of God and Christ there. There's a real smattering of humanity in this room. At the front of the auditorium is a gospel choir from one of the Baptist churches. They're a bunch of young people. I'm chuckling to myself walking in. These people don't fit together and yet they've come together." He says it makes him "very hopeful" to see people working together in this way.

The role of complex interorganizational networks is evident in the work of many other inner-city agencies. The ones that function effectively bring together people from the wider community, often to engage in short-term projects. In recent years such networks have been established to deal with housing needs, with food distribution, violence prevention, and job training. They have also been initiated to address special health needs, such as the AIDS epidemic.[20] Many AIDS patients are concentrated in inner cities, where resources for assistance during the final stages of the disease are scarce. A case study of one such organization further demonstrates the kinds of alliances that can be formed in urban communities and the factors that enhance and limit their effectiveness.

Laura Cantrell, a divorced mother of four (two in their teens), is the executive director of AIDS Network, a service agency that she founded in 1989 in the medium-sized city where she lives. AIDS Network provides emergency food, transportation, and emotional support to people with AIDS as well as an afterschool program for children whose parents are HIV-positive or have died of AIDS. The agency coordinates the efforts of approximately 125 volunteers. Besides Laura there are two part-time employees in paid positions; until a year ago Laura devoted full time to the organization without pay. The network now serves about 200 clients, a majority of whom are "buddied" with one of the volunteers who becomes their friend and supports them throughout their illness.

Most of the clients are desperate by the time they contact the AIDS Network. Laura explains: "They're very sick. They've been hospitalized and reached the point that they cannot make it anymore by themselves. A social worker will call and say, 'Will you come and see them?' So usually I'm seeing people who are frightened, very vulnerable. They've held it all together for as long as they can and now they realize they need help. Usually we're the last choice."

Volunteers are recruited throughout the city, many coming from suburban areas. Most respond to advertisements the AIDS Network runs in the newspaper; some come at the invitation of friends. They are screened to be sure they have the time to be involved and then attend an intensive thirty-two-hour training course. Because most of the clients die within a few months, the average length of volunteering is also relatively short. Only three volunteers have remained active since the beginning.

The program is truly an alliance of individuals and organizations from a wide spectrum of the community. The clients find out about it from social workers, case managers at hospitals or prisons, or friends. The volunteers become a network of people who attend support groups together and receive monthly newsletters and periodic requests for donations. Some of them know one another through churches and service clubs. It takes approximately $135,000 a year to operate the program. The funds come from individual donors, a charity ball, and a variety of small grants.

Although the clients include people from suburbs and outlying areas, most come from the inner city, and their situation has become worse in recent years. "In the old days the typical client was an upper-middle-class gay man with education, resources, and family," Laura says. "And we'd build a beautiful relationship, and we'd journey with them till they died." Those clients have become fewer. "Now I mostly have people who are minorities, poor, with a history of addiction, a history of incarceration, diabetic, illiterate, and HIV. They've got no tools to deal with life on the best days, and now with HIV they are completely helpless."

With the exception of volunteers who may have connections to civic organizations in the suburbs, the AIDS Network functions almost entirely in an environment composed of government agencies rather than other voluntary associations. Its ties to these agencies are clearly illustrated in Laura's response to a question about the program's sources of funding: "A little bit of the city's money, a little bit of the county's money, a little bit of the state's money, a little bit of federal money." Most of it comes directly in the form of small grants; some of it is channeled through hospitals that subcontract with the program because its services are cheaper than theirs. The social workers, case managers, and prison officials with whom the program interacts are representatives of government agencies.

Because the AIDS Network, like other such efforts that have appeared in inner cities, mostly functions in relation to government agencies rather than other civic organizations, it is heavily dependent on decisions that lie outside its control and outside the control of the community itself. The federal program from which it receives a share of its funding has recently been cut by 60 percent. Laura Cantrell is having to scale back her program by at least a third.

The dependence on government funding in the inner city differs dramatically from the independence of organizations in the suburbs. There, it is possible for busy people to participate casually in the established, autonomous institutions within their communities, attending meetings at service organizations or integrating volunteer work with their professional careers. In inner-city areas, in contrast, entities such as Union House or UIA are complex structures that span a large population with few resources of its own. Civic involvement in the suburbs seldom draws volunteers into direct contact with government agencies, except to hear an occasional speech by a politician or to send in a petition. The inner-city organizations cannot exist without close working relationships with government, not to mention public funding.

Yet in both contexts civic involvement defies the ideal of long-term involvement in membership organizations. In the suburbs it consists of short-term participation in volunteer projects that are facilitated by non-profit agencies or service organizations. In the inner cities it is more likely to consist of strategic coalitions involving networking among a number of nonprofit and public organizations. Both forms are adaptations to the porous institutions of which communities are now composed. Suburban residents do what they can despite divided loyalties and busy schedules. Inner-city organizations are faced with the problems that arise from corporations having fled to other places, from unemployment, and from disrupted families.

6

Surviving in
Small-Town America

SMALL TOWNS CONJURE UP IMAGES of idyllic serenity—settings where people know and care about one another, take an interest in their communities, participate actively in civic affairs, and suffer from boredom on summer afternoons. If, in reality, small towns are no longer quiet places where neighbors spend mornings sipping coffee together, they still provoke nostalgia for barbershop quartets and backyard barbecues. In these sentimental reveries, putting in a stint on the town council is unlikely to be regarded as a difficult task, and serving on the volunteer fire company may imply little more than polishing brass and rescuing stray cats.[1]

But small towns have been changing dramatically in recent years. Like suburbs and inner cities, they are becoming more porous. Growing numbers of them are populated by middle-class workers who drive longer distances to jobs in cities and suburbs. Although they tend to be more geographically remote than suburbs, many are threatened by the growth of nearby metropolitan areas. Some have a sharply declining economic base, as local shops are replaced by strip malls and discount centers, and as aging residents suffer from cutbacks in Medicare, or are alienated by new immigrants who come to take advantage of inexpensive housing. Virtually all small towns face a bewildering array of federal, state, and regional regulations, and they are becoming more closely connected to the wider world through satellite television and their own websites on the Internet.[2]

Small towns are increasingly populated by people who have *chosen* to live there, and residents accordingly have become more self-conscious about the pluses and minuses of village life. Residents often mention congenial social relationships, but seldom assign them primary importance. They more often mention access to nature, being able to plant a garden, go hunting, view wild turkeys in the woods behind their home, or visit neighboring farms. Some emphasize the emotional distance that living in a small town provides from their work in the city. They appreciate smaller stores and quieter streets.[3] Being involved in community organizations or having friendly relationships with neighbors is often regarded as a means rather than an end in itself. These commitments take time that might be spent in other ways, but they are useful for protecting the community against developers or maintaining its schools.

People in small towns are about as likely as those in suburbs and cities to feel that civic involvement is waning in their communities.[4] Oldtimers often blame newcomers for not taking a more active interest in established civic organizations. Newcomers sometimes regard these organizations as too traditional or too concerned with preserving the status quo that excludes them. But the perception of decline is also rooted in the small-town belief that problems can be solved if people work together to combat them. It is an adaptation of the motif of rugged self-sufficiency that has long characterized American individualism. Community sufficiency, as it might be called, means that neighbors, churches, civic organizations, and local politicians can collectively take care of most any problem that confronts them. As the residents of small towns reflect on their communities, they feel that civic disorder has gotten out of control: crime has gotten worse, drug use has surfaced, traffic is congested, businesses have closed, schools need to be refurbished. Believing that only they are responsible, they blame themselves. If people were not so indifferent, they say, things would surely be better. Yet they too feel disconnected from the larger problems confronting their towns.

People in small towns have their own reasons for becoming involved in their communities. They are less likely than suburbanites to emphasize personal quests, such as wanting to feel worthwhile, and less likely than inner-city residents to emphasize severe needs and grievances. They talk about expectations stemming from living in a smaller community where public behavior is generally noted. One man half-jokingly complains that he hated to see a new organization start because it was "just expected that you should be there." Suburban residents refer to friends or business acquaintances who mentioned an "opportunity" that "interested" them; small-town inhabitants say they felt an obligation to help a friend or to pay back what they had received from the community. Personal contact in the town breeds familiarity, concern, and service. Rather than being compelled by an abstract desire to help the needy, they are more likely to know the needy person or family and thus feel personally responsible for helping. These feelings are not always strong enough to propel people into action, but they reflect—and reinforce—the social bonds of the community and very often spur acts of caring.

The reasons given for becoming involved in small-town community affairs more often include the visibility of civic activities. It is not uncommon for people to admit that they enjoy being regarded as community leaders, having their names in the newspaper, and receiving service awards. Some acknowledge that their business depends on having friends in the community, and some describe community service as a way of building a favorable reputation. Their lives and those of their neighbors touch one another at many points. Because their images are at stake, they find it harder simply to walk away from membership organizations and they are more troubled when conflicts erupt. However, residents who commute to work in other places may care less about their local reputations. They drive to other towns for activities that interest them, or they become involved in national or international associations. They are influenced by larger cultural forces which enter their home through national media and urge them to change.

The uninvolved in these towns give many of the same reasons for not being more active as people do in suburbs and cities (especially being too busy). Those who commute some distance to work sometimes say they have neither the time nor the interest to get involved in local activities. But people in small towns also worry more than people in other places that they will be overwhelmed by too many responsibilities if they take on any. As the population is small to begin with, those showing an inclination to pitch in do run the risk of being frequently called upon. As one woman observes, "I barely walked in the door and they asked me to serve on two or three committees."

Increased mobility and communication have made it harder for residents of small towns to ignore the conflicts and inequalities in their communities. These tensions provoke a sense of unease that was not always as evident in the past. Observers of small towns before World War II found a complacency toward racial divisions, outcasts, and misfits that depended less on moral callousness than on mental frameworks capable of creating an implicit understanding of the social hierarchy.[5] African Americans or people from the other side of the tracks were considered inferior to the more affluent middle class. But today many small-town dwellers are less comfortable with traditional distinctions. Those who have lived elsewhere express concern about the prejudices they perceive among lifelong residents. Others have been unsettled by wider political debates about discrimination, welfare, and poverty. Their own views may range from far left to far right, but they are less sure that the disadvantaged can simply be left out of the equation when community affairs are discussed.

Small-town civic involvement has had to adapt to demographic, economic, political, and cultural changes. Centers for the homeless and for victims of domestic violence are being established in towns as well as in cities, and they provide examples of the forging of loose connections between the new and the older civic organizations. Unlike many suburban areas, small towns are still sufficiently integrated around local jurisdictions that civic involvement includes participation on the town council and the volunteer fire department and brings members of private community organizations into contact with these public institutions.[6] Unlike inner-city neighborhoods, small towns still have enough private organizations that public institutions do not have to shoulder the full burden of meeting local needs. Small towns nevertheless face challenges from large corporations that have set up shop in their environs and from external governing bodies that they are ill-equipped to handle by themselves. Citizens involved in town activities are finding themselves frustrated by these complex and large-scale bureaucracies.

Small towns are no longer as sealed off from the outside world as they once were. More people move in and out; information flows easily past municipal boundaries. The very existence of small towns depends on vital links with the world beyond their boundaries. But then small-town America has never been as isolated as nostalgic portrayals of it might suggest.[7] Indeed, the history of small towns is one of boom and bust, colored by the uncertain fortunes of river transportation, canals, livestock and crops, railroads, and fishing. People came and went much more than they merely settled in for quiet conversations at the barbershop or soda fountain. The flux of contemporary small towns is not dissimilar.

Yet town life is different now in one important respect. Because two-thirds of the nation's population lives in cities and suburbs, a large proportion of the newcomers to small towns are from those places.[8] They bring with them a very different experience of life than newcomers did at a time when most were from farms or other small towns. They are not accustomed to a close-knit neighborhood in which they will be expected to participate faithfully for the rest of their lives. Better transportation permits them to move across the community's borders as often as they wish, commuting to work, driving to church in another town, shopping in the suburbs, visiting friends and relatives in the cities. With many small towns adjacent to or surrounded by larger metropolitan areas, these passages may not involve long distances. Even if they do, telephones make it easy to stay in touch with people outside the neighborhood.

Newcomers report that it is often hard for them to become involved in community organizations. One of the problems is commuting. Many drive long distances to work, so when they get home they feel like relaxing instead of going out. Commuting also divides their interests. They feel less of a stake in what happens in their own community. They feel they do not belong, perhaps that they do not *want* to belong. Moving to the small town has been an escape from a more hectic life in cities or suburbs. Now they want to spend time in their garden or hunting and fishing. Some believe that they have little in common with long-time residents or that the oldtimers are happy to carry the load of civic activities.

Many small towns are thus divided between older and newer images of community service. Older, long-time residents are less likely to have children in school and more likely to be living on fixed incomes. They may have time to be involved in community organizations as volunteers. They may hold to the view that service clubs, churches, and neighborly relationships are the best way to keep the community strong. Newer and younger residents are more likely to have children in school and to be two-career families, perhaps commuting to work, and thus have less time to be involved in community organizations. They may turn out for meetings about issues that affect the schools or their developments, and they may recognize a need for professional services, such as special education teachers and emergency clinics. They are more likely to want services that require higher taxes, whereas older residents on fixed incomes are more likely to be worried about high taxes. These differing views often result in keen, if critical, attention being paid to local government. Some residents complain that town officials are selling out to developers and raising taxes, while others complain that "old boys" run the town and drag their feet when it comes to improving the roads or expanding the schools.

Besides the influx of newcomers, small towns are greatly affected by the penetration of their boundaries by chain stores and large discount organizations such as Wal-Mart. Although a majority of states have now passed laws against unfair pricing policies that chains like Wal-Mart could otherwise use to drive out local pharmacies and other small businesses, a growing number of service and retail chains that do not depend on raw materials (the way mines, steel plants, or agribusinesses do) can locate virtually anywhere. Some are attracted to small towns by low taxes, available space, and depressed wages, others by projected population increases.

The changing nature of civic involvement is evident in the way that some venerable institutions—like the town park—are now administered. As one visits small towns, a recurrent sight is a park that was built by the local Lions Club, whose emblem is prominently displayed on a nearby signpost, and that is maintained by volunteers. Residents can gather in the park for picnics, Fourth of July speeches, and softball games, and its physical presence serves as a reminder of the community's willingness to band together to do things for itself. But the small-town park is no longer the well-bounded setting it used to be; it is subject to various jurisdictions or interest groups and thus depends on civic involvement to draw resources from a variety of organizations.

David Schantz, age fifty-nine, is a physician who lives in a semirural township populated by retired people, farmers, shopkeepers, teachers, and a growing number of commuters who drive from fifteen to fifty miles each day to work. He and his wife moved here thirty years ago and raised their four children in a renovated two-story house. Dr. Schantz's practice is located in a small office complex a few miles from where he lives. For the past seven years he has been a member of the township's parks and recreation commission, serving twice as its chairman. In many ways he typifies what civic involvement has meant in small towns throughout much of American history. He is a long-time resident with a prestigious profession, and his work puts him in contact with most of the local population. As a self-employed person who earns a good income, he can afford to spend some of his time tending to the community's needs.

The parks and recreation commission is not a highly demanding form of civic involvement, but it plays an important role in a small township like the one in which Dr. Schantz lives. It came into existence seven years ago because the local Catholic diocese was experiencing declining economic fortunes and decided to sell a ninety-acre parcel of land. Several new housing developments had already been built, and there were rumors that Wal-Mart was scouting the area. Long-time residents were worried that the parcel would soon be filled with houses and shopping malls. To prevent this from happening, township officials purchased the tract and established the parks and recreation commission to oversee its use. Dr. Schantz attends commission meetings one evening a month and occasionally represents the commission at planning board meetings or at hearings with developers.

Developing the park has been a slow process because the township has not had funds for it, but after seven years the tract has begun to fulfill the commission's dreams. Two playing fields and a picnic pavilion have been built. With volunteer labor supplied by Boy Scout troops, an old house on the property has been renovated. A bicycle path has been constructed, and several hiking trails through the woods have been cleared. Each summer the commission sponsors a Friends and Neighbors Day that includes a picnic and games. The commission is also responsible for evaluating the plans of any developer who proposes to construct housing in the township and for suggesting ways in which parks, recreation facilities, and open space can be included.

Dr. Schantz believes the park and recreation commission is helping to maintain a sense of civic pride in the township. He feels the park is a tangible reminder that the community exists. Not only does it provide a space in which people can relax, it symbolizes that something other than working is important, and it brings families together and permits some community-wide activities (such as soccer games and the annual picnic) to take place more easily. "I saw this as an opportunity to give some time and to volunteer for my community," he explains. "I thought it was a good opportunity, and I'm very happy I did."

But the park has also made Dr. Schantz keenly aware of the complexity of small-town politics. It required official action to bring the park into being, and it took the initiative of voluntary groups in the community to prompt the town officials to take action. The need for a formal parks and recreation commission suggests to him that the community is in some ways not as strong as it used to be. Volunteers alone might have been able to create the park in an earlier era, but now there are fewer volunteers because of the aging of the long-term residents and what he perceives as apathy among newer residents. Also, it has taken more negotiation than he ever imagined to satisfy the state's environmental regulations, to make sure the township's legal liabilities are covered in case someone is injured in the park, and to evaluate the plans of developers. He is not sure the commission can continue to operate on a strictly volunteer basis and still have the resources to halt the expansion of new developments and shopping centers. He thinks about stepping down from his position on the commission, not so much because he has decided to pursue his own interests as because of uncertainty that he is up to the challenges presented by something as seemingly simple as a small-town park. Increasingly specialized regulations from federal and state agencies call for expert knowledge and skills.

For residents with less civic spirit than his, it is easy to become disenchanted with small-town politics. Indeed, many express distrust of local politicians and do so in a way that contrasts with similar expressions in suburbs and inner cities. Here it is impossible to view public officials as distant bureaucrats or as working entirely against one's own interests.[9] It is easier to regard them as well-intentioned bumblers who have more than a little trouble understanding that the twentieth century is nearly at an end (rather than only beginning). Newcomers are especially quick to observe the foibles of local officials: the yellow necktie, the plaid jacket, the screechy voice singing the national anthem, the cigar, the gaudy dress, the hillbilly accent, the nasal twang. To be cynical about politics is simply to feel that politicians are playing in Mr. Rogers' Neighborhood, rather than capably dealing with complex issues.

When newcomers get involved in local politics to save their communities from these entrenched bumblers, it is not uncommon for conflicts to arise that can produce as much cynicism as constructive change. The story of Alex Gunderson provides a case in point. He is a small-town resident who has jumped into the fray of trying to make his community a better place, only to find himself embroiled in controversy. As a youngster, he was a tough city kid who grew up fighting with his brother, and now at age forty-one, he is still fighting. An intense man with a neatly trimmed beard and penetrating eyes, he works as an auditor for a large corporation and argues like a lawyer. For the past five weeks he has been serving as a township supervisor.

Gunderson, his wife, and three grade-school-age sons live in a duplex in Midland Township, a community of approximately 6,000 people who live in small housing developments or on semirural tracts of an acre or two, all within a few miles of the post office, the feed store, the filling station, and the café. It is the kind of small town in which growing numbers of city dwellers and suburbanites have been seeking refuge in recent years. The

Gundersons settled here a decade ago, leaving the city in hope of finding a simpler life for themselves and their children.

What they found was a community under siege from developers, state laws, and local bureaucrats. Alex's first run-in with the system occurred about a year after they moved. With a second child on the way, he decided it was time to push out the back wall of his house and add on a room. He learned that doing so would be in violation of something called an "envelope" in the local zoning ordinance. To gain approval for the addition, he was required to draw up architectural plans, pay a $300 fee, and appear several times before the township supervisors. He won. But the experience rankled.

A few months later Alex read that a trash-hauling company was planning to build a large plant nearby to process trash and turn the energy into steam. He recalls: "Don't get me wrong. I'm really not one of those NIMBY [not in my backyard] kind of people." But the area had just been through a drought, and the proposed plant was expected to require millions of gallons of water. Alex worried that it would significantly lower the ground water level. He had also heard rumors that operations like these were controlled by the mob. Still angry at the township supervisors, he went to several of the hearings and spoke out. The plant was not built.

During the hearings some of his neighbors started to recognize Alex as a spokesman for their concerns and urged him to run for a vacant seat on the board of supervisors. Midland Township is one of 2,600 local jurisdictions in its state, including boroughs, municipalities, and townships. Some townships have five supervisors; the smaller ones, like Midland, have three. Traditionally, many had only one. The supervisors' job consisted of little more than overseeing the maintenance of local roads. Alex wasn't sure if he wanted to be a supervisor or not. At the last minute he decided to put in his name, did no campaigning, and lost by four votes.

Realizing how easy it might be to win a local election, Alex decided to try again. He admits it was an "ego thing" mostly; his competitive side had been kicked into gear, and his pride had been wounded. It took three more tries before he won. Each time, he learned more about local politics and came close enough to winning that he knew he had a chance. "When I finally decided to make the run this time and make it seriously," he laughs, "I had about ten reasons from the purely mercenary, egotistical reasons all the way to the purely altruistic, wanting to do good and everything in between."

Like many people, Alex Gunderson is not doing community service just from the goodness of his heart. He receives a small stipend for being a township supervisor, and modest as it is ($2,500 for the year), it comes in handy when paying the bills. He enjoys being visible in the community and having a reason to delve into subjects other than the ones he deals with day after day at his job. He admits he was sort of pressured into running by some of his friends. But, most important, he's still mad at the way things are going in his community.

One episode that pushed him to the brink of running for office was a confrontation between his neighbor and one of the supervisors. The neighbor, a longtime resident, had a storage shed on his property that the zoning inspector decided was in violation of codes. The man appealed, only to receive a $700 citation and a public scolding by one of the supervisors. Alex was infuriated. "[He] wasn't even allowed to present photographs he'd taken himself because they weren't being presented by a certified engineer as expert testimony!" Alex decided it was time to fight "the dictatorial, authoritarian attitude" of the supervisors.

He is also mad at Wal-Mart. As it has in many small but growing communities, Wal-Mart has been shopping for land in Midland Township. It has proposed a huge complex including a Wal-Mart store, a sixteen-screen movie theater, a restaurant, and several other discount stores. Alex fears the project would dramatically increase traffic congestion, reduce wages, and eventually force the township to raise taxes in order to build new roads. To make matters worse, the proposal has encouraged another developer to revive the plan to build a trash-to-steam plant.

In his desire to right wrongs in his community, Alex Gunderson even went after his fellow board members. Sensing that they were badly mismanaging township funds, he conducted his own audit and released his findings to the newspaper. The act constituted a breach of trust in the eyes of the other supervisors, who voted to censure him and immediately sent their own version of the story to the paper. Gunderson was stripped of his responsibilities, at least temporarily. He is unsure if he will be permitted to resume his civic activities in the near future. And he is still fighting mad.

Alex Gunderson's experiences in trying to change local government reflect a larger reality of small-town life. Many residents of these communities complain bitterly about their local governments, and they have several concerns: that local government is dominated by a few people who have been in office too long and are unwilling to keep up with the times;

that local officials are ineffective in dealing with such problems as increasing crime or traffic; that government functions are not being performed as efficiently or inexpensively as they could be ("it takes one man to fix a pothole and five more to supervise"); and that otherwise effective local agencies are being strangled by externally imposed regulations. That residents voluntarily bring up such issues means that they are aware of the importance of local government (more so than most suburban dwellers). But their complaints also express an undercurrent of worry about the integrity and well-being of the community itself. An offhand remark about the town supervisors, for example, leads into broader concerns about neighbors not caring for one another, residents not showing up at town meetings, and litter despoiling the countryside. The boundaries of the town have become so porous that residents question the town's very identity and their ability to attach to it.

The need for small towns to adapt to problems that stem from their integration into wider social and political jurisdictions is evident in the recent history of The Center, a shelter for battered women and children located in a town that is a sleepy, self-contained community except that it is within an hour's drive of a large city. Some of the women who come to The Center have been beaten by their husbands or boyfriends. Many come because their children have been sexually molested. Often they have nothing but the few clothes they were able to grab when they fled their homes. A typical case is a woman whose husband went crazy, beat her, and was then confined to a mental hospital. It all happened so quickly, she remembers. Suddenly there was no income, and within thirty days she and her children were evicted from their apartment. She stayed at The Center for three months. During that time she learned office skills, got a job that provided health insurance, and found affordable housing. An organization like The Center provides local residents with new challenges and new opportunities for becoming involved in their community.

Mary Carlson, age seventy-five, is retired from her job as a registered nurse. She and her husband live in a quiet village of older, middle-class homes. The population is under 9,000, but residents also shop, share some social services, and attend churches in a neighboring village of about 8,000 people. Most families have lived here long enough, as Mary has, to have close friends in the community. What she likes best about living here is that "I have a flock of friends and I know they're always going to be there, just as I'm going to be there for them." Some are women she worked with, some are neighbors, and some go to the same church she and her husband attend.

Four years ago one of Mary's sons came home (he lives in another state) to attend his high school reunion, and during his visit met a former class-mate who was in charge of The Center. His classmate described the organization and mentioned that it was in desperate need of volunteers. Mary's son volunteered his mother, and encouraged her to check it out.

During all the years Mary worked as a nurse she did no volunteer work for the community. Not only was she working full time, she was also raising four children and doing most of the household chores. When she retired she found an enormous amount of time on her hands. She also discovered that her self-esteem was plummeting. At work she had held an important position and had felt she was an important person. She enjoyed being needed by her patients, being able to meet their needs, and interact-ing with her co-workers. She now missed the feeling of being needed.

Mary Carlson was not drawn into The Center by her friends. It was a weak tie—her son's former classmate—that brought The Center to her attention. She had not been aware that it existed. Like most people's, her networks were more open than closed. This openness is evident, too, in the fact that she does not look only to her friends to meet her needs. She is, in a sense, reciprocating for some of the kindness people have shown her over the years, but she is doing so by reaching out to women who are not part of her own circle.

The Center defies the stereotypical notions that voluntary organizations are run strictly by volunteers and that in a small town they exist for the immediate benefit of the community. The Center enlists the help of a few volunteers, but it is a complex operation that includes paid professionals and partnerships with a number of other agencies. Although it has been a temporary refuge for some local women, it mostly serves women from a city some fifty miles away and its suburbs. Having been abused, they need to be at a place where they are no longer within easy reach of their abusers.

The Center is an old three-story house with twelve rooms. Mary isn't quite sure who founded it, but she says it was started at a time when the state was trying to encourage local communities to provide shelters for abused women and children. From the beginning it was a partnership involving resources from a number of different organizations. Its official address (which has to be separate from where the women are actually housed) is an office in the county's human services administration. The house was purchased below market value with a grant from the state. Volunteers turned it into livable space. Twelve churches in the area took responsibility for renovating the twelve rooms and for providing maintenance and repairs after the facility opened. The Center's directorship is a salaried position, paid for by a combination of state and county taxes, and the case managers assigned to the women at the shelter are also paid by the human services administration.

At any given time The Center houses approximately twenty-five to thirty women and children. They are permitted to stay sixty days and in special cases as long as ninety days, during which time they receive emotional counseling and, if needed, job training. They are provided with temporary transportation to attend classes and to look for jobs, and with help in securing low-income housing when they leave. Their transience is matched only by that of the volunteers and professional staff. For example, The Center has had five directors in five years, part of the turnover being due to changing expectations about training, and part to disagreements with the board.

Volunteers come and go because family circumstances and other commitments place unpredictable constraints on their time. Mary's husband helps occasionally, but she says, "He's like a lot of retired men, I guess; he'll do it if I ask him to come on a particular day to do something, but he says he doesn't want to commit himself to something long-term." Mary herself is more regular, but she too restricts her obligations. She comes in on Tuesdays from ten to noon so that the woman on duty can attend a staff meeting, but she makes it clear she absolutely has to leave at noon because of another meeting. "The main thing I've learned is to set boundaries," she asserts. If someone asks her to come to The Center and it doesn't fit easily into her schedule, she just says, "I'm sorry." She also draws a firm line around what she chooses to say. For instance, she sees aspects of The Center's politics that worry her, but she keeps quiet about them.

These loose connections work reasonably well because The Center maintains contact with a wide network of people and organizations both locally and throughout the region. It sends out an occasional newsletter to several thousand people to tell about special needs and upcoming events. The churches provide networks for recruiting new volunteers. Staff members speak occasionally at service clubs, and volunteers like Mary mention The Center to people in the community: "It's kind of an inside network. I'll tell a friend, 'They really have a need; couldn't you come and help with transportation?'" The Center also depends on connections with a nearby community college and with job-training programs, prospective employers, doctors, and realtors. Because each of its clients has different needs, the networks must be flexible and efficient.

Mary gives several examples of how these diverse ties make it possible for The Center to carry out its mission in the community. She says church people are often interested in helping the needy, but hold back because the needy are not like them or because they fear the needy may become involved in their church: "It's very hard for them to embrace someone who maybe doesn't look like them or doesn't look like they would like to be a part of their relationships." Regrettable as this may be, the way to work around it is for The Center to have loose connections to the church, using its volunteers but keeping its distance. Mary also says that The Center cannot draw enough volunteers from a single church, so it is helpful to have loose ties with a dozen congregations through the local ministerial council.

Loose connections have worked fairly well to keep The Center in business as a service to needy women and children, even though it intentionally keeps such a low profile that local residents are often unaware of exactly what it does. It is quite different from the volunteer fire company, which is more visible and serves the town's residents themselves, mostly by drawing from a fairly tightly knit group of long-term volunteers. Like Frank Purelli, these volunteers enjoy congregating at the firehouse, sometimes passing on their stories from one generation to the next. The people in small towns, like many in suburbs and inner cities, are increasingly alone, despite the friends and families who may live nearby, because they are single or divorced or because many of their close friends have moved away. Fire companies and other civic organizations are taking on the role of providing close, emotional support. The support of a surrogate family like this can be a powerful incentive to stay involved in a civic organization. But because most people, even in small towns, do not live in hermetically sealed enclaves, this kind of support can also empower people to become part of wider networks that connect them to others in need of assistance.

One man for whom the volunteer fire company plays this new role is Nelson Abram, a mechanic in his middle thirties who lives in a town of about 10,000 people. He is single, and the volunteer fire company has become his family, providing him with camaraderie and emotional support. For more than a decade he has spent most of his evenings at the fire station. On average he puts in at least twenty hours a week.

Like other volunteer fire fighters, Nelson Abram believes he is performing a valuable service. The fact that he and about thirty-five other men (and several women) are willing to volunteer means the village has fire protection without having to pay as much in taxes. For the poor people in the community this economical service is especially important. Nelson worries that many of the townspeople take the protection for granted. But there have been enough fires in recent years to provide periodic reminders of the volunteers' contribution. A few years ago, in fact, two boys were playing with matches one Sunday afternoon at the lumber yard; $9 million worth of property in the heart of town was destroyed, including the lumber yard, the hotel, two fire trucks, the funeral home, and the five and dime, before the volunteer company could put out the fire.

The support Nelson Abram receives from the volunteer fire company illustrates the complex relationship between civic participation and the kind of support that many people now think of when they talk about community. In the present view, community is less often simply the place one lives and more often an empathic bond that links diverse people together. It depends greatly on emotional attachment because it is recognized to be voluntary and thus intentional; in short, people feel they are part of a community when they perceive caring to be present. It is almost as if an emotional attachment has come to replace the geographic propinquity that used to tie people together.

Although Nelson Abram gets much emotional support from the fire company, he was not so lacking in social contacts that he turned to volunteerism just to make friends. He grew up in the small town in which he still lives. His parents live there, as do his older sister and her family and many of his friends from high school. In fact, it is through such relationships that the volunteer fire company recruits most of its members. In Nelson's case, his sister's husband started volunteering at the fire station, having become interested through a high school friend who was a firefighter, and it was his brother-in-law's influence that encouraged Nelson to join.

Once he started spending time at the firehouse, Nelson discovered camaraderie that was more a consequence of his civic involvement than antecedent to it. With three dozen volunteers coming in and out, there was always somebody to talk to. Often some of the guys would go out for a few beers afterward. Being a firefighter in a small town also gave Nelson visibility in the community. Many local merchants started to recognize him and strike up conversations about recent fires, for example, and he discovered that it was an "ego trip" to drive around town in the fire truck. "I guess it just gives me a sense of belonging," he explains.

Another activity has played an important role in small towns: the ladies' aid society, the sewing circle, the canasta group, and similar gatherings of club women. In the past they were occasions for mothers to get away from the children or to get out of the house while the children were at school. Their members tended to be women who did not work outside the home, and many of these gatherings were formally a part of local congregations, as in the case of women's missionary groups, or informally attached to congregations, as in the case of quilting bees. Although the stated purpose was often just to work on a project together, the members were able to discuss community issues, and sometimes these groups played strong roles in church decisions or in providing assistance to the needy.[10]

Such gatherings still exist, but in modified forms that reflect the changing conditions of small communities. Churches still play a role as the staging ground for some of these activities, but in other cases members are able to find each other without church help and need to do so in ways that transcend denominations and faiths. They find each other by word of mouth, but also by advertising in the newspaper, by speaking at civic associations, and even by creating home pages on the World Wide Web. These groups are directly influenced by the fact that many women work outside the home; members are thus empty nesters who have spare time, or meetings are held less often and at times when working women can attend. Participants sometimes commute from neighboring towns, giving the gatherings a regional flavor, and activities are influenced by television, by stores specializing in crafts, by craft magazines, and by shopping malls in the vicinity of small towns. Some members are long-term participants, but it is easy for members to come and go as their time and interests change. They participate chiefly to pursue some personal interest, and occasionally these interests are nudged in the direction of projects that contribute to the wider community.

Caroline Madison, age fifty-six, lives in a town of about 10,000 people; an empty nester, she works part time doing clerical temp work for local businesses, appreciating the money that supplements her husband's income but also enjoying the opportunity to interact with other people. Ten years ago she joined a local group called the Quilting Circle. Its purpose was simply to share knowledge and the love of quilting. Like similar groups that have sprung up across the country, it appealed to a rare combination of feminist, naturalist, religious, and nostalgic yearnings.[11] It allowed women to get in touch with a form of artistic expression that many of their mothers or grandmothers practiced, to do something with their hands, and to understand better how quilts were used to carry on family traditions within ethnic communities. Caroline Madison's Quilting Circle now consists of approximately one hundred women who are scattered across the entire county.

As the Quilting Circle has grown, its members have defined their mission in terms that emphasize its benefits to the community. Focusing on "education," they believe they are making citizens more aware of their past and thus contributing to a sense of community pride. They also consider it valuable to teach people a craft they can enjoy, and some members regard quilting in more idealistic terms as a way of combatting the pressures of a market economy, reducing stress, and returning to a simpler way of living. For some it is a reminder of the strong women who made the nation what it is, like the pioneer woman whose statement has become a kind of motto for the Circle: "I made quilts as fast as I could to keep my family warm and as beautiful as I could to keep my heart from breaking."

The group has had to become more formal than it probably would have been a generation or two earlier. It affiliated with the national organization early on because its members realized they could be sued if someone attending their annual show was injured in an accident; the national organization offered insurance to cover such potential liabilities. The national organization also trains judges to oversee competitions and provides certification to members who wish to teach quilting. Furthermore, because the Circle earns money by charging admission to its annual show, by taking a commission from vendors who sell food and beverages at the show, and by holding a raffle for one of its quilts, it has incorporated itself as a tax-exempt nonprofit organization.

One reason the Quilting Circle has been successful is that its members are very loosely connected to one another. A few, like Caroline Madison, devote a great deal of time to organizing the annual show and other events, but most members participate infrequently and on their own terms, and even Caroline gives only a couple of hours a week most of the year. Of the one hundred members, fewer than half typically attend the monthly meetings, but the half is not always the same, so most members do participate occasionally. And quilting is an activity that can largely be performed at home. Caroline's most memorable experience with the group was one Christmas when she organized an effort to make children's quilts for needy families. One evening in early November about thirty women gathered in the fellowship hall of a church, bringing scraps of fabric to exchange and receiving instructions about other materials, size, and when the quilts needed to be done. That was the only time the women met. Over the next six weeks they worked on their quilts while watching television in the evenings or when they had an hour or two to spare. Quilts began appearing on Caroline's porch or being delivered by Federal Express. By the week before Christmas twenty-seven quilts were ready to distribute.

Not only can people do quilting alone; they also express themselves through their quilts. As Caroline says, "Quilts become very, very personal." To be sure, the members learn from one another and sometimes work together, and of course they form friendships. But much of the activity (a large quilt may take four or five years to complete) is individual. Women in the group say candidly that working on the quilts is often a form of therapy, a time to be alone, to grieve, to reflect, and to think about their lives. For some, it is still a way to keep their hearts from breaking.

As the Quilting Circle illustrates, craft and hobby groups have at least held their own in terms of membership in recent years, despite busier schedules and changes in taste. They are seldom overtly altruistic or civic-minded; indeed, they are part of the self-interested leisure culture that worries so many critics of American society. For example, Caroline admits that she started quilting because she had devoted her life to her children and felt it was now time to do something for herself. Yet these organizations can play positive roles in their communities. The Quilting Circle found itself with extra funds, and its members were able to turn out more quilts than they could use themselves. It was hard for them to avoid becoming involved in charitable activities.

The Quilting Circle also illustrates that small towns are not isolated enclaves now under siege by outside forces. Small towns have always depended on being integrated into regional networks, and this integration has become more important than ever. The Quilting Circle is, in this sense, merely an extension of the ladies' missionary societies of the nineteenth century that collected clothing for needy people in Africa or provisions for soldiers during the Civil War. In today's more commercialized economy the Quilting Circle earns money from admission fees and vendors, but it also still makes contributions in kind, and it depends on the fact that people can easily travel, attend shows, and visit shopping malls, but also work at their own pace at home.

If the small town is to be praised as the epitome of community, it should be regarded in this broader sense. Few of the Quilting Circle members knew each other before they joined. They got to know their neighbors by making a deliberate effort to participate in something. In participating they did not become idealistic citizens or give up their personal autonomy; nor did their attention focus entirely on their immediate community. Small towns are loosely connected with other small towns and with various nonprofit organizations in the surrounding areas. At least some of these connections help address the ills of the wider community. The women who participate in the Quilting Circle have created a community within and across the boundaries of the small towns in which they live. They have a sense of participating in civic life, even if it is not always with their immediate neighbors.

Small towns do retain some of the community loyalties that many Americans attribute to them. But even here civic involvement is changing, and civic organizations are adapting to new realities. Public institutions such as park commissions and town councils must cultivate relationships with county, state, and federal agencies in order to be effective, and they are being drawn into controversies involving land management, environmental protection, water rights, interstate highway systems, chain stores, and new housing developments. Informal voluntary assistance to the needy is now augmented by formal nonprofit organizations, and service clubs are becoming more like self-help groups. With easier transportation and communication, local organizations increasingly form loose partnerships with groups in other communities and draw on a larger geographic area for members. Under these changing circumstances, the community organizations in greatest jeopardy are those which fail to bring in new leaders and initiate new programs. Residents' concerns that civic participation in their communities is dying are generally ill-founded, at least when innovative forms of involvement are considered, but it is also true that the character of community is changing.

Of all the changes taking place in small towns, the one that disturbs long-time residents most seems also to be the hardest for them to pin down with precision. It is their sense that a way of life has been lost, that people are somehow not what they used to be. It is similar to the feeling of things not being right that suburban residents express, but it is often tinged with a more poignant sense of nostalgia. Sometimes it is the sentiment that erupts in bare-teethed remarks about newcomers or public officials. It more often comes through as a troubled longing for the past.

Listening closely to their descriptions of how things are changing, one begins to envision what social scientists sometimes call a "moral order"—a pattern of implicit assumptions about proper ways of behaving—that was more a reality of small-town life than a mere figment of nostalgic imaginations.[12] The moral order told people not only what their place was in the community but why it was worthwhile to occupy this place. People could infer much about their neighbors from the time of day they did their shopping or who they drank coffee with at the local café. They knew who was a member of which church or club, and it was self-evident that membership implied certain duties. The moral order perpetuated itself with a long memory that kept track of favors owed and rules violated. Its watchful eyes discouraged citizens from straying too far from their civic obligations.

When a moral order starts to crumble, it leaves people wondering whether life can ever function as smoothly again. The formal regulations that replace implicit norms seem more intrusive. High taxes hit people in their hearts as well as in their wallets, evoking worries that taxation itself may be in violation of their moral principles. The people who used to be trustworthy now seem fewer, while the scoundrels seem to have multiplied.

In a small town called Hadleyville, some older residents see evidence of moral decay in what has happened to the Sportsmen's Club. It was once a thriving feature of the community, boasting a membership of four hundred men. It owned a plot of land too hilly on one end and too marshy on the other for farming but just right for hunting small game. The club was less a separate organization than an integral fact of civic life. The members held their meetings at the firehouse, where many of them served as volunteers. They let the Boy Scouts use their ground for camping and helped them earn their hunting badges. They gave the township supervisors free memberships and kept the local taxidermist busy.

As the Hadleyville residents remember it, the Sportsmen's Club blends imperceptibly with their assumptions about what makes a good community. During hunting season it was easy to tell the "real sportsmen" from the "slob sportsmen." The former were local men who paid their obligatory visits to the café on Main Street where they shared cautionary tales about where to hunt or not to hunt. The slob sportsmen visited the tavern at the edge of town, where their license plates clearly showed them to be outsiders and where they were sometimes overheard making comments disrespectful of local customs. The Sportsmen's Club symbolized good community in its own behavior. Members hunted in groups of five, walking in an orderly line ("none of this running here and there"), and they donated a Saturday morning several times a year to maintaining the property. Being a sportsman was a way to "be a man," as one member reminisces, because every man had learned how to hunt from his father and passed the skill along to his sons. They knew it was a sport that held little interest for the women.

The club's decline has given Hadleyville residents a way of talking about the erosion of their way of life. Membership has fallen precipitously. It does not work with the Boy Scouts; the local troop no longer exists. Some of the members now refer to the club as a "nonprofit organization." They fret that so few members are willing to help keep up the property, and some of the men are still ambivalent about the fact that 20 percent are now women. They keep the club solvent by holding raffles and selling lessons in marksmanship. They have to raise substantially more money than they did in the past to cover the rising taxes on their land and to pay for a hefty liability policy.

Like residents of many small towns, some people in Hadleyville find it hard to become emotional about the troubles of the Sportsmen's Club. To them the club seems better suited to a time of male chauvinism and cruelty to animals. Many of the sportsmen recognize the positive changes that are taking place in their community. But they worry. Although life is still good compared to other places they can imagine living, the changes evoke a vague discomfort. It is easier for them to allude to this discomfort metaphorically than to identify it directly. The town supervisors seem "nit-pickier" than they used to be. The number of slob sportsmen has risen dramatically. It is no longer legal to trap foxes. Most of the pheasants are gone. Small game is getting harder and harder to find.

Small towns are nevertheless adapting to changing times. Although their residents sometimes yearn for a simpler age with a better-defined civic and moral order, they are finding ways to forge ties to their neighbors and do constructive things in and for the community. The challenges are heightened by their decreasing isolation from problems in the wider world. Large discount stores and new housing developments threaten their familiar way of life. Still, the looser, more diverse, long-distance relationships that characterize their civic activities are helping them meet these challenges.

7

The Good Citizen

IF OUR SOCIETY IS BECOMING increasingly fluid and diverse, how are these conditions affecting our understandings of ourselves? Do we regard ourselves as people of strong moral character who can continue to fulfill our obligations as responsible members of our communities? Or are we losing our sense of who we are and starting to question our ability to perform our civic duties?

According to 90 percent of the public, good citizenship depends more than anything else on people who know what is right and wrong and are willing to stand up for their beliefs—in short, on people who have moral character.[1] Being a good citizen clearly implies more than voting or showing interest in politics and more than simply keeping one's property well maintained and not disturbing the neighbors. It means being firmly committed to high moral principles that include taking care of one's own needs as well as helping others. Part of being a good citizen depends on taking time to think through one's convictions and cultivating experiences that help develop one's personal talents. The other part entails being genuinely concerned about the needs of others and doing one's part to alleviate these needs. Being a person of character requires both self-knowledge and the courage, patience, and social skills needed to work with others.

An emphasis on character as the essential component of good citizenship is deeply embedded in our most cherished cultural traditions. Our religious heritage emphasizes that individuals carry an inner spark of divine goodness or undergo a redemptive experience that fortifies them both to do what is right and to serve the common good. Our tradition of civic republicanism, which is drawn as much from the classics as from the

Enlightenment and is taught routinely in the nation's schools, expresses similar ideas. In this tradition such virtues as personal honesty and integrity, humility, and a desire to serve others, as well as such practices as treating others fairly and being reliable in performing one's work, are important aspects of being a good citizen. In both traditions it is essential that a rudimentary knowledge of the nation's history and system of government be instilled in children at an early age and then reinforced as they mature and shoulder the duties of citizenship. This knowledge is of little value, however, unless it is internalized by people who understand their own strengths and limitations and recognize the benefits of trying to serve the wider community.[2]

In the past children learned to be good citizens through family experiences that taught them values and molded their character and through exposure to stories that illustrated courage, heroism, patience, and compassion. Lessons learned at home were generally reinforced by schools and churches, and by informal interaction among neighbors, participation in civic organizations, and military service or volunteering. In these familiar settings people gained experience that taught them patience and self-knowledge, and they learned social skills that were valuable for conducting community business, organizing meetings, and understanding democratic procedures.

The loose connections that now characterize so many of our communities raise doubts about our nation's ability to inculcate children with a clear sense of right and wrong or to reinforce the moral convictions of adults. As one older woman remarks, "The rules aren't as clear; life is more demanding." Scattered, ephemeral relationships expose people to different and even competing messages about appropriate standards of conduct. Whereas stable, communal, and bureaucratic organizations teach people to be loyal members who respect authority and fulfill responsible roles, short-term and variable contacts may encourage people to pursue their own self-interested activities.

Yet it would be wrong to assume that our understandings of citizenship cannot adapt to changes in society. Over the past two centuries Americans have learned to express their convictions on new issues and through new media, but they have retained the idea that courage to stand up for one's convictions is an essential aspect of being a good citizen. Even though communities grew larger and became more industrialized, people continued to believe that they should use their talents for the good of others rather than pursuing only their personal interests. Americans are now updating their thinking about citizenship and character to correspond with current social changes as well.

June Adams is a retired woman in her seventies who has been a peace activist most of her life. Her father worked for a munitions company during World War I, so she had many opportunities while growing up to discuss the pros and cons of war. June went to Vassar in the late 1930s and became embroiled in the debates concerning Germany and whether or not the United States should intervene. Shortly after graduation she married, and within a year her husband was drafted. He survived the war, but two of her brothers and a brother-in-law were killed. June's conviction that war should be resisted was now firmly in place.[3]

After the war she settled into the quiet life of being a mother and the wife of a college administrator. As was expected of her, she did volunteer work at the local hospital, served on the board of a private school, remained active in the Vassar alumni association, helped raise money for a family services organization in which her father was involved, attended church, and helped at the YMCA. She also wrote letters regularly to her representatives in Washington and to members of the state legislature. During much of this time her opposition to war remained dormant.

When the United States started building its military forces in Vietnam, June Adams's civic concerns shifted into high gear. She joined two peace organizations, a secular one and one sponsored by the Catholic church, stopped paying the tax on her telephone bill because she thought the monies were being used to support the war effort, kept a barrage of letters in the mail to Washington, and in 1972 worked actively for George McGovern and made a generous donation to his campaign. Several of these activities (especially the last), she was to discover later, earned her a place on Richard Nixon's list of enemies.

By the mid-1970s the peace movement had faded from public view. Most of those who had swelled the ranks of the two organizations June belonged to went on to other interests, but she stayed and has continued to be active. The groups help keep her informed, and she finds there is always something worth knowing about, whether it was the disarmament talks during the 1980s or the peace negotiations in the Middle East or opposing the Gulf War.

Her pattern of civic involvement fits the more enduring style of her generation rather than being an example of loose connections. Much of what she has learned about patience, courage, and civic responsibility can be attributed to her tenacious commitment to a few organizations. She has taken consistent and often unpopular stands on public issues, and she has put her convictions into practice.

Skip Lockhart reflects a very different form of civic involvement. At age forty-one he is a physician who earns a salary that places him among the top one percent of American breadwinners and who lives in a comfortable home in one of the richest sections of town. He is a devoted husband and father who likes to spend the few hours he is not working with his family. His time being so precious, he seldom ventures out to chat with his neighbors, and during the summer he and his family spend as many weekends as possible at their cabin in the mountains. His civic involvement consists mostly of doing pro bono work at the hospital. Through his profession he spent some time a few years ago with the Easter Seal committee. Because he is on call some weekends, he occasionally lends his cabin to other couples. He keeps in touch with his parents, who live in another city, by visiting them on holidays, and he has participated in a men's support group during some times of personal searching.

As a baby-boomer, a busy professional, and a suburbanite, Skip Lockhart is a clear example of someone whose ties to the community are relatively loose. Other than the large nondenominational church that he and his wife attend once or twice a month because they enjoy the music, he is not a long-term member of any community organizations. Although he has lived in the same neighborhood for a decade, wanting to be a good citizen has encouraged him mostly to be a short-term participant in activities outside his community. His medical practice does not provide him with the time and the predictable schedule that make it possible for June Adams to stay involved in the peace movement.

From her long-term involvement June Adams feels she has gained strength of character that has in turn helped her to be a better citizen. She has little sense of having made a great contribution to democracy during her long years of civic engagement. She can point out that the United States eventually got out of Vietnam and that the threat of nuclear weapons is not as great as it once was, but she is also discouraged that so many lives have been lost and that wars are always being waged in some part of the world. As she looks back on her life she is nevertheless grateful for the opportunity to have been involved in the peace movement and in so many other civic activities.

She is grateful because the people in these groups have challenged her to lead a better life than she might otherwise have lived. It would have been easier to sit and read or focus on her own family, but she would not have had to develop the character to face difficult issues in the community. "It's good to be at the edge, on the margins," she says, "having to raise difficult questions." She uses words like strength, faith, and patience to describe what she has experienced. There were often tensions in the peace groups she belonged to, and working through these tensions helped her understand her own convictions more deeply, as well as teaching her to appreciate other perspectives. The information and support provided by the groups helped her direct her energies in more useful ways (for example, she discovered that not paying the taxes on her telephone bill was a waste of effort), and kept her going at times when she was discouraged: "It's been good to have like-minded people, not people who were just clones of each other but who were interested in talking about the same sorts of issues."

The payoff was making a difference, if only a small difference, to the community and to the nation. "It's been a way of showing basic respect for man and woman. I wanted to make some effort, no matter how minimal or ineffective." Another payoff was the realization that courage and cooperation were virtues worth cultivating in their own right. She has been able to communicate these virtues to some of the people she has worked with or for whom she has volunteered. Probably the clearest evidence has been in her influence on her son. During the Vietnam war he declared himself a conscientious objector, and he too has remained active in the peace movement.

Although Skip Lockhart's civic activities have been more scattered, they have contributed no less to his personal growth than June Adams's activities did to hers. Just as it has been difficult for her to assess her contributions in terms of the difference they made in the wider world, so he recognizes that lending his cabin or helping with the Easter Seal drive may be of little consequence by some external standard. The results are clearly evident, however, in the kind of person he has become and in his outlook on what truly matters in life. He admits that he learned early to be a rugged individualist, to compete, to achieve, and to look out for himself. He would not have survived medical school without this tough, competitive orientation. But participating in civic organizations over the years has altered his perceptions of what is most important in life: "I realized that what is good in life is something I cannot attain by myself. I realized that it requires coming together. It requires an attitude of submission—and that's pretty strange in our culture. It means being submissive to one other, not a negative thing at all, but caring for one another, lifting up the other person, being willing to compromise."

Skip Lockhart admits that there are no easy ways to develop this kind of outlook on life. It is a process that requires self-monitoring, deliberation, and support. Being in groups has given him the opportunity to reflect on his decisions, to look at himself through the eyes of other people, and to detach from some of his own interests. It has forced him to think harder about the kind of person he wants to be.

More than voting, and more even than keeping abreast of political issues, citizenship in America has meant character—what the framers of republican tradition called civic virtue. It was a commitment to live according to high moral principles, knowing that these alone could make the nation better than it was. For people of June Adams's generation the resolve to live by moral principles often came from the hardships of war or economic adversity. Those of Skip Lockhart's generation have had to live with greater uncertainty about how to make the right choices. In both cases, character and civic virtue are crucial. Whether they belong to service clubs, as more people did in the past, or do sporadic volunteer service, as more people do now, Americans derive benefits from their activities: becoming knowledgeable about their communities, taking an active interest in social and political issues, gaining greater confidence in their own abilities, acquiring social and civic skills, and learning how to be patient and trust others to do their part (see Methods, Table 7). But it is also evident that their understanding of these traits is changing.

The understandings of character, its nature and meaning, are often different for people in traditional groups and for those in porous situations. For the former, strength of character is more often associated with belonging to a community that provides role models to emulate; because the community is fairly stable and homogeneous, there is likely to be a virtual consensus about the values and activities that constitute good character. For the latter, strength comes less from being a long-standing member of the community and more from voluntarily choosing to identify with a worthy cause or interest group.

Carmen Carlata, of Action X, says, "It gave me my focus in life." Her understanding of community is "not just defined geographically but by my

Latino heritage and young people in general and women also." In fact, participating in Action X differentiates her from most of the other people in her geographic community. It has helped her gain a clearer sense of her priorities.

A woman who volunteers for an urban ministry to teenagers says she is gaining a better understanding of herself from the difficulties she faces. Sometimes the other staff members serve as a supportive community that reinforces her commitment to help the ministry's clients. But often the other staff members are preoccupied with their own responsibilities or she has little time to interact with them. She then turns inward to find strength, sometimes by reflecting on the reasons she chose this activity. Phoning a friend is helpful as well.

Having character may mean being able to sort through the various messages one receives about how to behave. In a diverse community these messages are likely to come in all shades of gray, rather than being black or white. A Latino social worker in his mid-thirties who works with inner-city children says he routinely receives mixed messages about his professional activities from his supervisors, politicians, clergy, the local news media, and representatives of different racial and ethnic groups. He spends a lot of time listening to the various ideas and proposals, many of which include explicit criticisms of his agency. Being a person of strong character has come to mean ignoring many of these suggestions and doing what his training and instincts tell him is right.

The CEO of a large nonprofit organization makes a similar observation about being a good citizen: "I think it's more complicated now because there's so much information. The amount of static out there makes it more difficult to make decisions." Although he does not assume that being a responsible member of the community was ever easy, he says it is increasingly important to be able to entertain a wide range of opinions. A person of character must try harder to be inclusive.

Strength of character continues to imply that people are steadfast in their convictions, but its current definition also allows people greater freedom to change their minds. As one community leader says, "I pretty quickly develop a 'been there, done that' attitude." She associates personal strength with being secure enough to abandon familiar ways of doing things. In a rapidly changing environment that brings her into daily contact with new problems, she feels it is necessary above all to be flexible.

In addition to these shifting definitions of character, the changing nature of civic involvement is related to new understandings of the skills that good citizens should have at their disposal. Traditional skills, such as how to lead a meeting using democratic procedures and how to secure cooperation from others, are still important. But civic skills are increasingly shaped by looser civic connections to include knowing how to work with the media, understanding how to cultivate trust among strangers, and finding ways to turn self-interested concerns into tasks beneficial to the community. Most people learn a complex array of civic skills.

An example of this is Nancy Fielding, the founder of a group called the Garden Club. Nationally, such clubs are not as popular as they once were.[4] And on the surface there is little reason to consider Nancy Fielding's club, which she started as a way to pursue her own interest in flowers and shrubs, a form of civic participation at all. Yet the story of its founding demonstrates a great deal about the skills needed to initiate a successful group of this kind. The Garden Club is a lesson in grassroots democracy and in the ways norms of mutual assistance develop and lead to other forms of civic involvement.

Because those who joined the club were entering into a kind of contract with each other to help and be helped, they needed to know as clearly as possible what to expect. The pooled experience of the initial members played an important part in establishing the guidelines. They realized, for example, that some potential members might think the club was a way to get their leaves raked or other routine yard work done. They wrote into the rules, "The focus of this particular club is to give women or homeowners real concrete help in their flower and shrub beds." They wanted the club to focus on flowers and bushes, and thus to attract people who thought of themselves as gardeners. They also knew they did not want to emphasize participation in competitive flower shows.

The Garden Club has worked well because it is driven by members' needs. They participate because they want help with their gardening and the group provides a way to secure this help. The one-page newsletter, along with photocopies of clippings from newspapers and magazines, is an added inducement, as is the telephone chain members use to let one another know of events such as sales. The meetings are fairly democratic and informal, even though Nancy has continued to provide leadership. "The life of the club," she says, "was driven by the needs of the women, which fostered group ownership."

Indeed, part of the skill required to organize a club like this is knowing the importance of teaching others the same skills so that they feel a sense of ownership and, more than that, are able to take over some of the leadership roles. Nancy Fielding recognizes that her interests or available time may be different in a year or two, so she is delegating responsibilities to other women in the club. She has enlisted volunteers to handle the newsletter and is encouraging several women who know more about gardening than she does to assume more prominent roles. She has published an article about the club in a leading garden magazine and has developed a "starter kit" with sample letters, ad copy, by-laws, rules, vouchers, and clippings to send in response to the dozens of inquiries that come in from all across the country. Her own needs enable her to understand those of others, and she is eager to help other women find the same support and satisfaction in their own garden clubs as she has found in hers.

The Garden Club is but one example of the hundreds of thousands of self-help groups that have been started in the past few years. Few have operating procedures as highly formalized as Nancy Fielding's, but most have devised norms that facilitate cooperation and deter misunderstandings. In the process, members learn valuable lessons in grassroots democracy, such as how to lead a meeting, how to be a participant, and how to resolve differences and come to an agreement. The Garden Club was organized almost entirely for self-interested purposes, and yet it has also benefited the wider community.

As the members talked, they learned about problems in the community and recruited one another to serve as volunteers. One replaced another member on the citizen's advisory committee for the local post office; another started volunteering at a program for the blind after hearing about it through the club; yet another persuaded all the members to help "beautify" the grounds of one of the public buildings. To be sure, these are small contributions, but they are performed in the spirit of civic-mindedness. They are a product of the "social capital" that members of such groups create when they gather to help one another. Most important, the Garden Club provided its members with skills that would help them function as good citizens in future endeavors.

The abilities people develop in civic organizations are often called "transferable skills." Such skills as leading a meeting, phoning strangers, and knocking on doors to raise money can be learned in one organization and then used just as easily in another. This transfer is possible because civic organizations deliberately imitate one another, building on their members' experience in other organizations, and because utilizing standard techniques makes it easier for newcomers to participate. People often have to make and break relationships in order to accomplish civic tasks, and these skills facilitate the forging of loose connections.

Today it is not enough to learn the transferable skills that may be common in traditional membership organizations such as service clubs and churches. Increasingly, good citizenship is also defined in terms of innovative skills that include networking, dealing with diversity, initiating new projects, and filling niches in an already crowded institutional environment. An example is provided by Delores Buchanan, who in her early fifties inadvertently became the founder and president of a small foundation that helps families who are in financial difficulty because of children with serious medical needs.

Delores Buchanan married during college and quit school to raise three children, who are now grown and live in other parts of the country. Her second husband, whom she married five years ago, has no children. He works for the government and she runs a one-person advertising and graphic design agency from a spare bedroom. They live in a modest Cape Cod built in the early 1920s. The suburb consists mostly of longtime residents, some of whose parents also lived in the community, and many have taken pay cuts or started driving farther to work because of plant closings in the area.

Five years ago, shortly after she and her new husband moved to the neighborhood, Delores was working at a real estate office, and with the local economy depressed, nothing was selling. Thinking that they needed to do something to give the office a higher profile in the community, Delores and a co-worker started brainstorming. Mostly they came up with gimmicks, such as sponsoring a raffle or handing out pencils and balloons. But an article in the newspaper seized their imaginations. It was about a seven-year-old girl in another town who had been stricken with leukemia and needed a bone marrow transplant. The story filled Delores with sympathy for the family; she also saw an angle. Raising money for the bone marrow transplant would benefit the family and create good publicity for the real estate office. She was to discover that it would also teach her to be a better citizen.

After meeting with the girl and her mother, Delores promised to do what she could to raise a thousand dollars. She contacted the newspaper editor, who agreed to publicize her efforts. She then contacted the girl's teacher, who enlisted students to raise money by collecting cans for recycling. Prompted by the teacher, a teacher at the high school sponsored a car wash. Delores got the man who ran the donut shop and the woman who ran the pizza parlor to put collection cans near their cash registers. Someone read about the campaign and offered to donate a free week at a summer cabin in the mountains if Delores would include it in a raffle. She printed raffle tickets and set up a table in the shopping mall.

The action expanded soon after a man in a black motorcycle jacket stopped at the table to purchase a ticket. He told his friends in his motorcycle gang and they told their friends. One of them was a musician who decided to put on a benefit rock concert, which proved so successful that a second concert was scheduled a few months later. Another wrote a short story for a national bikers' magazine, and before long Delores was receiving checks from all over the country.

Instead of the thousand dollars she had expected, Delores found she had $200,000, more than enough for the operation. The girl and her parents went off to a large medical center in another state for the operation. But it was unsuccessful, and the girl died a few months later. Delores was devastated. Meanwhile, however, the state agency that had initially denied the girl Medicaid funds reversed its decision and paid for the entire operation. Delores now had to decide what to do with the money.

She offered it to the girl's parents, but they were moving away to escape their grief and wanted nothing to do with it. Enough of the money had been given in cash or anonymously that it was impossible to return it. The Leukemia Foundation, the American Cancer Society, and several other charities immediately put in bids for it, but Delores was reluctant to see it absorbed into the coffers of a large bureaucracy. She lay awake at night, prayed, and finally visited a lawyer who explained that it would cost at least $3,000 to set up a foundation to disseminate the money.

Delores did not have $3,000 (and did not feel it was appropriate to draw money from the fund). She decided to see if she could raise it. One night she made a list of fifty people she knew: her hairdresser, college classmates, friends of her first husband, people who had helped with the campaign. The next day she began calling them. By the time she got to number twenty-two on the list she had her $3,000.

The foundation is called Angels and Friends in honor of the girl who died and the friends who raised money for her. Delores is its president, her husband is secretary-treasurer, several friends serve as officers, and the twenty-two donors are listed on the letterhead as charter members. It is not widely known, but people hear about it through friends of friends, and Delores has briefed the human services department and the directors of several children's hospitals about it.

The effort did not save the girl's life, nor did it save the real estate office. Ironically, the regional manager had already decided to close the office before Delores came up with the idea of seeking publicity. But the money has made a difference in other cases. One was a little boy Delores spotted one day at the county welfare office with his dad; she knew immediately that he was undergoing chemotherapy. She left her card with his welfare caseworker, who phoned an hour later to say she was an answer to his prayers.

Delores breaks into tears as she tells her stories. Cynics may respond by pointing out that such efforts do little to heal the larger problems of our society. Yet the relationships that were established or strengthened in the course of raising the money are important in themselves. People with no previous ties have come to know and trust one another. Delores says her own views of the community have improved—and she is no longer as frightened when she sees someone in a motorcycle jacket with tattoos and a bandanna.

The history of Angels and Friends defies many of the stereotypes of small, informal support groups and self-help efforts. It was not a small group at all, nor did it emerge to meet the emotional needs of its members. It nevertheless originated in self-interest: Delores's wish to publicize the real estate office. Through its fundraising efforts it became a kind of support group for the leukemia-stricken girl and her family, and it was a private self-help effort geared to handle a problem that was not expected to be dealt with through public agencies.

It is an example of how relationships are forged in a society where traditional forms of community are no longer reliable. The newspaper became an important tool for developing connections. Delores contacted strangers, such as teachers and merchants, knowing nothing about them personally but understanding that they held roles in organizations that might be served by getting involved. The most tightly knit group, perhaps ironically, was the motorcycle gang. But it, too, was loosely connected, and its national publication proved instrumental in spreading the story.

Delores's resistance to giving the money to an established charitable organization points to the antibureaucratic sentiment that promotes smaller, entrepreneurial activities like her own. Her efforts would largely be missed by standard sociological surveys, insofar as she does much of the work herself and has little need for frequent meetings or large membership lists. The volunteer time that went into recycling and car washes and raffles would be about all that most surveys would register.

Angels and Friends is an example of how good citizenship can be cultivated by an activity characterized by loose connections. It has promoted a few lasting relationships (Delores and her husband keep in touch with the girl's mother), but most of the people who contributed did not know one another then nor do they now. They participated briefly and for one specific purpose: to help a dying girl. Nevertheless, there have been secondary benefits. The twenty-two charter members have something in common that they did not have before. Several contributors have enlisted one another's help to serve on the board of the local hospital. There is a level of personal confidence and a sense of pride in the community that were not there before.

Being a strong enough person to take the initiative to make a difference in one's community is critical to good citizenship. One must be able to take responsibility for oneself and make difficult decisions when the need arises. This kind of strength does not necessarily precede civic involvement but emerges as people face the challenges it presents. People do not serve the good of the community best by focusing all of their attention on other people and neglecting themselves. They need to focus some of it on themselves. Thus, the antidote to American individualism is not a collectivist orientation that always puts the community first; it is an orientation that strikes a balance between individual needs and community needs. Love of neighbor is best accomplished when it satisfies one's own needs as well.

Social observers who express concern about a therapeutic mentality that encourages people to focus on their own feelings and to worry about taking care of themselves assume that such an orientation necessarily shifts attention away from the interests of the community to a narcissistic interest in the self.[5] But it is important to recognize that the kind of therapy that strengthens individuals' sense and understanding of self can make a positive contribution to civil society as well.

Consider what a young blind woman says. In the past few years she has become a therapist and has redirected much of her attention from volunteering in the community to working with individuals in therapy. Many of her clients are women who have been socialized to care for others to the point that their husbands and sons have found it easy to avoid taking responsibility for themselves. She is aware that teaching women to take less responsibility for others may have negative consequences for volunteer agencies, but she also finds that her clients and their families become stronger in the process of learning the appropriate boundaries between themselves and others: "It's a paradox. I try to get them to focus back on themselves, and then they are better able to relate to others."

This is essentially what June Adams and Skip Lockhart accomplished without the aid of professional therapists. Stretching themselves thin in service to others, as an activist and as a physician, forced them to look more closely at their motivations. In each case, having a small group was helpful because it gave them an opportunity to talk about their personal needs. What prevents such discussions from turning entirely inward is that members remain involved enough in civic activities to realize the need for a balance in their lives. This realization necessitates being honest about the struggles, the tensions, and the unfulfilling aspects of community life.

Rather than throwing their energies wholeheartedly into the problems of others, Americans have responded, in part, to the message of therapy to help themselves first and let others solve their own problems. It is evident from the large numbers of people who are detached from their communities that these lessons are having an effect. But there is a kind of healthy detachment that is part of good citizenship that protects people from despair or burnout. Most people engaged in civic activities admit that the involvement has given them plenty of grief, instead of simply filling their lives with happiness. In the Civic Involvement Survey, among those who had volunteered in the past year, 61 percent said other people had let them down, 42 percent had experienced conflict with other people, 63 percent had felt discouraged or frustrated, and 37 percent had become burned out. Faced with such realities, many volunteers say it is more effective for them to realize their limitations and not expend all their energies and emotions, rather than attempting to ensure that everything somehow gets done.

Sara Mermel illustrates this point in a candid comparison between Hadassah and working in special education: "All my professional life I've worked in special ed. Problem families. Kids with handicaps. Parents mentally ill, brain damaged, stroke patients, families in crisis. It's more difficult in Hadassah!" If doing community work is more difficult than working with seriously impaired people, then it takes some emotional work to do it right; the self cannot be ignored, but must be guided reflectively. "I'm learning humor," Sara Mermel says. "I'm learning that to work too hard is not good for my health. I'm feeling the effects of it physically and I've got to delegate and detach from the things that can't get done. Just let them go." She has come to realize that not everybody has a "compulsive organizational nature" like hers. "So I have to just say, 'Well, that's all that person can do. Forget about it.' I have to learn to let go of the things that can't be fixed."

Self-knowledge can limit one's civic involvement, and thus promote the more ephemeral kinds of connections that are coming to characterize American communities. Sara Mermel is pulling back, telling herself she needs to do so to preserve her mental and physical health, rather than pouring her life into the work of Hadassah. When millions of Americans pull back in this way, it becomes harder for civic organizations to perform effectively. Yet it is also fundamental to a democratic society that people share the burdens of responsibility for their communities. Properly understood, emotional detachment that includes limiting one's commitments can encourage people to recognize that they must work together, each doing a small part, rather than attempting to manage or manipulate what the final outcome may be.

One of the most common lessons learned by people who are active in civic affairs is the importance of being patient. Martha Wilson, who devotes a few hours each week to the PTA, says that patience is the main virtue she has had to work at developing in her PTA experience. She means this in several senses. Patience means the kind of deep, inner resolve that comes from exercising the will, something almost like courage, in the traditional sense: she feels she has become a better person, a more patient person. It also means being savvy enough to know what to say and what not to say: she has learned little scripts to recite, even though she may not feel very patient at the moment. For example, her instinct sometimes is to blurt out, "That's a ridiculous idea," but instead she says, "Well, that's interesting." Patience also means the kind of forbearance that comes from adopting a democratic stance toward other people. Martha's motto is that "everybody's important" as far as the PTA is concerned. She explains: "They might not head a committee, or they might not be on the board, but their opinion is just as important as mine, because their child goes there. I guess that's it, to be able to consider all kinds of different ways of looking at something, and really give them some thought."

Patience involves not only learning to wait for others but also respecting their needs and interests even when doing so may make it take longer to accomplish tasks. A young man named Rene DuMont discusses the lessons he is learning from his youth training program. Coming to understand that the congressman who sponsored the program was worried about being reelected, he says, helped him from feeling too let down. He realizes that the concerns of school principals and merchants may also affect the program. He says, "[I've learned] patience in dealing with people and the issues of other people. I think it's so easy for things to not go your way and for you to dismiss what's happening as, 'Okay, it's them against me or they're inconsiderate or it's their loss,' as opposed to just thinking things through and sort of being patient to sort of make sense of what's happening."

Being involved in a single membership organization over a long period is likely to require certain kinds of patience: a willingness to wait on other people, to put up with their foibles, and to forgo immediate outcomes in the interest of longer-term goals. People with loose connections often speak of patience as an awareness that one may have to shop around to find the right person for a task. Patience also means moving on to another person when the first person fails, or taking the time to put together a coalition of people who can complement one another's abilities. As one man explains, "Patience means being willing to enlist the help of others until you find the right combination to do the job."

For many good citizens being patient means understanding that each person has unique gifts which demand respect. Acknowledging individual differences may conflict with the view that good citizenship requires everyone to pitch in with volunteer work, help with political campaigns, and participate actively in service clubs and associations. This view is often expressed by political scientists and community leaders who believe that every person should be an active member of a civic organization, take enough interest in politics to keep up on the important issues, and donate volunteer time to helping the needy. The opposing view is more often articulated by people who have an organic image of society that includes the notion of each person contributing a little to the common good by using his or her unique gifts to the fullest, whether that be raising children, working in a chemistry lab, or pumping gas. One woman expressed this view when asked what she had learned from more than a decade of community service: "That life is short and I'm not going to spend my time anymore doing things for which I'm not specially qualified. I will stay with the areas where I'm a little more gifted."

The view that everyone should be doing the same things is valid up to a point; for example, few would deny that every citizen should vote and do so knowledgeably. The alternative view is compelling, however, because it accords greater respect to people's diversity. Rather than assuming that those who are pursuing their own interests are necessarily bad citizens, it recognizes that people contribute best to the common good when they develop their particular skills and talents. Citizenship, like democracy, is in this respect messy. It requires those who exhort everyone to join a service club to keep on with their exhortations, but it also requires those who are genuinely fulfilling their civic responsibilities in other ways to ignore these exhortations.

People who are active in their communities often emphasize that civic involvement must be kept in perspective. In keeping with their more flexible view toward relationships, they argue that we owe responsibilities to the communities in which we live, but that we also exercise these responsibilities by performing well at our jobs, spending time with our families, and taking care of our personal needs. The diversity of contemporary civic organizations gives us opportunities to participate at many different levels and to take on longer- or shorter-term commitments as our circumstances permit. This diversity requires people to spend time reflecting on their lives, to choose wisely, and to set their own limits.

Sara Mermel talks eloquently about setting limits: "I've learned that I have limited energy. I've learned that I'm exhausted and that some of the stress issues have affected my health, seriously affected my health. I have to learn to set some limits and restore some balance to my life. I get caught up in it and the work itself becomes addictive. Work, the challenges of the problems, and my lists have a reproductive system all their own. They give birth to more lists when I'm not looking!"

Although she sets limits, Sara insists that balance in life includes doing something of service to other people. An underlying, enduring commitment to be of service is the antidote that keeps her notions of detachment, patience, and balance from leading to easy withdrawal from civic action when the going gets tough. Virtue of this kind is what some people refer to as a "flat-out commitment." It is not contingent on accomplishing some goal for the community or for oneself. Nor does it depend on deriving satisfaction from the involvement itself. The commitment is a kind of pledge people make with themselves to be involved and to stay involved through thick and thin, much like the commitment they make when they take a marriage vow.

Matilda Martin has made such a commitment to her community. It grew from having been on welfare and from her religious upbringing. She remembers vividly being near death on one occasion. She prayed to God, unsure what kind of God she was praying to, but sensing the power within herself to make a resolution. She resolved that she would devote her life to improving the community in which she lived. She made good on this commitment partly through her inner resolve, but also because the people at Union House gradually drew her in, helped her develop the skills she needed, and supported her emotionally when her resolve diminished. "Along the line, I've had people here who have encouraged me," she says. "I say to myself, I'm tired, I'm going to throw in the towel. But then I don't."

Jacob Merrick talks about virtue in terms of having a perspective that transcends self-interest. For some people this outlook comes from family or from being involved in civic organizations; for him it came through his participation in churches. "I think we're basically selfish," he admits, "and so I'm going to look out for my own ass first and not the next guy's. I think most people don't get motivated to get out of that unless they're involved in a faith experience somewhere." He elaborates: "A faith experience puts one in awe of divinity, of a God that cares about this creation, and all of a sudden one looks a whole heck of a lot smaller." He thinks selfishness can then diminish enough that people can consider the needs of others.

The kind of faith experience he has in mind does not supply rigid answers or generate a commitment to absolutes; it is more a humbling experience that opens people to the mysteries of life. His own encounter with the sacred, which occurred in high school, explains much of his present commitment to serving the community. He was drawn into the high school youth group (at the Presbyterian church he still attends) and found it a place where he could ask many of the questions about life that were beginning to plague him. More than a hundred students from twenty different high schools gathered every Sunday evening.

What Jacob experienced there is expressed clearly in one of his current volunteer activities. Despite the fact that he is overwhelmed by the low-income-housing project for which he volunteers and by serving on the hospital board and chairing a fundraising drive for another organization, he recently agreed to head his church's search committee for a new youth pastor. He's looking for somebody who will rekindle the enthusiasm he experienced when he was in high school: "Doggone it, I'm going to go on this committee and we're going to get the very best person we can. And not somebody with all the pat answers. It's not what we want. It's somebody who's going to encourage the kids to feel free, to ask all their questions and to explore all the issues in a place where normally people perceive that you've got to do the right thing and be the right way and you can't have doubts in church. Holy Mackerel. I want the kids to think, and this is the place where they can come and ask the questions and not be afraid."

If civic virtue is its own reward, as the saying goes, that reward is nonetheless real. Many people describe it as an intense feeling of satisfaction. It is especially sweet when people know with certainty that they make a difference in their community or when somebody in particular has been helped. As with any other job, part of the satisfaction is simply in having learned some valuable skills and put them to good use. Nelson Abram, the volunteer firefighter, expresses it well: "The biggest thing I've gotten out of it, I guess, is a good feeling of helping my neighbors when they've needed it, a feeling of accomplishment. Going out and tackling the job and getting it done. Those are the biggest things. Those are really the rewards that you get for being a firefighter."

Along with greater self-esteem, one gains greater insight into one's own strengths and weaknesses. Contrary to the idea that such insights are too individualistic to be of any value for civic involvement, many people talk about having learned humility. They do not think any less of themselves, but they think more highly of others, recognizing that other people sometimes have a better way of dealing with problems.

Katherine Stevens, a woman in her forties who works with something called the Hospitality Network, recalls the night a teenager became violent and the police had to be called. As a teacher, she had always felt capable of dealing with difficult situations involving students, but this was more of a challenge. The young man was behaving angrily, pacing back and forth, refusing to speak to anyone, and acting as if he might do more than just break another window in the church basement. Katherine saw that the police had better skills for dealing with the situation than she did:

"The policemen, kind of one at a time, gave the different women jobs, to go call the pastor or go wait at the door for somebody who was coming, and eventually had him alone in the room and talked to him, and actually got him to talk to them about what was bothering him, how he felt betrayed by his father, and he was really angry with his stepfather, and he had gone from being a great kid to being called names and stuff, and being belittled. I couldn't get that out of the kid. I could not, as a coordinator, get him to open up to me, and sometimes you need somebody else who's good at that. They were working with him, asking him personal questions, and not just saying 'You're in trouble because you broke a window.' They were looking at 'Why did you? What's going on in your head?' To see that somebody else's style worked better than mine, and somebody else happened to be better for the situation, it was okay to call in somebody else to work their magic."

Some people learn humility by realizing that there are problems too big for them to solve alone, others by discovering that their instincts for helping others are sometimes wrong. One woman was tempted to put her own money into the organization's budget every time there was a shortfall, but she eventually realized that the organization needed to find ways to become self-sustaining. In another case, a man's instinct was to propose solutions himself and ask the committee to rubberstamp his ideas, but he learned that letting others present their ideas was equally important (and more effective).

Within homogeneous communities people sometimes discover that their fellow members of civic organizations have different personality styles, different needs for structure, and the like. But it is those who venture out of their homogeneous neighborhoods who seem to be prompted to reflect most about themselves. Jeremy Alexander, a white businessman who serves on the board of an inner-city development corporation, has had to confront racial tensions directly, and says he has come away with a better understanding of his African American colleagues and a clearer sense of his own feelings about race: "I think I understand both the black community and the white community a whole lot more through seeing it from different eyes, and from working side by side with the new executive director, who's African American."

Civic participation also makes many people feel better rounded or gives them a way to keep their priorities in clearer perspective. Serving the community is a way of demonstrating to themselves that they are not simply leading a life of self-gratification, even though service may also be gratifying. They feel that they are pursuing different values than they normally do through their work: cooperation rather than competition, or being of service rather than making a profit. Often they are interacting with different kinds of people who help remind them of higher values.

Laura Cantrell, who founded the AIDS Network, illustrates that trying to be a good citizen can evoke a vivid awareness of one's higher values. She was not raised within a religious tradition, and she joined the Episcopal church largely to please her husband. When asked her current religious preference, she says only that she believes in God. Yet the language she uses to describe what motivated her to become involved with AIDS patients is that of religion: "I was going to my upper-middle-class Episcopal church, doing what women did. I did volunteer work while the kids were in school and socialized with my friends. I was in a prayer group and I used to pray (it makes me smile now), 'God, I want to know you more.' I'd take communion and pray, 'God, I want to know you more.' Well, one night I had a dream in which I heard someone say, 'Come to my people with AIDS.' I told my husband I'd had the strangest dream and it was probably something on television that had been bothering me. That night I had the same dream, only this time I was awake. And the next night I had it again. 'This is really weird,' I said to myself. 'I'm not the least bit mystical. I'm an Episcopalian, for God's sake!'"

A year later Laura was indeed working with AIDS patients, and now, after nearly a decade, she still finds religious language the only way in which to describe her experiences: "This is where I found God, alive and well and full of strength. Clearly, words are inadequate to describe how I know that exists, but I found it with people with AIDS, and the way others cared for them, people with AIDS, in their profound suffering, yet a strength in that. I used to believe intellectually that life was sacred. When you watch people fight to hold on to something, then it ceases being an intellectual thing, but a very holy thing. I learned this is where God is. That life is in fact holy, and that we, together in that relationship, those with HIV and those of us who care for them, change the suffering. We do this and it changes the suffering."

Many people—nurses, social workers, lawyers, peace activists, business executives—describe their involvement in their communities in similar language. To them being a good citizen is amplified by the sense that life itself is at stake, that human suffering is at issue, that there is a profound underlying morality to which they are compelled to be true, and that perhaps they are even gaining a faint glimpse of what it might be to realize the full measure of their humanity. In these instances good citizenship requires reflecting on the deeper meanings of the human condition.

Whether they live in rigidly bounded or porous social circumstances, those who become active in civic affairs emphasize a strong connection between being a good citizen and being a person of character. The complex problems of today's world require people to make difficult choices about how much of their time to devote to work, families, and communities, and scattered commitments sometimes make it harder for them to develop a clear sense of their own identity and interests. Yet these scattered commitments continue to reinforce—and depend on—their learning to work with others, gaining self-knowledge, developing patience, and grappling with the reality of human suffering.

8

The Question of Trust

AS SOCIAL RELATIONSHIPS BECOME easier to move into and out of, people find it harder to depend on others' presence and help over an extended period. Certainly it is more difficult to know what to expect from others when much of our interaction takes place with strangers. Going through a divorce or being laid off from one's job can erode one's faith in human nature. And many Americans have lost confidence in their leaders as a result of scandals that have been widely publicized.

In a national survey in 1994, only 34 percent of Americans felt they could trust other people. This figure was twelve percentage points lower than it had been in 1972. During roughly the same period, the proportion who had "hardly any confidence" in those running the executive branch of the federal government rose from 18 percent to 42 percent.[1]

But what exactly are people talking about when they say they do or do not trust others? Social scientists define trust more in terms of what it does than in terms of what it is.[2] It encourages us to conduct business with other people even if we do not know them well; if we trust them we are confident that they will treat us fairly. Similarly, we are likely to feel more secure in our beds at night if we believe our neighbors are honest and of good will.

Being able to transact business and feeling secure are vital to the functioning of any society. Consequently, it is worrying when surveys suggest that we are less trusting than we were in the past. If we harbor suspicion toward our neighbors we may be less likely to join with them in efforts to improve the community. Feeling that our leaders are only looking out for themselves may cause us to withdraw our interest from elections instead of participating in electoral politics.

It appears, however, that the meanings of trust are changing, and that Americans are finding creative ways to restore their confidence in others. When people use their own words to describe what they mean by trust, rather than responding to preconceived questions in surveys, they reveal that trust is a malleable idea that still holds resonance for them, and that reflects the complex circumstances in which they live. In simple, tightly bounded communities people may have been able to rely on others because they knew their neighbors well enough that they could anticipate their behavior. Nowadays, when people are more loosely connected with one another, they often have to expend greater effort to discover whom they can count on.

The members of civic organizations worry a lot about questions of trust. They often join organizations hoping to create relationships that will make them feel better about their communities. Especially when they come from different backgrounds and do not necessarily share the same values, participating in an organization together becomes a way of discovering that they do have something in common.

Janet Stetson, age thirty-eight, is a housewife who lives in a medium-sized city. She is married, has worked in a profession, and now devotes full time to caring for her nine-year-old daughter and four-year-old son. Her main form of civic involvement is the PTA at her son's elementary school. She is now serving a term as vice president of the PTA. Of the 400 children who attend the school, only 30 have parents who are active in the PTA (all are mothers). But these few put on several fundraising drives each year that pay for all the class trips as well as some extra books and equipment and any costs associated with putting on assemblies. In addition to the fundraising committee (which is the largest), there are eleven other committees, including one to promote school spirit, one to coordinate homeroom mothers, and one that operates the school store.

As chair of the school spirit committee, Janet recently organized a Blue and White day to promote interest in the school colors and a mascot day to encourage familiarity with the school's mascot (a panther). Just before Christmas she organized a school-wide contest to guess how many pieces of candy were in a big jar. She is currently preparing a new display for the showcase in the school's foyer and putting up a bulletin board to promote interest in the library, and she is planning a curriculum fair that will give parents a chance to visit the school and get a better sense of what is being taught in all the classrooms. A conservative estimate is that Janet spends at least five hours a week on PTA activities. She also spends between five and ten hours each month attending the PTA's executive meetings.

Not all the PTA mothers are motivated by the same values. Some of the women are involved because their children have pressured them into it, and others, especially the long-term leaders, seem to relish the power and the visibility. Janet had decided not to run for a PTA office because she was too busy and didn't consider herself qualified. At the meeting, however, someone nominated her from the floor. Although Janet was ambivalent, she felt a sense of responsibility to the school and to the other parents and the children.

Building trust among the parents who take part in PTA activities is Janet's main reason for being involved. Several years ago she noticed, in talking with parents of her daughter's classmates, an enormous wariness about what the school was doing. On the one hand, any time a program was changed, there was "a lot of back-biting." For example, the teachers canceled the annual Halloween party and had a harvest party instead, prompting widespread complaints from parents their children were being denied one of their favorite holiday traditions. On the other hand, parents did not have enough confidence in themselves or in the school administration to experiment with some ideas and programs that were being used effectively in other schools (such as afterschool programs for latchkey children). Janet believed that parents would trust the school more if they became more involved; they would better understand the reasons for decisions, and they would be acquainted with the people making these decisions. Dissent would then be based on knowledge rather than fear and ignorance.

She asserts that one of the most important changes as a result of her being a PTA officer is within herself. As she has come to know other parents better, she has learned to trust them. She has gained a better understanding of certain decisions, she has made some friends, and she has been heartened by meeting other parents who care about the school and are willing to work for its improvement: "It's just been nice to kinda get to know other parents in the school who really care, and to see what they're doing, and, I think, making some new friendships. I'm getting some companionship, or camaraderie, and while I'm doing the work, it's not just me working, it's other people pitching in, and we're able to laugh, and tell stories, or whatever."

Janet's experience exemplifies the way trust evolves in many community organizations. As people interact they learn more about one another's values, perhaps realizing that they are all intensely interested in their children's education or that they shop at the same stores and watch similar programs on television. "Just that interaction, whether it's a pancake breakfast at the firehouse or a meeting at Rotary," says a man who is working to promote civic involvement, "allows you to gain deeper trust in people by understanding where they're coming from."

People who find this kind of trust and dependability in civic organizations sometimes express it simply as a sense of belonging. As its members interact over a period of time, a group develops a culture or style of its own that supersedes changes in membership or the idiosyncracies of individuals. Members come to share a common history and common assumptions. A woman who has participated for eight years in a civic group devoted to discussing controversial political issues captures this sense of trust well: "You just know when you're saying things, that you're saying it within a common framework that is understood."

When trust consists of having a "common framework" based on long-term association, members may come to trust one another but have no reason to trust outsiders. In Janet Stetson's case, fewer than 10 percent of eligible parents are active in the PTA, so its ability to promote trust among parents does not reach far. Parents who have little contact with the PTA do not trust the proposals its leaders make. And yet they may not have the time or energy to get to know the PTA. Janet is willing to spend long hours working for the PTA, but many parents are too busy. Then, too, outside mothers may not find common ground with those inside the PTA. A generation ago most women in Janet's town were married to farmers, did not work outside the home, and were white middle-class Protestants. Now she lives in an occupationally diverse community divided between those who have careers and those who do not. The population includes a greater variety of religious, racial, and ethnic backgrounds. It is not surprising that trust rooted in shared values has proven difficult to maintain.

In response to these problems, leaders of civic organizations are devoting more of their attention to public relations in the hope that greater communication will inspire confidence in the organizations' activities and promote goodwill in the community. Janet's school spirit committee tries to get people from the wider community to identify with the school. Grace Bishop uses local television to show the city that Partners for Peace stands for shared values. But relying on mass media is often of limited value. In diverse communities unifying slogans are hard to find. A man who heads an organization with the words "individual responsibility" in its title says many people don't trust it because they assume it is promoting a conservative economic ideology. A man who does public relations for a large civic organization says it is hard to stay on people's "radar screens." "You're on and then you're off," he complains. "You're always competing with other organizations that have their own agendas." Another leader finds it better to keep a low profile than to worry about trying to promote common values in the wider community.

Community organizations search for trustworthy people, those who perform reliably, to sustain their work. Such people can be counted on to be at meetings, to do what they say they will, and to support the organization, even though there may be differences of opinion. This trust is based on a rational assessment of someone's past performance and the likelihood that the future will hold similar performances. One man says a trustworthy person is somebody who "walks the walk and talks the talk; somebody whose deeds reflect their words; somebody who when they tell you something, you can take it to the bank. They're dependable, consistent." Providing a negative example, a lawyer describes a former intern as someone who cannot be trusted: "He would miss meetings. He wouldn't call up ahead and let you know why. That kind of thing. He wouldn't get things in on time, would always be late and with excuses." In the Civic Involvement Survey, only 23 percent said they would be very likely or somewhat likely to trust "somebody who misses appointments."

Participation in civic organizations stimulates trust because members see one another over a long period of time and learn which other members are dependable. Each person discovers what to expect about the others. One person always volunteers to serve as treasurer, and so the group trusts that person to be available and in turn trusts that it will be possible to fill the treasurer position. Or a member always raises questions about how a policy is going to affect single mothers, and so the group comes to expect that this is an issue with which it has to deal. Such expectations may be perceived negatively (as when other members groan to themselves and think, oh no, not that refrain again), but at least people feel they can predict, even anticipate, this concern. Participation also familiarizes members with those who cannot be trusted (the person who is always late, or the person everyone knows cannot finish a job). The overall functioning of the group is facilitated because members learn whom they can count on for what, and by the same token know how to avoid problems.

Leaders of civic organizations deliberately cultivate the idea that their members, individually and collectively, are reliable. Antonio Perez, who heads an organization that collects food and clothing for homeless teenagers, says he tries to show the community that it can count on him to do what he says: "We make sure that we hand in all the receipts, that we buy everything that we're supposed to buy, that no money is missing from any part of this." Diane Mason, who runs a mental health clinic, elaborates on a similar idea of trust: "I always keep my word. I'm consistent. If I say I'll do something, I do it. I do my best not to make promises I can't keep. I think that's the most important thing with people trusting you: you don't make a commitment you can't keep, people have to trust you, because you keep your commitments."

But it is difficult for organizations to be completely reliable in an increasingly diffuse society. Most are faced with so many contingencies that it is impossible for them to carry out programs or activities exactly as planned. Sometimes Antonio Perez cannot provide food because the pizza parlors that have promised him leftovers have none. Diane Mason tries to keep her own promises, but has found that she often cannot depend on the college students who volunteer at her clinic to show up. Another leader notes that his organization has lost two directors in recent years, both of whom tried to interpret government rules correctly but ran into different interpretations among their boards of trustees. Other leaders say it has been difficult for them to convince the public that their organizations are dependable because the public has already formed impressions based on experiences with other organizations.

People talk about the difficulty of being dependable in their personal lives. The CEO of a company that has grown to 125 employees has always regarded himself as a trustworthy person, but he is having more doubts than he used to. Employees tell him things, expecting him to remember and follow through, but with so many employees he forgets. Despite his good intentions, he sometimes is unable to live up to his expectations of himself. A lawyer who has five children and tries to juggle his work, his wife's interests, coaching soccer, and being a member of a service club also admits that he is seldom as dependable as he would like. Even at work, he says, "You have a client and you're supposed to do something for them, and you just get so bogged down that you just don't get an opportunity to do it." Another man says his daughter regards him as untrustworthy because he has been unable to keep many of his promises to her.

Most Americans continue to consider themselves basically trustworthy, and yet it is not uncommon to acknowledge personal limitations. A majority of Americans (57 percent) say they have too much to do. More than a quarter (28 percent) say they change their minds fairly often. Approximately one-fifth (19 percent) say they don't trust themselves sometimes. And one-sixth (16 percent) say they have trouble fulfilling their responsibilities.[3]

Not surprisingly, surveys reveal that trust of others is less common among people who do not trust themselves than among people who trust themselves, and that the kinds of people who regard themselves as untrustworthy are the same kinds who believe it is necessary to be careful in their dealings with others.[4] For instance, a woman who blames herself for her husband's leaving her wonders if she is trustworthy; she also doubts other people's trustworthiness. Yet people suggest that the act of trusting encourages others to be trustworthy. "If you trust other people," one man observes, "they'll usually rise to the occasion."

The connection between porous social conditions and mistrust is evident in many people's comments. Maria Castillo, who grew up in South Central Los Angeles, remembers her neighborhood being more cohesive when she was a child: "We could really communicate with our neighbors. There was more of a bond between people and you were more able to trust people." Since then the community has become more ethnically diverse and many of the local organizations that used to anchor the neighborhood have closed: "You can't really trust anyone, there's no one trying to work with each other. It's just everyone for themselves."

A man who has served in the military perceives a similar change: "I've seen a lot of strange things in life. [This is] certainly not the Mayberry kind of life I had when I was growing up, and I'm certainly a lot more careful with people." A young mother who laments that people don't have the time to get acquainted with their neighbors says, "Let's say I'm going to sign my son up for Boy Scouts. You never gave it a second thought that anything would happen to your children in one of these groups. So now you have to take a second look and say, 'Okay, who's the Boy Scout leader? Is he known in the community? How is it structured?' I really take a hard look at everything before I let my son participate in anything."

As it has become harder to depend on other people or to trust them because of the perceived absence of shared values, individuals and organizations have started to redefine what they mean by trust. A man who runs a job-training program has devised a ritual to determine if someone is trustworthy: he tells them a rumor he has allegedly heard and tries to gauge their reaction. Another man has redefined trust to mean being true to himself; this helps him feel better when he has to violate others' expectations. A woman says she trusts everyone, but she means she believes they are basically good; it is their "methods and motivations" that she doesn't trust. Other people say they seek feedback from friends because they can no longer decide whether they themselves are trustworthy.

As people adapt to a porous society, they also invent their own ways to decide whom they can trust and under what conditions. One widespread assumption is to distrust anyone who may be motivated by economic gain. Another is to distrust people who live in places where crime and drug use are common. Still another is to figure that a certain percentage of social relationships will violate one's trust. For instance, some people invoke the "80-20 rule" and assume that approximately 20 percent of those around them cannot be trusted.

For those who insist that it is still possible to trust most people, an additional set of mental devices comes into play to explain why their trust is sometimes violated. Noting their own problems in being dependable, some point to unpredictable family schedules as explanations for others' untrustworthiness. Some affirm that it is "rational" to trust others, and then excuse untrustworthy behavior by emphasizing emotional states that may cause people to behave irrationally. Others affirm the value of trusting as an act of faith, arguing that life goes better if one assumes the best in people.

In many instances trust is possible to define only in the context of intimate relationships, leaving people without guidance about how to trust strangers. Even in intimate relationships trust ceases to be a matter of shared values or of dependable fulfilling of social obligations. Indeed, one of the most commonly used definitions of trust associates it with the kind of understanding that is cultivated in self-help groups—where members report exceptionally high levels of trust for one another. By this definition, a trustworthy person is someone who openly and honestly discloses his or her opinions and feelings. In the Civic Involvement Survey, a striking 89 percent (almost the same proportion as those who said they would trust people in their neighborhoods) said they would be very likely or fairly likely to trust "somebody who shares their personal feelings with you." For many people this kind of trust emphasizes the value of the soul mate, the confidant, the intimate friend. In a diverse society, people may trust others who share their feelings more than those who simply happen to live in their neighborhoods (see Methods, especially Table 8).

Carmen Carlata, the founder of Action X, explains how she cultivates people's confidence in her: "I'm very open with my life story. I'm always very open about whatever my agenda may be and what I'm thinking and what I'm feeling." Another woman trusts people who tell her what they are feeling because she then knows where they stand: "You're not having to wonder, 'Are they playing games with me? Is this a social thing that they're doing?'" A man whose volunteer work puts him in daily contact with strangers says he usually cannot get them to tell him their true feelings, so he tries to "read" their feelings in other ways: "It's body language sort of stuff. It's the tone of their voice, the way they hold themselves. Obviously what they say, whether what they say is something that sounds truthful or not. Whether they tend to exaggerate."

Some leaders try to cultivate trust in their organizations by encouraging people to disclose their opinions and feelings. A member of a hobby group of about fifteen people who had not known each other before joining the group talked about trust in these terms: "People would share their problems or concerns or things that they were pleased with and the reception that it would get at the meetings helped to create trust. The problems that they were experiencing were not trivialized at the meeting." In this case, meeting in homes added to the trust that developed from members talking about common interests. Rotating meetings from house to house gave them a chance to feel that they knew the other members better because they had glimpsed the private sphere in which they lived.

The difficulties that arise when trust is defined in terms of being open about feelings are evident in Sara Mermel's comments about Hadassah: "People are very quick to feel a sense of exclusion. It is a basic insecurity in many, many women. 'Am I wanted? Am I accepted? Do the people want me here? Do I have a place here?' What I want to do is let them know that [excluding them] should not happen and must not happen, and if it does happen, I will apologize for it for whoever made them feel that way. I will call and say, 'I don't know what that person said and he or she didn't mean it that way, but however you interpret it, I apologize for it because it shouldn't have happened. No one should ever feel the way you felt about this.'" In fact, a lot of the time she devotes to Hadassah is spent doing repair work: "There's a lot of repairing that has to go on, because people don't always have the people skills they need in organizations and it knocks the crap out of you."

Sara could have chosen other examples of misunderstanding, conflict, and hurt feelings. The important point is her comment about repair work. Trust has to be worked at, fixed, repaired. It is not simply maintained by people participating in organizations or by being reliable. When trust is defined as the aim of disclosing feelings, the leaders of organizations may indeed find themselves spending a great deal of time doing repair work.

Fluid or unpredictable social conditions increase the likelihood that trust will have to be maintained through repair work rather than through reliable performance. Under such conditions people often do not know one another well enough or long enough to guess what others are thinking or feeling. Open communication about their thoughts and feelings becomes more important. In Sara's case, someone had to be candid about feeling excluded, and someone else—Sara—had to be willing to say she wasn't aware of everything that happened but was nevertheless sorry about it.

Repair work of this kind is time consuming, and defining trust in terms of expressing one's feelings also increases the possibility that people may abuse the language of feelings to avoid fulfilling civic obligations. This is a concern of social critics who speak of a "therapeutic culture" that encourages a narcissistic withdrawal from public life by focusing too much attention on the inner needs of individuals.[5] Sara Mermel tells about a young woman who refused to participate any longer in Hadassah activities because she had been offended by another member: "I called her and asked, 'How come you never did help with the fashion show?' 'Oh,' she said, 'because Karen said something to me about not giving my $100 donation and then she found out I didn't have to because I was a new member.' I said, 'Well, that's all right. She corrected the error, didn't she, when she found out?' She said, 'But, Sara, it was the whole way she talked to me.' I said, 'What do you mean?' She said, 'She really didn't welcome my help and she wasn't apologetic when she found out that I didn't have the dues.' I said, 'So will you come?' She said, 'No.' I said, 'Because you still feel that you weren't treated properly?' She said, 'That's right. I wasn't.'"

Sara was already having trouble with the donation policy that had become an issue between the two women. The chapter had a long-standing policy of soliciting $100 donations from its members if they wished to attend the annual fundraising luncheon, but younger members found it difficult to pay this much, so a lower rate had been approved for new members. Not everyone knew about the new arrangement, and there was some confusion about who was eligible for it. Some of the confusion represented a genuine conflict between old-timers who wanted to preserve the existing rules and others who wanted the chapter to include newcomers more easily.

It nevertheless appears that the young woman used her wounded feelings as an excuse for not becoming involved in Hadassah events in the future. No amount of cajoling from Sara was capable of changing her mind. Civic groups could scarcely function effectively if everyone were as thin-skinned as this woman. Her particular grievance also suggests that there was a lack of trust in the group. Had the women trusted each another, they would have been more forgiving in their positions.

There is no reason to suppose that such grievances have ever been absent from civic organizations. Faithful members might be expected simply to bury their feelings and get on with the work of the organization. And yet this is precisely the point at which it is helpful to understand the social circumstances in which civic organizations are embedded. In a tightly knit community, members might have suppressed their feelings and remained loyal to the organization for several reasons: they had to continue living next door to the person who offended them, they had to stay active in the organization if they were going to move up its ranks and achieve greater status in the community, they knew the offending party well enough to discount the incident as atypical behavior, they knew there were other occasions for getting even, or perhaps they knew other members well enough to vent their grievances to them.

In a porous social environment, it is much easier to walk away from the situation and vow never to participate again. It is unlikely that one will have to see the offending party again, and there are many other organizations in which one can become involved. Telling the organization's president that one was offended permits one to withdraw from responsibilities without seeming to be untrustworthy. One may also feel genuinely offended because the offensive remark is the only basis one has for judging the other person.

When problems of this nature arise, civic organizations have two options for attempting to rebuild trust. One is to raise the ante, as it were, arguing all the harder for loyalty to the organization and giving members stronger incentives for being faithful. The other is to engage in the kind of therapeutic repair work that Sara Mermel has been doing. The former strategy is not likely to work well when organizations already have declining resources or when there are lower-cost options elsewhere in the community. Getting people to disclose those feelings which block their participation may in fact be the more effective strategy.

The therapeutic approach probably cannot be escaped if civic organizations are serious about cultivating trust. Some of their members' trust of others is likely to be based on the fact that the others show up at the right time and do their jobs. But civic organizations also require explicit moments in which trust is discussed. This is one reason small groups are sometimes more effective than large, impersonal organizations. Small, informal settings provide opportunities to reflect on grievances and to express them candidly. Civic organizations may not be able to address the underlying personal problems in a way that group therapy might, but clearing the air may allow members to work together more effectively.

Trust that depends on constant repair work is of course fragile. It happens more easily in first-hand, intimate encounters than in large-scale organizations. We depend on being able to talk out our grievances with a few other people, and so we remain suspicious of everyone else. It also works better in homogeneous groups, where we can give ourselves credit for having chosen trustworthy friends.

Sara Mermel reveals the limitations of this kind of trust. She says she trusts most people, but when asked why, she explains, "I've learned to choose as colleagues and friends and associates those people who I intuitively feel have integrity and work well on whatever it is that we have to do together." Implicitly, this is an admission that there are people who cannot be trusted but who can just be avoided.

What saves this attitude from becoming narrow and exclusionary is an awareness of the circumstances in which we now live. That few of us have full control over our daily schedules is more than an academic insight; it also has practical value. Sara Mermel expresses it best: "I find that most people are well intentioned. They do care and they will not intentionally let you down. And when they do, there are usually circumstances in their lives that have prevented them from following through on things that they said they would do."

These considerations about the precarious role of feelings as indicators of trust also provide insight into some problems that have arisen in the political sphere. Civic involvement brings people in some communities into direct contact with politicians, and these contacts are not always productive of trust.[6] Indeed, people have learned to be wary of politicians, and so it is all the more difficult for them to know whether specific officials can be trusted. These difficulties can lead to greater reliance on feelings, and this basis for trust is likely to be quite limited. Politicians need to be judged in terms of their performance and their ability to carry out campaign promises; they may evoke strong feelings, but these feelings cannot possibly serve in the same ways that they do among people who know one another well.

Trust that is deeply influenced by personal feelings is much harder to maintain in large-scale settings than in small groups. Indeed, the emphasis on this kind of trust bodes ill for how we relate to impersonal institutions. Rather than being willing to trust the leaders of these institutions because their organizations have been reliable at getting their work done over time, we listen to our feelings and let ourselves worry because we do not know these leaders personally or are concerned about some off-hand remark they made that seems offensive. Television encourages us to think this way because it brings a remark to our attention, perhaps a sensational remark that can be debated by commentators whose feelings serve as surrogates for our own. Television produces pseudo-intimacy with public officials. We think we should be able to trust them in the same way we trust our parents and friends, but it is ultimately impossible for us to interact with them in the same way, leaving us with a feeling of betrayal.

The reality of this problem—and some insight into how it can be overcome—is vividly evident in the case of Ashley Beckman, age twenty-five. She has recently graduated from a prestigious law school and is working as a law clerk for a federal judge. Ever since high school Ashley has toyed with the idea of becoming a politician herself. But her attitude has been on-again, off-again, sometimes placing her in a love-hate relationship with politics. Although she has had more opportunities to do political volunteer work than many people her age, she illustrates why it is difficult to trust politicians.

Ashley Beckman exemplifies the porous social circumstances that are conducive to loose connections within our communities. She was raised in an intact upper-middle-class family, but she has learned that a bright young person with the economic resources to realize her ambitions must take advantage of the permeable boundaries that define communities and organizations. She has learned that a way to set herself off from the crowd and to secure more cultural capital for herself is to move in and out of organizations, picking up transferable knowledge and skills that will make her more valuable in future activities. In high school most of the girls in her class were involved in athletics, music, or drama; Ashley was an indifferent lacrosse player and an enthusiastic member of the hockey team. She abandoned these normal adolescent pursuits to volunteer for the campaign of a man her father knew who was running for mayor in the city adjacent to the suburb in which she lived. Ashley's family is Jewish and encouraged her to participate in activities at the synagogue, but they also believed it was important to build bridges to other religious and ethnic communities. The mayoral candidate was African American. Ashley broke with her community of origin when she was eighteen and was accepted at a prestigious university. She thought nothing of moving three thousand miles away from her parents to attend this university.

Her college experience, too, illustrates how organizations encourage their members to participate in wider networks. The university permitted students to spend a full semester in the nation's capital, doing internships instead of taking classes. Ashley spent the semester pursuing her interest in politics, splitting her time between working for a member of the Senate Judiciary Committee and helping at a nonprofit public advocacy center. When she graduated she moved several thousand miles again to attend law school, deliberately choosing one that offered a flexible curriculum. Its flexibility gave her time to help with several local political campaigns. At the moment she is working as a law clerk, but this position will end in three months, and she will move on to a different job.

Ashley's civic involvement has been a series of loose, short-term commitments. The mayoral race she volunteered for in high school involved a few hours of work each week for a few weeks in the fall. In Washington she deliberately split her internship between the senator's office and the advocacy center because she wanted to have a more diverse experience. Back home one summer, she volunteered to help with a senator's reelection campaign. In law school she rearranged her study habits one fall so that she could put in three forty-hour weeks helping a woman who was running for Congress. In her present position she is not permitted to engage in partisan politics, so she is helping a nonpartisan women's caucus, and she expects to shift from that to partisan activity as soon as her position ends.

The common thread in all these activities is politics, but she has worked for both Republicans and Democrats, done so in four states, helped with partisan and nonpartisan groups, and never spent more than a few weeks on any activity.

Such experiences inevitably shape one's understandings of trust. Ashley Beckman's short-term, varying activities have not undermined her own trustworthiness in the eyes of the political candidates for whom she has worked. They have become accustomed to short-term volunteers, and even the projects she worked on in Washington, including several confirmation hearings, were sufficiently limited that short-term involvement was sufficient. As long as she shows up and does what she is asked, the candidates are pleased to have her help.

But Ashley's confidence in the candidates—and in the political system—has been shakier. She mentions three factors that trouble her. One is what she has learned about specific candidates and officeholders. Although she admits that negative campaign advertising has been responsible for some of this information, she believes enough of it to wonder about the trustworthiness of many people in public office. She can recite scandals that lead her to believe there are ruthless, immoral people in American politics, and she suspects she is no different from a majority of the public who have these concerns. A second factor has to do with the nature of politics itself. She wonders if the political system as a whole is as focused on compassion and helping the needy as she would like it to be. Sometimes it seems more like a game that people are using to maximize their power or wealth or to gratify their own egos. The third factor is a kind of veneer that seems to be part of the political style. Politicians, she believes, are good at shaking hands, smiling, talking, hiding their true feelings, and espousing the party line, all of which makes her wonder about their sincerity.

These concerns help illuminate why confidence in political leaders has plummeted in recent decades and why voter turnout has sunk to low levels. Ashley Beckman has thought more about politics than many people, and her concerns are shaped by who she is, by how she understands trust, and by her loose connections to the political system. Living in as many different communities as she has, she has had to be a strong person who looks mainly to herself for guidance. She is worried about feeling the pull of many different reference groups, and so she resolves her questions about personal authenticity by paying close attention to her feelings and by talking about them with her boyfriend and a few other soul mates. It is not surprising that she raises questions about the personal identities, the sincerity, and the authenticity of politicians. As she imagines herself being a politician, she wonders if she could be one and still be true to her feelings about herself. She is concerned about the integrity of particular officials and candidates because she does not know them well, and even the ones she does know are acquaintances that move in and out of her life within a few weeks. She is thus vulnerable to what she sees about them on television.

Like Sara Mermel, Ashley Beckman engages in repair work to deal with her mistrust of the political system. She has volunteered for several campaigns as a way of checking out her fears, perhaps settling once and for all her question of whether or not politics can be a way of caring about people. The recent congressional race she volunteered for did much to restore her confidence. Ashley got to know the woman who was running for office, often meeting her at five in the morning and driving her to a breakfast engagement. Through her friendship with this woman, Ashley came to believe it is possible to be an authentic, caring person and still be in politics.

Ashley's other tactic is to reflect on her own doubts and make a conscious decision about what kind of feelings will work best for her, given the uncertain circumstances in which she lives. She has decided that trusting people, even politicians, is a more workable tactic than being cynical. She knows that her faith will be shaken by an occasional scandal, but she prefers to think that most people, most of the time, are trying to do what is right and good. That decision quiets some of her own doubts, makes her feel better about herself, and permits her to take risks.

It is little wonder that trust has become problematic in the public life of our society. Not many of us have the time or inclination to become personally acquainted with officeholders. We sit back, watch public leaders portrayed on television, and wonder what kind of people they must be. Our emphasis on intimacy and feelings and our fears about our own inauthenticity focus our attention on the personal attributes of officeholders, leaving us with questions about their trustworthiness. We are unwilling to trust them simply because they get the job done, partly because we are unsure what job needs to be done, and partly because we realize that good results are hard to predict.

Civic involvement is one antidote to these problems. By getting involved with some small group, whether it is our bowling team or church or AA group or chapter of Hadassah, we are able to establish first-hand relationships with a few other people and thus come to believe that some people are good and decent. The fact that these groups feature loose connections means, however, that doubts will still be present about who can be trusted. Misunderstandings and hurt feelings make an enormous difference when our conceptions of trust focus so heavily on emotions. Repair work is thus needed to mend these feelings and to heal broken relationships.

There is wisdom in the view that trust, after all, is an item of faith. The decision to trust people, to believe that most people most of the time are trying to do what is right, ultimately has to be made in the face of much evidence to the contrary. It can be made on philosophical or religious grounds, but it can also be made strictly on the grounds that trust is a better basis for one's life than cynicism. In the Civic Involvement Survey, 71 percent said they mostly agreed with the statement, "If you trust people, they will usually rise to the occasion." Whatever the reasons, trust may sustain us through the dark times when we are unsure that anything can be done about the problems in our communities.

If trust is difficult to maintain within a civic organization composed of women of the same social background or between volunteers and politicians who know each other, it is all the harder to establish when civic activities deliberately aim to transcend the barriers that separate diverse groups.

Jeremy Alexander, age forty, heads a company that sells prefabricated doors and windows to contractors. His business has grown to the point that he makes a lot of money, lives in a luxurious suburban home with his wife and two children, and has time to devote to civic activities. Several years ago the realtor who sold him his house happened to mention a nonprofit organization in the inner city that needed some doors and windows for a building it was renovating. Jeremy got in touch with the director and eventually donated some doors and windows. Today he is the chairman of the organization's board.

The organization, the Westside Development Corporation, functions mainly as a center to raise money for and to coordinate community services in one of the poorest sections of the city. One of its activities is home repair. In the last few years approximately 600 homes have received some kind of repair, mostly provided by volunteers from the suburbs who come with their hammers and paintbrushes on Saturdays. Another activity is renovating homes and selling them at low interest to local families. The organization also provides job training and runs a child care program to give parents a chance to receive job training or instruction in better parenting. Its annual budget is approximately $400,000.

Trust was an issue almost from the beginning of Jeremy's involvement. The board members and volunteers he knew from the suburbs generally trusted one another, as did the board members, volunteers, and clients from Westside itself. But the two groups had little basis for trusting each other. One was virtually all white, the other mostly black; one was middle and upper income, the other was lower income. The people from Westside weren't sure they understood the motives of people from the suburbs; the suburbanites weren't confident that they knew the Westside well enough to be of genuine assistance. Jeremy recalls wondering "whether we were a bunch of do-gooders that came in and were doing this for ourselves rather than for the people of the community."

After a year on the board, Jeremy began to sense that board members were tiptoeing around the important issue of whether to support Westside through external resources or to work harder to help people in the community become self-sufficient. There was also a reluctance to address latent racial tensions: "Those were issues that, I think, were in the minds of many on the board, but we didn't talk about race. We were very friendly and there was a lot of care and love and affection amongst the players on the board, but the toughest issues weren't discussed. There wasn't any reason for it to flame up at any point. We didn't have anybody that felt that that was their objective on the board to make that the issue."

An opportunity to address these deeper concerns arose when the board needed to choose a new executive director for the development corporation. As long as they had been discussing particular programs, board members had been able to focus on smaller issues, but the search for a director forced more candid thinking about the larger identity of the corporation, its mission, and its role in the community: "As we went on our search, we came very close to hiring a woman who was very skilled but she was white. The issue came about from the black members of the board as we came down to making that choice. It hadn't been stated before, but it had to be, in their mind, an African American, somebody more representative of the community, and the community is 90 percent African American."

The discussion was not without strain, but it led to a more intimate sense of understanding among the board members: "What was surfacing was a heart-felt thought process. We were at the threshold of becoming a real community organization versus an ad hoc group that was there and providing services. We went through a tremendous growth process certainly amongst the search group, which was about five of us. We interviewed more people on a second wave after we decided that the first candidate, the white woman, wasn't appropriate for us. It was a very frustrating process. We came close to hiring a woman who had a lot of background and skills and it would have been in retrospect, I think we all feel, a mistake. So we had an opportunity to grow through that process. And then we finally were blessed with having two very good black candidates appear at virtually the same time."

Trust resulted from the civic involvement of people on the board in three important ways. As the board members talked candidly about race, the climate of trust on the board itself increased. This climate was more than one individual feeling better able to understand another individual; it was more a sense of esprit de corps, of being in it together, of having a common experience on which to build. In addition, people in the community were better able to trust the corporation. They felt that it was concerned with their interests, not so much as a service organization, but as an entity that represented them and was congruent with their own identity. The third kind of trust was self-confidence among the board members; they trusted themselves better as a result of having gone through this difficult decisionmaking process.

Trust as self-confidence was evident among the white board members, such as Jeremy Alexander. His fear that he was a "do-gooder" from outside who was there to make himself feel better diminished. But it was even more evident among the African American board members. Some said later that they had been intimidated by the white businessmen from the suburbs who seemed to dress right, talk fluently, have connections, and know all the right answers. They felt so intimidated that they went along with decisions they did not agree with. But once the mood on the board changed, they were better able to participate as equals.

Trust cannot be hurried or produced artificially, especially when civic activities draw participants from diverse backgrounds. Trust can develop more effectively when people address difficult issues rather than simply focusing on routine tasks. Civic organizations are often places where these difficult issues emerge, because the good of the community, rather than

self-interest, is at stake. Some nonprofit professionals and volunteers interact over long enough periods that trust can evolve. These organizations
also suffer the danger, however, of becoming exclusive and homogeneous,
especially because they are voluntary, and thus permit people who are
dissatisfied to go elsewhere rather than stay and express their points of
view.

Developing trust under porous social conditions requires more than
simply getting acquainted. The board members of the Westside Development Corporation knew one another and were friendly. But they also
needed to know more about one another's vision for the organization, and
thus to feel that they were truly working together for a common purpose.
Jeremy Alexander says this kind of trust came about mainly through the
process of interviewing candidates: "We decided that we would have all
the interviewers give a little spiel [about the corporation]. It was a wonderful exercise, because everybody had to verbalize what they thought the
organization was and we did get some new perspectives. We were listening
to ourselves as much as we were listening to anybody we interviewed. I
found myself becoming more adept at understanding what we were all
about, and I think everybody else did, too."

When people have been trained to be cautious in their dealings with
strangers, as most Americans have, or when there is an atmosphere of
dissension to be overcome, deliberate effort is likely to be needed to generate trust. Such effort may consist of joining a civic organization that includes people from backgrounds different from one's own. It may require
talking openly about one's feelings or doing repair work to mend broken
relationships.

Under porous social conditions, trust also depends on common courtesy. In asymmetrical, exploitative power relationships, people may be
inclined to treat their subordinates crudely or their superiors with pseudo-
respect. In contrast, the voluntary relationships that characterize most
civic associations are likely to fall apart if common courtesy is violated too
often: people will simply leave. Trust, then, is more than some generalized
faith in other people; it is rooted in specific acts of kindness, perhaps as
simple as saying "thank you" or asking people for their opinion or compli-
menting them on a job well done.

A firefighter makes a special point of this kind of respect, pointing out
that it is sometimes difficult to practice when people have been awakened

in the middle of the night and are "stressed out" and tired from fighting a fire: "Everyone gets on edge at two o'clock in the morning, and you've got to be a bit of a diplomat at times. You've got to keep the guys wanting to come out when the whistle blows. So you really can't be screaming at them, you can't be saying, 'Why did you do this?' and call them all kinds of names. I always found that it was best to use a thank you as far as trying to get guys motivated to come back again. I did that one particular daytime call. The guys took off of work, we came and put the fire out. We got back to the station, and as the guys were on the way out, I said, 'Hey, thanks for coming, guys. See you next call,' or whatever. This one guy who also runs with another company stopped and he said, 'You know, my chief wouldn't have said that. Nobody says that in our company.' And he says, 'I'll be happy to come back.' One of the things that I've learned is you've got to respect other people, you've got to motivate them to want to do this job and keep their motivation. Because there's really no other pay, at least at this point, at least not here."

It is clear that trust remains an important aspect of civic involvement, even though the nature of this involvement is changing. Surveys showing that trust in people (or in human nature or in the leaders of institutions) is declining pose worries for the future of civic involvement. If people do not trust one another, they may take a cynical attitude toward civic participation, and if they do not participate, they may have no opportunities to overcome their mistrust of others.

Porous institutions make it harder for people to trust one another. Loose connections make it hard to establish trust even when people take part in community organizations. Coming from different backgrounds, they may not know other participants well enough to trust them. To be effective, they may need to cultivate weak ties with strangers in other organizations, rather than focusing full attention on people in their own circle. Not being able to control their own schedules, they are likely to worry about being dependable. Fluid social conditions also erode trust among people who lack resources to fend for themselves or to cultivate dependable social relationships. Of all demographic predictors of trust, measures of resources such as a good education, a good income, a home, a good neighborhood, and stable family relationships remain the strongest.[7] Having experienced layoffs, divorce, cuts in medical insurance benefits, and crime, many Americans find it difficult to believe that people can be trusted. As one welfare mother remarks, "You may be a very caring person, but you just can't trust people because you never know what may be wrong with them or how they're going to react."

But for many people trust is a robust concept. Like civic involvement, its meanings change as people adapt to new situations. The emotional bonds that tie soul mates together have come to be part of people's understanding of trust in civic organizations and even in politics. The benefit of this understanding is likely to be that people recognize the need to become acquainted and to share their feelings. The drawback is likely to be an overemphasis on intimacy that gets in the way of trusting strangers simply because they are good at getting the job done. Trust is above all an aspect of relationships that requires effort and engagement, rather than simply a background trait that people bring to their civic involvement.

Under porous conditions it is more important to understand the complexities of trust. Negotiation is always part of the deal. People decide whether or not to trust someone by watching how people like themselves respond in similar situations. In long-term relationships, these observations accumulate and are often reinforced implicitly. In more loosely bounded settings, civic groups are more likely to have to confront the problem of trust directly by making explicit decisions about whom to trust and under what conditions to trust them. Indeed, one of the most important roles of voluntary organizations is to provide a space in which the rules for making these decisions can be formulated.

This role is evident in civic groups that routinely deal with strangers in situations where there is reason to expect that trust will be violated. Homeless shelters and food distribution centers are typical of such groups. Organizations generally develop their own methods for making decisions about trust. For example, one has devised a rule that in effect says ask no questions the first time someone comes in, but if they come in again get more information. Another's rule requires collecting extensive information on the first visit and checking with other organizations to make sure the request is legitimate. Still another has adopted a policy of honoring only a certain number of requests from the same person in a specified period.

Civic organizations contribute to the social construction of rules about trust in this way. They provide opportunities for people to come together to define the conditions under which behavior will take place *as if* trust were present. In a society of strangers, this function is especially valuable. Just as traffic lights regulate the interaction of strangers in automobiles, the formal and informal rules established by civic organizations regulate the interaction of strangers in many other public spheres.

Besides defining rules, civic organizations are also deliberately cultivating trust among the wider constituencies and networks on which their success depends. Some of what they are learning is straightforward, such as to treat people fairly, be honest, and carry through on their promises. Some insights are particularly applicable to the fluid circumstances in which civic organizations now find themselves. For example, several people emphasize the importance of acknowledging failures. As the head of an organization dealing with inner-city problems puts it, "We're dealing with high-risk problems all the time, so if we never have a failure, something's wrong; it means we really aren't doing our job." A foundation official says she favors proposals from organizations that include failed programs rather than only ones that demonstrate success. A similar view comes from a community organizer: "I try to be as honest as I can be, and when I make a mistake, I'm the first one to say I've made a mistake. The good news is we're allowed to make mistakes, and we say that to each other."

Above all, specific understandings of trust appear to be changing as a result of loose connections. Long-term members of organizations that attach high importance to loyalty emphasize their trust of other members. They talk about a generalized trust of other people that derives from their sense of representing and serving these people; for example, Rotary and Kiwanis members often view their organizations as representatives of a dominant culture that embraces everyone and inspires the best in everyone. In contrast, people who have looser ties develop ways to interact sporadically with people they may not trust or redefine trust to focus more on their feelings about themselves. Some also display the classic symptoms of marginality: they know they are outsiders and expect to remain so, even though they may be involved in a number of activities. Making moral capital of their situation, they speak of the value of remaining marginal and describe marginality itself as a protection against gullibility. One man summarizes this view well: "Being cynical is a valid position. You can see things from the inside and the outside. You can ask the questions that nobody else is able to ask." For people like this, a certain level of mistrust is not inimical to civic involvement; it is simply a way of adapting to complex social realities.

If, as surveys suggest, trust is declining, then the more complicated ways in which people are grappling with issues of trustworthiness and dependability are particularly important. Living in a porous society does not mean that we must relate to one another with suspicion and misgivings. Establishing loose connections with other people can also be a way of building trust. Doing so requires deliberate attempts to communicate and to demonstrate that we are reliable.

9

The Larger Picture

ALTHOUGH THE DEMISE OF CIVIL SOCIETY is a specter that has alarmed many social observers, a close look at civic involvement today reveals that many Americans still care deeply about their communities and make efforts to connect with other people. But these efforts generally do not take the same forms as they had in the past because of the increased diversity, fluidity, interdependence, and specialization of contemporary life. The new, loosely structured forms of civic involvement often leave people with the sense that they are not doing enough to help others and that their communities are coming apart at the seams.

Of course there are serious problems in our society, such as crime, homelessness, and domestic violence, and these problems could be addressed more effectively if more Americans became involved in community organizations and took a more active interest in political affairs. Yet the main difficulty in generating greater civic engagement is not some moral malaise but rather a profound change in the character of our institutions. Whereas earlier conventions and ways of life created well-defined roles that tended to characterize and restrict people for their entire lives, today's more flexible roles create institutions that allow for and even require more negotiation and change. In the process of adjusting to these new institutional realities, we have had to invent new ways of being involved in our communities.

Porous institutions favor civic activities that are more loosely connected. In place of enduring membership organizations, we now see a wide variety of activities that involve short-term or sporadic commitments and task-specific relationships that bring together individuals and organizations from different sectors of the community. Civic involvement is increasingly identified with the nonprofit professionals, the volunteers, and the self-help groups that form the basis for these loose connections, and the mix of organizations (and their relationships with public officials) differs considerably from suburbs to inner-city neighborhoods to small towns. In short, broad social and cultural patterns interact with specific kinds of communities to produce different repertoires of civic involvement.

Despite the best efforts of particular individuals and organizations, limited or unanticipated outcomes leave many problems unresolved: peer mediation happens in the schools, but ethnic and racial tensions in the wider community remain unaddressed; church people bag groceries to help the poor on an emergency basis, but social programs that would provide training for new jobs languish because of inadequate support from voters; a few highly motivated people staff the boards of community development corporations, but they become overburdened because others in their neighborhoods remain uninvolved. It is thus imperative to consider what measures may be taken to strengthen civic involvement.

Because a strong civil society depends on citizens who interact with one another, one of the most basic questions is whether Americans still have meaningful connections with significant others—people with whom they can share their lives and to whom they can turn when in need. Such connections may have little to do with politics, voting, or taking part in community organizations. But they are the elemental condition on which all other forms of civic involvement are based. People who do not have friends and family are less likely to hear about opportunities or needs in their community. They are less likely to trust others. They may also feel alienated or be so isolated that they need public assistance, rather than being able to rely on help from other citizens. That people seem not to know their neighbors as well as they did in the past, and that neighborhood soda fountains and taverns and bowling leagues are less abundant, are thus worrying developments not primarily because these were places in which political issues were discussed but because they helped forge bonds among people.

Yet today's loose connections are real and substantial. Even though they may be more sporadic or span greater distances than in the past, they do link people together in a community of interest. Although it is true that many Americans do not know their next-door neighbors and live alone or in blended families, most do have friends and associates who care about them and with whom they interact in meaningful ways.[1] Most Americans can still depend on friends and family to help them during personal crises and to celebrate major events: attendance at weddings and wakes has not diminished, and high proportions of the public visit friends and co-workers who are hospitalized.[2] Most people who join self-help groups do so because they are invited by someone they know, rather than because they are completely isolated; most people maintain ties to family members and soul mates through personal visits and telephone calls; and it is common for working men and women to develop close attachments with co-workers. Indeed, the workplace is for many a more significant source of personal attachments than the neighborhood. Similarly, the Internet has fostered electronic communities of interest that help keep geographically scattered family members in closer touch and that permit people to exchange ideas and information about such diverse topics as new books, religious beliefs, politics, and genealogical interests.

A middle-class Californian in his thirties is fairly typical of those whose lives include a loose network of personal attachments. Like many Americans, he is disconnected from his neighbors, and yet he manages to stay involved with a wide range of significant others. He and his wife live with their two sons in an upscale neighborhood about three miles from the city in which he works. This is his seventh address, including one in another state and one in another country (he says he has moved around less than most of his friends). He is on speaking terms with several of his neighbors, and he sees them periodically at community-wide picnics or Little League games. But his significant connections are more scattered. "Most of my friends live outside the community," he says. He keeps in touch with them by telephone and an occasional visit. He also communicates with several by e-mail, even though he prefers hearing their voices or seeing them in person. He likes the fact that he can be thinking of a friend at work and just spontaneously send that person a greeting. He says it is "less arduous" than picking up the phone. If he were faced with an emergency, he would turn to one of his friends (since he lives far from his family). Keeping these relationships, he says, is "critical."

This man is not deeply attached to any particular place. He knows he and his family could move to another community fairly easily, because he has already done so many times. But he is involved with people. He does volunteer work at his son's nursery school, participates vicariously in his wife's Junior League activities (sometimes helping with its fundraisers), plays pick-up basketball at the gym, attends Mass about once a month, and enjoys the camaraderie of his colleagues at work. By virtue of owning a house, he has become interested in local politics, paying attention to zoning laws and what is being done to keep the streets safe. His best friends, parents, and siblings form a virtual community that stays with him wherever he goes. Noting that he played Little League as a boy, was in a fraternity in college, hopes to coach Little League when his sons are old enough, and expects to do more volunteer work at some point, he says he has made a commitment at the moment to spend his evenings and week-ends with his family. Because his wife also works long hours at her job, he feels that one of the ways he can contribute to the eventual good of his community is by being a good parent.[3] Despite his devotion to personal interests at this stage of his life, he looks forward to contributing to the larger public interest at a later stage when he has fulfilled his commitments to those nearest and dearest to him.

Many Americans lead lives similar to this man's. They move an average of six times during their adult lives, switch jobs and change churches periodically, and often do not belong to voluntary organizations or do volunteer work. Their lack of involvement sometimes worries them and earns the scorn of people who believe the society is suffering from selfishness and apathy. They are nevertheless connected to other people. They belong to formal and informal groups or have circles of friends who exchange visits, help one another, and constitute caring communities. They keep in touch with soul mates by telephone and e-mail. They send record numbers of greeting cards each year, and they crowd the airlines and highways making holiday visits. The looseness of their connections means they often have a vague feeling that something is lacking, such as the familiarity that developed in the tightly knit neighborhoods in which their parents and grandparents may have lived. But loose connections also fit most comfortably with the demands of their own lives. These connections allow for many acquaintances which may be more superficial and require little care to maintain. A large number of contacts often proves useful in finding a new job or a good restaurant. Such connections also enable one to disengage when work or family responsibilities require a shift in commitments, and to establish new connections with relative ease.[4]

The ease with which many people establish new connections is itself an important social development. Loose connections are possible because of social arrangements that facilitate them. A society in which many people remain unmarried well into adulthood and divorce and remarriage are common is able to function because specialty organizations have emerged to help people deal with these realities: escort services, marriage counselors, dating agencies, divorce courts, and support groups, to name a few. Similarly, group therapy sessions, marriage encounter retreats, and support groups provide ways for strangers to come together and help one another much as threshing circles and artisans' guilds did in the past. Such arrangements make it possible for people like the man in California to know they are not entirely alone, even though they have moved away from their communities of origin.

The disadvantage of many loose connections is that they may be purely instrumental, thus failing to nurture the casual socializing that leads to deeper friendships. The diffuse, nonpurposive activities of social clubs and service organizations were intended to facilitate such socializing. But networks based largely on socializing take enormous amounts of time and seldom have any obvious purpose. They put people in contact with others who may not share their interests or their political orientations and who are probably not their soul mates. Such networks include the neighbor who talks too long about his arthritis and the invitations to play poker when one would rather relax at home.

When social networks of this kind erode, something important is lost. Such networks have been the key to many of the best community efforts in the past, and they are still needed. The junior committees on which blue-chip nonprofits rely for fundraising and volunteering depend on these networks for organizing black-tie parties. Grassroots movements in small towns and suburbs get started because of these networks. As the founder of one such movement observed, "If you want to start an organization or get people involved in it, the biggest thing is getting to know the people in your community." But, he lamented, "People tend to be very isolated these days. They communicate by telephone or fax or watch television. They don't go over to their neighbor's house for dinner as often."

Enduring commitments to membership organizations such as civic associations and service clubs are not disappearing. Although memberships in many have declined, many others have adapted to changing times. Rotary is sponsoring short-term projects that require members to participate for only an hour or two at a time. Hadassah is initiating small groups that resemble those of the self-help movement. Churches are cooperating with other congregations so that projects can be divided into smaller tasks performed by more volunteers. PTAs are attracting busy parents by deemphasizing committees and focusing more on public meetings.

Traditional civic associations are likely to continue to serve as anchors for the informal ties that characterize new forms of civic involvement. These informal ties are often not as loose as they seem because they run through organizations that have long played a stabilizing role in their communities. A citizens' task force can be small and loosely structured because it meets in a building maintained by a volunteer fire company. An innovative advocacy group can get started by soliciting donations from the members of established churches. Nonprofit organizations also anchor new forms of civic involvement. Staff members supply professional expertise and coordinate the efforts of short-term volunteers. Many small organizations use the tax-exempt status of established community organizations rather than going to the expense of incorporating themselves. Buttressing established community organizations and helping them adapt to the changing needs of their members and clients is clearly a way of strengthening civic involvement.

If we wish to reinforce civic involvement we must recognize that the pattern of community connections has become more complicated. The service organizations that emerged at the end of the nineteenth century modeled themselves on corporate bureaucracies, with local chapters resembling the branch offices of a large hierarchical structure. At a time when large memberships were a way to impress national leaders, these arrangements often permitted indifferent citizens to have a considerable impact on public policy. Today public opinion polls make it possible to identify constituencies in different ways, and the mass media and nonprofit organizations provide alternative ways of influencing policy. In a richer environment of organizations, the efforts that succeed are not always the ones with the largest memberships. They are just as likely to be those run by people who know how to forge strategic alliances and assemble the right combinations of information. A coalition to combat violence in the schools makes a positive difference, not by asking members to make a long-term commitment to socialize regularly, but by bringing concerned citizens, teachers, clergy, law enforcement officials, outside experts, and media together on strategic occasions.

In many instances, successful civic organizations are ones that deliberately reconcile themselves to the porousness of their environment and capitalize on the loose connections of their participants. They rotate leadership roles to give more people experience in leading meetings and thus have reserves to fall back on when their most active participants leave. They form committees or task groups that bring diverse participants together, thereby drawing on the different networks of the participants. They give routine or highly specialized tasks to paid staff members, leaving some of the more interesting work to help motivate volunteers. They also make ample use of mechanisms for reaching into diverse sectors of the community, including the media, seminars, and personal contacts at businesses, schools, hospitals, service agencies, and churches.

Organizations also succeed by giving people a sense of belonging—or of having a voice—rather than stifling an egalitarian or democratic spirit as a strict hierarchy may do.[5] In a porous environment, successful organizations find innovative ways of cultivating this sense of belonging. They make less use of initiation rituals, secret handshakes, special insignia, and restrictive membership criteria than many of the older organizations. Instead, they hold roundtable discussions, maintain e-mail networks, and invite input from selected individuals and representatives of other organizations. Many intentionally stay small enough to give their core participants a sense of ownership of their activities. Many focus on specialized issues or are targeted to subpopulations, such as people with disabilities, minorities, or youth. Ideals of volunteering and self-help are promoted to encourage people to think of themselves as being involved because they want to be and because they are making a contribution.

Although the horizontal relationships that bind together neighbors and friends or members of civic organizations are important, vertical relationships that bridge different groups must also be cultivated. In the nineteenth century benevolent associations and service clubs linked people at the grassroots level with national leaders by developing national federations. Vertical relationships of this kind are often difficult to sustain, especially if they include people from all social strata rather than only the privileged few. These relationships are especially needed at present because people distrust organizations from which they feel distant. Many perceive the national government as particularly distant. Most Americans say they are content with the way democracy works, and it is useful to recognize this level of satisfaction. But most Americans also believe the government is increasingly being run by special-interest groups rather than serving the needs of ordinary people.[6]

Vertical relationships that connect people from different social strata do

not seem to occur naturally or easily in today's society. Americans generally choose friends who are like themselves, live in neighborhoods with
people of similar incomes, and join community organizations with relatively homogeneous memberships. Because civic involvement is more
common among people in upper and middle income brackets, it is the
exception more than the rule for voluntary organizations to include people from different social strata. Many people believe it is more difficult for
poor people to participate in community affairs than it was in the past.
Commonly mentioned are such problems as not having time or energy
because they are working two jobs, not having transportation or daycare so
they can conveniently attend meetings, and feeling uncomfortable because they are not as well educated or knowledgeable as people who have
more privileges in life. Organizations that work to encourage disadvantaged segments of the population to participate in civic activities, rather
than focusing only on participation by the better educated and the
wealthy, are performing a valuable service.

If vertical relationships are uncommon in many voluntary associations,
they are the norm for many nonprofit organizations. Nonprofits are thus a
resource for building vertical relationships that empower the disadvantaged. As the leader of one observed to an audience of fellow professionals,
it is easy to see the status differences in nonprofit organizations by thinking
of a few words to describe oneself and then a few words to describe one's
clients. Such asymmetrical relationships may make the more privileged
aware of the needs of those with fewer resources. There is also a danger. It
is easy for these relationships to devolve into arm's-length or paternalistic
transactions. A board meeting such as that described by Jeremy Alexander
in which people from different racial backgrounds, neighborhoods, and
social strata attempt to interact as equals may truly be the unusual occur-
rence.

Interviews with inner-city residents reveal how essential it is for effective
vertical relationships to be established. People like Carmen Carlata and
Darryn Walters are able to contribute to their communities by finding out
which agencies are responsible for various services, by applying for grants,
and by informing citizens of their rights. The decline of voluntary associations in many inner-city neighborhoods has made vertical relationships all
the more crucial to bring together ordinary citizens and public officials. In
a more complex environment of competing public and private agencies,

vertical relationships are needed to supply vital information about needs and opportunities.

Middle-class people recognize the need for vertical relationships—in their case with public officials—to keep their communities strong. Many feel alienated from national officials because they can see no way of influencing politics at that level; even their votes seem inconsequential. In contrast, those who attend town meetings or volunteer for neighborhood associations say they have earned favors or cultivated relationships that they can call on when a problem in their community needs to be addressed. They sometimes feel frustrated that their efforts do not produce desired results, but they also feel they have a better understanding of how to exercise their influence.[7]

The importance of vertical relationships points clearly to the fact that many forms of civic involvement depend on the resources people have at their disposal, not simply their good intentions. In addition to such obvious resources as free time, energy, and transportation, civic involvement requires organizations in which to be involved, and these organizations need funding. Much of this funding comes from private donors and from foundations. The strength of civic involvement depends on the continuing willingness of donors and foundation officials to support innovative community activities. Government is also a major source of financial support. Many volunteers recognize that their efforts would not be possible without government funding—a view that squares with the large proportion of funding for nonprofit organizations that in fact comes from federal, state, and local government agencies.[8]

In addition to its role as a source of funding, government is the means through which community organizations accomplish some of their most important objectives. Although (especially in suburbs) much volunteering is done without direct awareness of public policy, many volunteers are shifting their involvement toward efforts to bring government resources to bear on the problems in their communities.

A man who had devoted his Saturdays for three years to working for Habitat for Humanity decided to give it up: "I'd work all day and feel good about it. Then on the way home I'd be driving through all these bombed-out areas. You could fly over that section of the city in a helicopter and you wouldn't even be able to see what Habitat had been doing. It was just a drop in the bucket. I just came to the point where it was unbearable to continue." He now spends his time working with the Black Network for Progress. It is an educational organization that focuses on racism, African American pride, and urban development. Through direct contact with his senator and some business leaders, it was instrumental in pushing the federal government to demolish high-rise tenement buildings and allocate funding for housing like that which Habitat has been building. It remains to be seen how effective this plan will be. He knows Habitat will still need to play a role, but for the moment he believes his efforts to mobilize public support are more worthwhile.

The larger climate in which civic participation can flourish is increasingly conditioned by political and legal initiatives. The health of American democracy depends to a large extent on statutes that promote fairness when personal trust may be lacking, that encourage equitable distribution of economic resources, and that maintain checks and balances among the branches of government. Civic participation appears to be a necessary but not sufficient means of maintaining these political and legal conditions. The porousness of institutions does not in itself imply that these conditions are eroding. But porousness may make governing more complex and create greater opportunities for exploitation: the traditional checks and balances of America's democratic system may not work as well when so many economic transactions take place across national boundaries or when the mass media disseminate heavily edited information to people who have little interaction with their neighbors. It is important that civic participation not focus only on doing good for needy individuals but also on the laws and regulations pertaining to whole populations.[9]

The corporate or for-profit sector will continue to be a major force in shaping the character of civic involvement. Its role is evident in local communities through such organizations as the Chamber of Commerce and Jaycees or in the memberships and meeting places of Rotary, Lions, and Kiwanis. In the 1970s corporate civic responsibility was encouraged through such efforts as the Environmental Defense Fund, Businessmen for the Public Interest, the Council on Economic Priorities, and the Corporate Accountability Research Group. Stockholder initiatives and occasional boycotts were used to raise awareness of corporate responsibility and major firms such as AT&T, General Motors, the Bank of America, and Boise Cascade introduced public policy committees and community projects as a way of responding to public concerns. Foundations that derive their earnings from corporations have also played an increasing role in financing the work of nonprofit organizations and volunteer efforts.[10]

The corporation has also become one of the major places where people make friends and interact with casual acquaintances (as one woman observes, "It's the prime social aspect of my life"). If civic involvement depends on social ties, the corporation is central in facilitating such involvement. Corporate cultures that reward volunteering and make civic activities more visible have the potential to encourage the relationships that lead to civic involvement.

As people talk about their civic activities, they mention corporations but less often than nonprofit organizations, government agencies, service clubs, and churches. Corporations train people to handle managerial responsibilities and connect them to influential members of the community, both of which prove helpful to the volunteer efforts of employees. Corporations also contribute to service agencies through foundations, in-kind donations (such as leftovers from bakeries and restaurants), direct financing and loans for community housing projects or minority and low-income business initiatives, and participation in community projects such as clean-up days and the Special Olympics.[11]

Compared to the resources at their disposal, the role of corporations in civic activities is relatively small. Funding for nonprofit organizations comes largely from government grants and individual donations rather than from corporate philanthropy, and although many corporations participate in United Way campaigns and encourage employees to do volunteer work, they seldom give employees time during work hours to participate in community projects. Some employees even report taboos against talking about politics or civic concerns at work. For their part, executives point out that large donations of time or money to civic projects are difficult to reconcile with market pressures that require corporations to keep output at competitive prices. They speak of the need for public programs, laws, and other regulations to ensure that social needs are addressed broadly and fairly.

Corporate leaders need to be aware of the considerable influence of business conditions on the porousness of American life. Much of the looseness of civic participation is linked to the ways in which market capitalism has developed in the United States since World War II. Residential mobility often results from corporate transfers or business closings.

The educational system encourages young people to break ties with their hometowns, develop broad connections, and participate in national labor markets. Divorce is sometimes the outcome of conflicts in two-career families, and is often an option because of dual earnings. Local service organizations are hurt by the divided geographic loyalties of long-distance commuters. Family bankruptcies and leisure time devoted to spectator sports and television are partly a function of the credit-card and entertainment industries and corporate advertising. High unemployment and declining service organizations in inner cities are related to the flight of corporations to suburbs or rural areas, not to mention their quest for cheap labor in overseas markets.

Of these developments, the movement of corporate capital, headquarters, and jobs has probably had the most significant impact on the character of civic involvement; it has also made it harder for nonprofit organizations to work in tandem with corporations. When top decisionmaking roles are transferred to other communities or other countries, local leaders are left with no corporate officials who clearly have local or regional interests as a priority. As one leader complains, "I used to be able to walk into the president's office at [such-and-such corporation] and have an answer when I left; now that they've merged and no longer have a headquarters here, I don't know who's in charge."

The corporate sector is thus deeply implicated in the changing nature of civic involvement. The unraveling of communities, families, and commitment to service organizations is as much attributable to markets as it is to morals. Public discussion about ways to solidify social relationships and restore communities must not be limited to debates about government agencies and individual volunteers. It must also take into account the economic forces to which corporations are subject and the ways in which corporate leaders can respond imaginatively to them.

Religious organizations can help encourage civic participation by taking an active role in their communities. Many people are motivated by religious beliefs, and some have learned about community projects through their churches or synagogues. Many believe their congregations are doing all that is possible, but they wish that more could be done.

If churches are going to do more for their communities, they will have to cooperate with one another. Individual congregations often are too small or are faced with declining finances and thus cannot mount more than token efforts to minister to the wider community. In the past they might have been assisted by denominational bodies or formed alliances with other congregations from the same denomination. These possibilities are less available now because denominational resources and loyalties have weakened. Large congregations may be tempted to keep close control over their own resources rather than working cooperatively with other organizations. Their reach into the community will thus be limited.

Forming loose coalitions and alliances among congregations is a way to amass greater resources, as cooperative food pantries and homeless shelters illustrate. Interfaith coalitions demonstrate that the members of their various congregations are also members of a single community and are willing to work together for its benefit. As one man (a member of an African American church) puts it: "When you talk about, 'My church is doing something in community X,' that's an isolated effort. Continue doing those isolated things but on a grander scale. Churches, mosques, and synagogues need to combine their efforts, and they need to do like the churches did in the 1950s and 1960s and develop a plan to attack these larger issues."

Religious organizations can also work effectively with nonreligious agencies to address community issues. Development corporations that provide funding and expertise in community planning can cooperate with religious organizations who provide volunteers to serve on oversight boards or to wield hammers at construction sites. Religious organizations sometimes make an important contribution just by providing space for public meetings at which community concerns can be discussed.

Congregations in suburban areas and small towns are often involved in projects that benefit less advantaged communities as well as their own. But it is low-income, inner-city people who voice the strongest pleas for congregations to do more. One inner-city resident characterizes vividly the kinds of work that congregations should be doing: "When you have a church and drug dealers are selling drugs on its corner, the church needs to pull its congregation together and they need to think about an active way to develop a plan of action that solves the problem. That means attacking the issues on a political front, like writing or protesting. It means doing whatever they can on an economic front to empower people so that they don't have the need to sell drugs. It may mean standing on the corner all night themselves to prevent people from doing it. You can't say that it's wrong for people to sell drugs, and not challenge them. Any organization that believes in God can never, never, under any circumstance, justify their inaction with regards to social injustice."

Another relationship that bears close scrutiny in efforts to strengthen civic involvement is that between civic associations and the mass media. In today's world citizens depend heavily on the media for their knowledge about civic issues. This is why some observers are concerned that the media may be eroding the role of community organizations. On the one hand, too much dependence on the media seems to keep people at home watching television rather than participating in their communities. One woman who thinks civic participation is declining in her community explains, "I think television has a lot to do with it; people congregate around their television sets instead of around the village green"—a perception that seems to be confirmed by evidence that those who watch more television are less likely to be involved in civic activities. On the other hand, television has become a way in which people learn about the needs of their communities, and many leaders of civic organizations feel they need to use the media to advertise their work and to help solicit donations and volunteers.[12]

In an era of public relations specialists, one way civic organizations can make use of mass communications is by disseminating information to the media or working with media specialists to publicize a particular message or event. Large bureaucratic organizations relate to the media as one megalith to another, sending out special envoys to control what the media report. Jack Schmidt thinks Rotary should be doing more to cultivate the national newspapers and to get its message on television. Sara Mermel says the same thing about Hadassah: "What we really need is a full-time person working on public relations, getting an article in the paper at least once a week about what's happening; working with the media needs to be done by someone who knows how to do it; it doesn't just happen." Another community leader has learned by trial and error how to deal with the media; at first she was troubled by the penchant for headlines and sound bites, but now she gives reporters a pithy image within the first two minutes of her conversation with them, and it generally appears as a headline.

The urban partnership in which Jacob Merrick is engaged is a loose network that cannot control the information it disseminates to the media, but its regional base encourages it to work with the press and local television stations to publicize issues that affect the entire region. An organization does not have to be large to do this effectively, as is illustrated by Nancy Fielding's use of the local newspaper to solicit members for the Garden Club and subsequent use of gardening magazines to spread information to interested people across the country. Another organization found it hard to get publicity in newspapers or on television, so it has turned to sending faxes and using the Internet.

Whether large or small, civic organizations need to use their limited resources wisely in dealing with the media. The acid test is how successfully they control their own information. Civic organizations need to communicate a different kind of information from that found in newspapers and on television. Many community leaders have local and specialized knowledge of particular problems that is not suitable for the mass media. It is a more practical form of knowledge, showing them how to tackle community problems instead of simply airing these problems. Civic organizations can be especially effective when they are able to disseminate information that motivates people to take responsibility for social problems, rather than simply feeling despondent about them. Leaders like Grace Bishop and Jacob Merrick devote a great deal of attention to setting up seminars and providing other occasions for such information to be disseminated.

The strengthening of civic involvement requires above all that people value their role as citizens and the responsibilities of citizenship. It was not without reason that the architects of American democracy looked as much to moral philosophy as to political theory. Good democracy has always depended on the virtue or character of its citizens. And virtue is a kind of strength, an awareness of who one is and what one's capacities are, that transcends simplistic views of citizenship that reduce it to such acts as voting or reading political columns in the newspaper.

In a loosely connected society it is often more difficult for people to know their civic role because their sources of identity are so varied and ephemeral. They are likely to be rewarded for presenting different sides of themselves in different situations. It is for this reason that the self has come to be problematic, taking more time to repair and requiring more effort for reflection. Civic engagement puts people in new situations where they may be forced to think harder about their identities. Personal repair work is likely to go hand in hand with civic engagement, rather than conflicting with it.

Evidence from people who are involved in their communities suggests that personal virtue does not simply precede civic involvement but is an attendant feature of it. People who take an active part in civic organizations typically feel they have grown because of the experience. They gain information that gives them confidence in negotiating with complex political realities, or they learn to muster reserves of courage to speak at meetings. Some who participate in activities that take them out of their own neighborhoods are especially likely to find their self-images recast by these engagements.

People who feel they know themselves and believe they are trying to do what is right generally believe they can trust others to do so as well. Some who have doubts about themselves say they nevertheless try to behave dependably and hope that others will respond by doing the same. Civic organizations can help restore trust by paying more explicit attention to it. When social ties are loose, deliberate effort must be expended to establish expectations about the conditions under which trust is warranted.

Behaving politely and respectfully is a crucial aspect of the interpersonal relations on which trust depends. It is more than a semantic coincidence that has led social theorists to emphasize the integral relationship between civility and civil society. To behave civilly involves showing fundamental respect for the dignity as well as the rights of another human being. Civility is rooted in a prior commitment to the worth of others even if those others have different beliefs or interests from one's own. But civility is also demonstrated in the decorum with which personal relationships are conducted. It includes common etiquette, such as letting others finish speaking, respecting their opinions, and avoiding incendiary language.

Loose connections tempt citizens to behave in a less civil manner because relationships are more likely to be transitory and casual than enduring and dependent on good will.[13] It is precisely for this reason, however, that civility is more important in fluid or sporadic relationships. Adhering to widely acknowledged patterns of decorum becomes a way to signal one's trustworthiness to strangers. Intimate relationships can more easily be repaired when violations of decorum occur. Loose relationships lacking familiar contact need additional behavioral evidence to engender respect and trust. Civility demonstrates respect, a commitment to the humanity of another person that may sustain the relationship despite tension and disagreement.

People who are active in community organizations or in their neighborhoods often mention small manifestations of civility that have impressed them: a mayor who shows up on time to play softball at a community picnic or someone who sends a letter of appreciation to a business that has tried to resolve a community conflict. Sometimes the examples seem trivial, such as paying someone a small compliment as a way of healing a grievance, or staying on the telephone a few minutes longer despite needing to do other things. But they clearly are not trivial to the people involved. They are remembered, not so much as ways people show kindness to one another, but as reasons people believe they can *trust* one another. Often it is the small token of caring, even more than getting the job done, that convinces people it is worthwhile to take part in civic activities.

Because of the porous nature of our society, many people are not attracted to civic organizations and are unlikely to join, no matter how much good these organizations do in their communities. The reasons vary from feeling too busy to believing that the participants in such organizations have a different kind of personality. Individualism, however it is defined, is often a major aspect of these reasons. Yet it is a form of individualism that people see as respectable rather than as a selfish absorption with themselves. As one woman observes when asked why she does not join organizations: "I do not want to be steered along my path. I don't want to be part of a herd. I don't want to be made to feel guilty. I don't want to be part of a social group that I might not enjoy."

It is unlikely that someone like this will overcome her deep antipathy toward membership groups in order to become involved in her community. Indeed, she finds other ways to engage with community needs, such as responding to the call of a neighbor who has been burglarized, keeping in touch with friends and family by phone, donating money to a battered women's shelter, participating in a pick-up musical group, and above all working long hours as a speech pathologist. In any given month she embodies the nonprofit professional, the volunteer, and the soul mate in her practice of civic involvement. She illustrates the diverse ways in which people can play responsible roles in their communities, even when they are not attracted to civic organizations.

That individuals can contribute in so many different ways means that a great deal of responsibility falls on the individuals themselves. This is where moral resolve becomes important. It consists in taking responsibilities seriously, but also in recognizing the social realities with which one is confronted. Nothing in this woman's personal makeup guarantees her continuing involvement in civic affairs or prevents her from becoming so self-absorbed that she ignores the problems that beset the needy in other communities (or her own). She is not drawn out of herself by participating in groups that expose her to people of other races or income brackets, and she is not compelled to listen to speakers talking about unpleasant topics by virtue of obligations to any service organization. Yet several important realities of her life reinforce a certain level of civic participation.

The first reality is her work. As a speech pathologist, she understands something of the contribution of nonprofit organizations, clinics, schools, and government agencies to the well-being of society. She works in a city among people who are quite different from the ones in her suburban neighborhood. Her work puts her in routine contact with a wide variety of organizations, including mental health programs, hospitals, and agencies for the elderly. She is intensely interested in public policies that affect her own and similar organizations; in this she is a self-interested citizen, but one whose interests are also geared toward the provision of social services.

A second is her upbringing. She works in a nonprofit organization partly because her parents taught her the value of caring for other people and her teachers reinforced this value. As a young woman she developed an interest in community needs that continues to be expressed in her work and in some of her leisure activities. Although the daily reinforcement of these values in her work is important, she learned much of what it means to be a good citizen earlier in life.

A third reality is her exposure to the mass media. Being a college-educated professional, she has been trained to keep informed about what is happening in the society. She admits to being uninterested in much of what she reads or sees on television, but she pays attention to the statements of public officials, follows election campaigns, and talks about current events with her friends and family. The media, as well as her job and her upbringing, prompt her with ideas about how to be a responsible citizen.

Critics of contemporary civil society want more than these nominal forms of civic participation. They point out that many people do not work in nonprofit organizations, that those who do may become insular and self-interested, and that having good values and being a media consumer are probably not sufficient for the effective functioning of a spirited democracy. But criticisms of democracy must also take into account the ways in which people do participate in their communities. Rather than calling only for greater personal resolve or for a sweeping cultural reorientation, it may be more useful to work through these existing modes of participation.

Nonprofit organizations, schools and families, and the mass media are among the significant institutions through which careful deliberation about public values can take place.

A difficult issue in a society characterized by loose connections is the dilemma of how to make decisions about different levels and kinds of civic involvement. This dilemma has grown in direct proportion to the freedom of choice that is so deeply valued in American culture. Tightly bounded communities and organizations compelled their members to be involved in civic activities. The moral force came from the outside (from the expectations of other members), rather than having to arise from within. People attended meetings, helped with pancake feeds, or voted because it was customary. They knew that respect, offices, and mutual aid flowed to those who fulfilled these customary expectations. Loose connections in porous institutions depend more on individual deliberation. Sporadic contact is less likely to provide occasions for reflection about enduring values and identity. Messages from competing sources (including internalized messages) provide justifications for alternative responses. For example, helping out, advancing one's career, thinking of oneself as "nonpolitical," being a faithful friend, taking care of one's own needs, pursuing one's interests, and doing what one enjoys can often be found in a single person's language about engaging (or not engaging) in particular civic activities.[14] Even long-term members of service organizations are likely to be faced with conflicting messages from all these moral languages.

It is in relation to the moral dimension of civic involvement that concern about the balance between self-interest and social commitment can best be understood. Moral choices are never made in pure isolation, but are influenced by social context. Contexts that reinforce languages of self-interest, personal happiness, and pleasure are abundant. A consumer economy encourages people to think in these languages in order to sell entertainment, therapy, fast food, expensive automobiles, vacations, and the like. Contexts that reinforce values of service and sharing are often submerged relative to those emphasizing gratification. Thinking seriously about service or about the complexity of public issues is less likely to provide immediate gratification than focusing on the messages of advertising. Participation in volunteer organizations, community service programs, churches, or town meetings is thus important as a way of reinforcing the languages of civic involvement, as much as it is a means of actually contributing to the community.

A popular interpretation of America's social ills blames the newer, more loosely connected forms of civic involvement themselves. Observers who believe traditional membership organizations are the only way to sustain American democracy suggest that any substitute for these organizations inevitably will have undesirable effects. In this view, the increases in crime, drug use, and divorce and the decreases in voting and trust in public officials are evidence that nonprofit professionals, volunteers, and self-help groups are failing to provide vital social bonds or normative commitments that were reinforced by service organizations, fraternal associations, women's clubs, and neighborhoods. But this argument does not take adequate account of broader changes in social institutions. By ignoring these larger changes, it assumes that loose connections are the cause of social problems, rather than recognizing that loose connections and social problems are both results of other developments.

Interpreting current social problems as caused by loosely connected civic involvement implies that the way to solve them is to bring back commitment to membership organizations. These organizations, however, were embedded in a particular set of social arrangements. Loyalties were reinforced in the post-1945 era by (among other things) the memory of a massive war effort and the continuing fear of communist aggression, by segregated neighborhoods and discriminatory club policies that kept memberships homogeneous, and by a virtual taboo on civic organizations open to both men and women. It is unlikely that those who advocate a return to strong membership associations would be willing to promote fears about national security, racial segregation, and gender boundaries in order to bring about such a return.

Failure to understand the ways in which loosely connected forms of civic involvement are related to one another produces inadequate proposals for addressing social problems. Some critics favor emphasizing volunteerism, viewing it as more effective than the efforts of professionals who work for the so-called welfare establishment or are paid by government programs. This argument implicitly recognizes that people's willingness to volunteer is crucial in social conditions that make it hard to mobilize strong membership associations. But it falters in its insular conception of volunteers. It does not recognize that the appeals that encourage people to volunteer come in large measure from nonprofit organizations.

Another argument emphasizes changing social conditions, stressing not increasing porousness but government bureaucracy and regulatory intervention. In this view, private initiatives have been driven out by public programs. People who depend on welfare checks and people who sit back and wait for the government to solve national problems are both examples of how bureaucracy stifles civic responsibility. This argument ignores all the other changes in American society in the past half-century. New information technologies, corporate downsizing, the relocation of businesses from center cities to suburbs, and rising levels of education, to name a few, have promoted porousness, which has in turn generated some of the social problems to which public and private agencies alike have attempted to respond.

Another popular view attributes worsening social conditions to moral failure on the part of individuals. One variant decries the immorality of teenagers who become pregnant or use drugs, or that of homeless persons who do not find jobs or families who are on welfare. Another variant blames middle-class Americans who pursue their own interests and seek pleasure rather than participating in civic affairs. These arguments are correct that porous social conditions often give individuals greater discretion about how to lead their lives and thus pose moral questions that individuals need to ponder seriously. But the arguments are overly narrow when they ignore the social conditions that reinforce certain moral choices rather than others. Calls for marriage partners to resist divorce, for example, can be cast in more effective terms if they consider not only the moral resolve of the partners themselves but also ways in which corporate policies on employment and family leave might be altered to lessen the pressures on working couples.

To acknowledge that loose forms of civic involvement are embedded in porous social conditions is not to deny the weaknesses of these arrangements. It is fair to say that many social problems have increased *despite*—not because of—the efforts of volunteers, nonprofit organizations, and public agencies. Nevertheless, it is also fair to say that these kinds of civic involvement perpetuate certain responses to social problems and perhaps preclude consideration of others. Nonprofit professionals are often the first to admit that having to submit grant proposals to more than a dozen sources of funding is inefficient, even though they may recognize that competition and decentralization are preferable to depending on a single government agency. Volunteers observe that their efforts are often ineffective, compared to those of paid professionals, if only because they do not have the requisite skills. Discussion is needed of ways in which civic organizations can adapt to these conditions.

American democracy continues to be a frustrating endeavor, just as its architects expected. As the twentieth century moves to its end, social observers are right to worry about the health of democracy and to question whether or not civic involvement is declining. As the society has become more diverse, the need for active engagement in our communities has increased. But it is also helpful to note that civic involvement has been changing. Despite the persistence of many clubs and service organizations from an earlier era, millions of Americans are experimenting with new ways of reaching out to their communities. The new forms of civic involvement have been shaped by the information technologies, the market forces, and the cultural redefinitions that have made our society more fluid. Part of the challenge confronting all civic-minded Americans is to understand these changes so that efforts to promote civic involvement can be both realistic and effective.

Methods

Notes

Index

Methods

The primary material for this book was collected through in-depth qualitative interviews and a national survey. The qualitative interviews were designed to elicit information about respondents' involvement in particular community organizations, their perceptions of developments in the wider community and society, and their personal values, beliefs, and lifestyles. The survey supplemented this information, providing data from which generalizations about civic involvement in the adult U.S. population at large could be made.

The qualitative interviews were conducted in eighteen states: California, New Mexico, Oklahoma, Kansas, Minnesota, Florida, South Carolina, Kentucky, Tennessee, Virginia, West Virginia, Michigan, Ohio, Pennsylvania, New Jersey, New York, Massachusetts, and Maine. Respondents were selected to ensure approximately equal numbers of men and women, older and younger people, and residents of inner-city areas, suburbs, and small towns; a range of occupations and educational levels; and representation of racial, ethnic, and religious diversity. Respondents were identified through snowball or network methods involving multiple starting points, including referrals from clergy and other community leaders, civic directories, published lists of community organizations, newspaper articles, and personal contacts. Five trained researchers conducted the interviews using a semi-structured instrument that I designed and pretested.

Information was drawn from approximately 250 respondents. Of these, 165 were selected with advance knowledge that they were active in a community organization or civic activity. Their interviews generally took between three and five hours. Thirty others were selected as examples of ordinary citizens who in most cases were not involved in any community activities. Their interviews focused more on their perceptions of their community and the wider society as well as on their attitudes, beliefs, backgrounds, and daily schedules, and generally lasted between an hour and a half and two hours.

The remaining interviews were conducted as part of another project that provided information about respondents' attitudes toward their community, the groups in which they participated, and their volunteer activities. All interviews were tape-recorded and transcribed. Respondents were asked to choose pseudonyms by which they wished to be identified. Other identifying aspects of the information they provided that might compromise their anonymity, such as the names of their organizations or communities, have been altered.

The qualitative interviews asked questions about respondents' background and demographic characteristics, civic activities, community, social attitudes, religion, work, and family. The version for respondents involved in a community organization asked detailed questions about their organization, including its mission and main activities, size and history, sources of funding, expenditures and clients, relationships among staff and volunteers, interaction with other public and private community agencies, and any problems it might be facing. These interviews also included questions about respondents' histories of involvement in the organization, their current positions, what had motivated them to become involved, and what they liked and disliked about their involvement.

The version for other respondents asked about the size and character of their community, how they defined their community, what they liked and disliked about it, their perception of its main problems, what organizations were addressing these problems, how they perceived the community in terms of civic participation and community pride, their own history of residential mobility, their civic activities, why they had dropped out of any community organizations, which organizations they would or would not consider joining, the barriers that prevented them from becoming more involved, how they interacted with their neighbors, their religious activities, their association with friends and family, and their daily schedules.

The survey was conducted in January and February 1997 among 1,528 randomly selected respondents representative of the noninstitutionalized adult population of the United States. Field work was subcontracted to the Gallup Organization. Each respondent was interviewed in person for approximately thirty minutes using fixed-choice questions that focused on the following areas: perceptions of problems and quality of life in the respondent's neighborhood and community; involvement in innovative and traditional forms of volunteer community service; membership in traditional and innovative civic organizations; participation in and location of community meetings; multiple measures of trust of others and of oneself; likelihood of volunteering under various personal and family circumstances; perceptions of the meaning of good citizenship; personal religious involvement; attributes of respondent's congregation; perception of congregation's involvement in community issues; congregation's links to other religious and secular organizations; and standard demographics.

Some results are summarized in the text. In the Introduction, the discussion of the correlates of community satisfaction is based on the following analysis: Respondents were asked whether each of ten items was a problem in their own community and, a few questions later, how satisfied they were with the quality of life in their community ("On the whole, are you very satisfied, somewhat satisfied, somewhat dissatisfied, or very dissatisfied with the quality of life in your community?"). Using canonical discriminant function analysis to predict whether respondents would say "very satisfied" versus any of the other responses, we found that "people not caring about each other" ranked highest of the ten items (coefficient of .771), followed by "crime," "racial or ethnic conflicts," and "drugs." (The other items were "a lack of jobs," "problems in the schools," "too many people moving into the community," "traffic problems," "threats to the environment," and "gangs.") Further analysis of the correlates of community satisfaction is presented in Table 1.

On trust (Chapter 8), in the Civic Involvement Survey 62 percent said they mostly agreed that "most people can be trusted." But 71 percent agreed that "you can't be too careful in your dealings with people." Moreover, of those who thought most people can be trusted, 66 percent agreed about the need to be careful in dealings with people; and of those who agreed that you can't be too careful, 58 percent still thought most people can be trusted. Overall, 48 percent of the respondents gave consistent answers to the two questions (agreeing with one and disagreeing with the other), while 47 percent gave inconsistent answers.

In the Civic Involvement Survey, as in other studies (especially Putnam, "Bowling Alone," and Kohut, "Trust and Citizen Engagement in Metropolitan Philadelphia"), the effects on trust of lower incomes and education and of being a member of a minority group are evident. Agreement that "most people can be trusted" is negatively associated with having an income below $25,000 (odds ratio of .776), being male (.774), being African American (.308), being Hispanic (.547), being under age 35 (.666), and being unemployed (.462); it is positively associated with having attended college (1.624). Other factors in the logit regression model were not significant: central-city residence, small-town residence, low-income neighborhood, being age 50 and older, knowing only a few of one's neighbors, and being unmarried.

In contrast, agreeing that "you can't be too careful in your dealings with people" was unrelated to most of the foregoing variables; the exceptions were being young (1.302), having attended college (.683), knowing few neighbors

(1.199), and being unmarried (1.274). An interpretation of these findings is that "trust in the generalized other," as it has been called, is lower for those who belong to a segment of society that is disadvantaged compared with the majority; while being careful about dealing with people is more an indication of the caution that younger people are taught to exercise and that people who do not have strong relationships (with neighbors or spouses) may need to exercise. An additional finding that may account for some of the decline in generalized trust is that women who work outside the home or who are students are less likely than those who keep house to say that most people can be trusted (the odds ratio among women for keeping house is 1.611, controlling for age, college attendance, and being African American or Hispanic).

Table 1 presents the results of using logit regression to predict the likelihood of being "very satisfied" with one's community. The main results are as follows. Residents of central cities are significantly less likely to be satisfied than residents of suburbs (but residents of small towns are not significantly more likely to be satisfied, controlling for other factors). Living in a low-income neighborhood is strongly associated with not being satisfied. Other demographic characteristics associated with low odds of being satisfied are being male, African American, or Hispanic. Older people are more likely than the middle-aged to be satisfied. Of the community problems asked about, crime, too many people moving in, a lack of jobs, and people not caring about each other are significantly associated with low satisfaction, controlling for other variables shown in Model 3 of Table 1.

Table 2 presents the percentages of respondents in the Civic Involvement Survey who participated in various voluntary activities, the median hours they volunteered, and the kinds of persons or organizations with whom they came in contact. Table 3 presents three models to explain the total number of persons or organizations with whom volunteers say they come into contact. The first model shows that people who devote more hours to volunteering are likely to have higher numbers of contacts. The second model shows that a number of personal characteristics of volunteers also influence their likelihood of having higher numbers of contacts: these characteristics include being a college graduate, holding membership in at least one voluntary group, being employed, not living in a low-income neighborhood, being a church member, and having children. The third model shows, however, that the best predictor of how many contacts a person has is the number of volunteer activities in which that person participates; this result is strong despite the effect of personal characteristics, and it largely explains away the zero-order effect of time spent volunteering.

Table 4 presents the results of logit regression models in which the dependent variable is whether or not respondents feel they could count on neighbors for help if someone in their families became seriously ill. The first model shows that central-city residents are only about 65 percent as likely to believe they could count on neighbors as residents of suburbs (whereas residents of small towns are 50 percent more likely to give this response); in addition, those in low-income neighborhoods are about half as likely as others to give this response (meaning that residents of low-income, central-city areas are only about a third as likely as suburbanites to feel they could count on their neighbors). The second model introduces controls for respondent's income, gender, race or ethnic group, age, and employment status; it shows that each of these personal characteristics is related to the likelihood of perceiving help from neighbors, but that the effect of living in a low-income neighborhood remains significant. The third model introduces the effect of having attended college, showing that the effect of living in a low-income neighborhood remains significant.

Table 5 repeats the analysis; here, the dependent variable is being a member of any voluntary organization. Living in a low-income neighborhood remains significant when most characteristics of individual respondents are taken into account; the neighborhood effect ceases to be statistically significant when college attendance is controlled, but the odds-value remains below one (meaning that neighborhood has a dampening effect on memberships). The strength of the college variable suggests two possible explanations for the lack of civic involvement in low-income, inner-city areas: that civic organizations appeal to college-educated people, and that college-educated people have fled inner-city areas.

Table 6 shows no significant effects on church membership of the area (central city, small town, or suburb) in which people live or whether or not they live in a low-income neighborhood; unlike the results in Table 5, these also show that church membership is not heavily influenced by college attendance.

Table 7 relates to the discussion in Chapter 7 of the personal benefits associated with involvement in bounded and loosely connected settings. It compares the likelihood of people saying that by helping others they have learned new things about their community, become more interested in social and political issues, gained self-confidence, developed new skills, and found that they had more confidence in other people. As a measure of the more tightly bounded form of civic involvement, I examine the effects of being a member of a civic or service club, and for the more loosely connected kind of activity I examine the effects of having done any kind of volunteer work during the past year. I also control for age, gender, and having attended college (each of these variables is significantly correlated to the dependent variables).

Three sets of logit regression models were used: a model that included the controls and club membership, a model that included the controls and volunteering, and a model that included the controls and both club membership and volunteering. For all five dependent variables, the main pattern is as follows: being a member of a civic or service club (examined separately) has powerful effects, increasing the likelihood of experiencing each of the benefits by at least 2.341 and as much as 7.894; volunteering (examined separately) has as powerful effects (and in four of the five comparisons, stronger effects), yielding odds-ratios from 3.805 to 7.410; and when the two variables are entered simultaneously, volunteering is the stronger of the two. These findings support the suggestion in the text that loosely structured activities can generate many of the same personal attributes that have been associated with civic organizations in the past. Other examples in Chapter 7 illustrate some of the specific ways in which people gain personal confidence, learn civic skills, or become more interested in their communities.

Table 8 presents the social correlates of saying one is very likely to trust a person "who lives in your neighborhood," "who shares their personal feelings with you," and "who does volunteer work in the community." Trust of neighbors is highly contingent on social location, as indicated by the statistically significant relationships for eight of the twelve variables in the logit regression model. People who live in cities and in low-income neighborhoods are relatively unlikely to trust their neighbors, as are men, African Americans, Hispanics, and unmarried people, while older people and those who have attended college are more likely to do so. Trusting someone who shares feelings with you is more universally possible: only three of the twelve relationships are significant. Residents of small towns are relatively likely to say they trust such people and men are relatively unlikely to do so; because generalized trust is lower among young people, it is important that young people are above average in their likelihood of trusting people who share their feelings. The table also shows the likelihood of trusting someone who volunteers. Here, only one of the twelve relationships is significant (the one for older people). This finding lends some support to the idea that volunteering is a type of civic involvement that Americans with many different social characteristics admire; it also suggests that the presence of volunteers in communities may generate trust.

TABLE 1. Correlates of community satisfaction (logit regression)
Dependent variable: On the whole, are you very satisfied, somewhat satisfied, somewhat dissatisfied, or very dissatisfied with the qualtiy of life in your community? (very satisfied vs. else)

	Model 1	Model 2	Model 3
Area			
Central city	.587*		.701*
Small town or rural area	1.104		1.059
Neighborhood			
Low income	.256*		.305*
Respondent			
Income < $25,000	1.055		1.069
Male	.883		8.14*
African American	.304*		.379*
Hispanic	.504*		.569*
Under age 35	.780		.817
Age 50 and over	1.657*		1.657*
Unemployed	.638		.690
Attended college	1.037		1.041
Serious problems in community			
Crime		.601*	.678*
Drug abuse		.767*	.780
Too many people moving in		.773	.719*
Traffic problems		1.025	1.048
Threats to the environment		1.083	1.142
Problems in the schools		.836	.843
A lack of jobs		.523*	.618*
People not caring about each other		.680*	.668*
Gangs		.862	.841
Racial or ethnic conflicts	.731*	.893	

Number = 1,528

* Significant at or beyond the .05 level of probability (Wald test).

TABLE 2. Descriptive information on volunteering
Question: During the past year, have you spent any time volunteering
for any of the following?

Type of volunteering	Response: yes (%)
Church-related activities	27
Distributing food to the needy	20
Activities related to schools	20
Youth activities	18
Informal volunteering	15
A neighborhood crime watch program	10
A neighborhood or homeowners' association	8
A political campaign	7
Environmental projects	7
Arts or cultural activities	7
Community organizing	7
A shelter for abused women or children	5
AIDS-related activities	4
A violence-prevention effort	4
Building houses for the poor	3
None	48

Median hours volunteered each week	Hours
All respondents	1
All volunteers	2

Through volunteer work, had any contact with	Response: yes (%)
Your neighbors	59
Teachers	49
Clergy	47
Nonprofit organizations	41
Health professionals	29
Social workers	24
Government officials	22
Lawyers	21
Service clubs	19
Corporate executives	14
Banks	14
Community development corporations	9
None of the above	5

TABLE 3. Correlates of contacts from volunteering (ordinary least squares regression)
Dependent variable: number of different contacts, volunteers only

	Model 1	Model 2	Model 3
Hours volunteered	.303*	.234*	.065*
College graduate		.132*	.065*
Group member		.361*	.149*
Employed		.051*	.034*
Low-income neighborhood		−.049*	−.030*
Church member		.097*	.044*
Have children		.058*	.006
Number of volunteer activities			.652*
Adjusted R-square	.092	.299	.614
Number = 775			

* Significant at or beyond the .05 level of probability (F-test).

TABLE 4. Odds of being able to count on neighbors (logit regression)
Dependent variable: If you or someone in your family became seriously ill, do you think you could count on . . . your neighbors . . . for help? (Yes)

	EXP (B)		
	Model 1	Model 2	Model 3
Area			
Central city	.657*	.858	.862
Small town or rural area	1.504*	1.581*	1.691*
Neighborhood			
Low-income	.543*	.628*	.653*
Respondent			
Income < $25,000		.731*	.828
Male		.788*	.779*
African American		.512*	.555*
Hispanic		.698*	.744
Under age 35		.744*	.752*
Age 50 and over		1.392*	1.530*
Unemployed		.975	1.011
Attended college			1.714*
Number = 1,528			

* Significant at or beyond the .05 level of probability (Wald test).

TABLE 5. Odds of membership in any group (logit regression)
          Dependent variable: Currently a member of at least one voluntary
          group or organization

	EXP (B)		
	Model 1	Model 2	Model 3
Area			
Central city	.582*	.831	.835
Small town or rural area	.823*	.986	1.112
Neighborhood			
Low-income	.613*	.728*	.794
Respondent			
Income < $25,000		.373*	.461*
Male		1.036	1.024
African American		.736*	.884
Hispanic		.618*	.696*
Under age 35		.654*	.664*
Age 50 and over		.586*	.691*
Unemployed		.558*	.588*
Attended college			2.974*
Number = 1,528			

* Significant at or beyond the .05 level of probability (Wald test).

Note: Groups included: fraternal; civic or service; veterans; political; environmental; labor unions; sports; youth; school service; health, fitness, or exercise; hobby or garden; school fraternities or sororities; ethnic, racial, or nationality; farm; literary, art, or music; discussion or study; professional or academic, church-affiliated other than church membership itself; consumer or buying; therapeutic or counseling; any other groups.

TABLE 6.   Odds of church membership (logit regression)
Dependent variable: Are you currently a member of a church or
synagogue (yes)

	EXP (B)		
	Model 1	Model 2	Model 3
Area			
Central city	.996	1.011	1.013
Small town or rural area	1.174	1.135	1.155
Neighborhood			
Low-income	.916	.935	.948
Respondent			
Income < $25,000		.751*	.780*
Male		.646*	.645*
African American		1.504*	1.549*
Hispanic		1.214	1.240
Under age 35		.698*	.701*
Age 50 and over		1.553*	1.596*
Unemployed		.427*	.432*
Attended college			1.174
Number = 1,528			

* Significant at or beyond the .05 level of probability (Wald test).

TABLE 7.   Effects of club membership and volunteering (logit regression models, controlling
for age, education, and gender)

	Dependent Variables:				
	Learned about community	Interest in social issues	More self-confidence	Learned new skills	Greater confidence in others
Entered singly					
Volunteered	7.410*	4.714*	5.064*	3.805*	3.727*
Club member	7.894*	4.733*	2.899*	3.007*	2.341*
Entered together					
Volunteered	6.871*	4.364*	4.856*	3.607*	3.600*
Club member	4.398*	3.048*	1.715*	1.987*	1.518*
Number = 1,528					

* Significant at or beyond the .05 level of probability (Wald test).

TABLE 8.   Correlates of trust (logit regression)

| | Odds of being very likely to trust somebody who | | |
	Lives in your neighborhood	Shares personal feelings	Does volunteer work
Central city	.495*	.870	.866
Small town or rural area	1.163	1.367*	1.282
Low-income neighborhood	.586*	1.093	.800
Income < $25,000	1.156	1.082	1.099
Male	.792*	.764*	.824
African American	.686*	.779	.998
Hispanic	.607*	1.062	.807
Under age 35	1.035	1.412*	1.092
Age 50 and over	1.520*	1.125	1.309*
Unemployed	.816	.802	.986
Attended college	1.271*	1.024	1.231
Unmarried	.689*	.903	.975
Number of significant coefficients	8	3	1
Number = 1,528			

* Significant at or beyond the .05 level of probability (Wald test).

Notes

INTRODUCTION

1. Unless otherwise indicated, survey figures are from the Civic Involvement Survey that I conducted in 1997; see the Methods section for details. On perceptions of selfishness see Robert Wuthnow, *God and Mammon in America* (New York: Free Press, 1994); on caring about others, Robert Wuthnow, *Acts of Compassion* (Princeton: Princeton University Press, 1991).

2. See esp. Charles Taylor, "Liberal Politics and the Public Sphere," in *New Communitarian Thinking: Persons, Virtues, Institutions, and Communities*, ed. Amitai Etzioni (Charlottesville: University of Virginia Press, 1995); Jean L. Cohen and Andrew Arato, *Civil Society and Political Theory* (Cambridge, Mass.: MIT Press, 1992); John A. Hall, ed., *Civil Society: Theory, History, Comparison* (London: Polity, 1995); Ernest Gellner, *Conditions of Liberty: Civil Society and Its Rivals* (London: Penguin, 1994); Adam Seligman, *The Idea of Civil Society* (New York: Free Press, 1992); Keith Tester, *Civil Society* (London: Routledge, 1993); Peter L. Berger, Richard John Neuhaus, and Michael Novak, eds., *To Empower People: From State to Civil Society* (Washington: AEI Press, 1996); Robert Hefner, ed., *Democratic Civility: The History and Cross-Cultural Possibility of a Modern Ideal* (New Brunswick: Transaction, 1998).

3. Robert D. Putnam, "Bowling Alone: America's Declining Social Capital," *Journal of Democracy* 6 (Jan. 1995); idem, "The Strange Disappearance of Civic America," *American Prospect* (Winter 1996) (http://epn.org/prospect/24/24putn.html); idem, "Tuning In, Tuning Out: The Strange Disappearance of Social Capital in America," *P.S.: Political Science and Politics* 27 (1995).

4. Everett C. Ladd, "Civic Participation and American Democracy," *Public Perspective* (June–July 1996). Sidney Verba, Kay Lehman Schlozman, and Henry E. Brady, *Voice and Equality: Civic Voluntarism in American Politics* (Cambridge, Mass.: Harvard University Press, 1995).

5. Paul F. Cromwell, Roger G. Dunham, and Paul E. Cromwell, *Crime and*

Justice in America: Present Realities and Future Prospects (Englewood Cliffs, N.J.: Prentice-Hall, 1996); James Q. Wilson and Joan Petersilia, *Crime* (San Francisco: ICS Press, 1996); Lawrence B. Joseph, ed., *Crime, Communities, and Public Policy* (Urbana: University of Illinois Press, 1996).

6. Sheldon Danziger and Peter Gottschalk, *America Unequal* (Cambridge, Mass.: Harvard University Press, 1996); Michael Tanner, *The End of Welfare: Fighting Poverty in the Civil Society* (Washington: Cato Institute, 1996); Rebecca M. Blank, *It Takes a Nation: A New Agenda for Fighting Poverty* (Princeton: Princeton University Press, 1997).

7. In the Civic Involvement Survey, 55 percent said "racial or ethnic conflicts" were a problem in their community (19 percent said they were a serious problem); among nonwhite respondents, 32 percent said they were serious.

8. Christopher Lasch, *The Culture of Narcissism: American Life in an Age of Diminishing Expectations*, rev. ed (New York: Norton, 1991); Drew Western, *Self and Society: Narcissism, Collectivism, and the Development of Morals* (Cambridge: Cambridge University Press, 1985).

9. General Social Survey (University of Chicago, National Opinion Research Center, 1996); Family Circle Family Index Project (1993); National Commission on Children (1990); General Social Survey (1982).

10. E.g., William J. Bennett, John J. Di Iulio Jr., and John P. Walters, *Body Count: Moral Poverty and How to Win America's War against Crime and Drugs* (New York: Simon and Schuster, 1996).

11. Barrington Moore Jr., *Injustice: The Social Bases of Obedience and Revolt* (White Plains, N.Y.: M. E. Sharpe, 1978); Zygmunt Bauman, *Between Class and Elite: The Evolution of the British Labour Movement, A Sociological Study* (Manchester: Manchester University Press, 1972).

12. Karl Dietrich Bracher, *The German Dictatorship: The Origins, Structure and Effects of National Socialism* (New York: Holt, Rinehart and Winston, 1972); Michael Stephen Steinberg, *Sabers and Brown Shirts: The German Students' Path to National Socialism, 1881–1935* (Chicago: University of Chicago Press, 1977).

13. I conceive of connections as social ties among individuals, between individuals and organizations, or among organizations. Looseness is a variable that describes ties in terms of the degree to which they exhibit one or more of the following characteristics: brevity of the relationship, infrequency of interaction, specific episodes of interaction that are short or occur at unanticipated intervals, interaction that is limited to specific roles or tasks, ease with which the relationship can be initiated or terminated, lack of connectedness with third parties, and low likelihood of occurring within closed networks. Although the data on which this book is based do not lend themselves to precise quantification, the conceptual basis for distinguishing loose connections is well established in the literature on social networks; see, e.g., Richard M. Emerson, "Exchange Theory, Part I: A Psychological Basis for Social Exchange," in *Sociological Theories in Progress*, vol. 2, ed. Joseph Berger, Morris

Zelditch Jr., and B. Anderson (Boston: Houghton Mifflin, 1972); Richard M. Emerson, "Social Exchange Theory," in *Social Psychology: Sociological Perspectives*, ed. Morris Rosenberg and Ralph Turner (New York: Basic Books, 1981); Robert Perrucci and Harry R. Potter, eds., *Networks of Power: Organizational Actors at the National Corporate and Community Levels* (New York: Aldine De Gruyter, 1989); Samuel Leinhardt, ed., *Social Networks* (New York: Academic Press, 1977).

1. BREAKING APART, COMING TOGETHER

1. Jeffrey A. Charles, *Service Clubs in American Society: Rotary, Kiwanis, and Lions* (Urbana: University of Illinois Press, 1993), 158.
2. The decline of fraternal orders was already receiving comment in the 1970s: see Alvin J. Schmidt and Nicholas Babchuk, "Formal Voluntary Organizations and Change over Time: A Study of American Fraternal Associations," *Journal of Voluntary Action Research* 1 (1972).
3. Information supplied by Holly Hass, Rotary International, April 1996. In our interviews, members of local Kiwanis chapters, Lions clubs, Federated Women's Clubs, and Masonic lodges uniformly reported membership declines and spoke about discussions their groups were having about how to adapt to changing conditions.
4. Jack Schmidt's observation about the difficulty of attracting young people is supported by the Civic Involvement Survey, in which 3.4 percent of respondents aged 18–34 were members of "civic or service clubs," compared with 6.7 percent of those aged 35–49, and 8.6 percent of those 50 and over.
5. Since 1960 the proportion of all single women who are in the labor force has grown from 44 percent to 65 percent; the proportion of married women, from 30 percent to 61 percent; and that of married women with children, from 28 percent to 69 percent. U.S. Bureau of the Census, *The American Almanac, 1995–1996: Statistical Abstract of the United States* (Austin: Reference Press, 1996), table 638.
6. Robert D. Putnam, "Bowling Alone: America's Declining Social Capital," *Journal of Democracy* 6 (Jan. 1995).
7. Frank Purelli's interest in firefighting as an alternative to his job corresponds with findings of Alexander M. Thompson III and Barbara A. Bono, "Work without Wages: The Motivation for Volunteer Firefighters," *American Journal of Economics and Sociology* 52 (1993), whose survey of 354 volunteer firefighters suggests the relationship of volunteering, alienation, and self-actualization.
8. Kenneth Perkins, *Volunteer Firefighters in the United States: A Sociological Profile of America's Bravest* (Farmville, Va.: National Volunteer Fire Council, 1987); Malcolm Getz, *The Economics of the Urban Fire Department* (Baltimore: Johns Hopkins University Press, 1979).
9. Vincent Paul McNally Jr., "A Most Dangerous and Noble Calling: The De-

velopment, Organization and Operation of the American Volunteer Fire Service" (Ph.D. diss., Temple University, 1979); Ernest Earnest, *The Volunteer Fire Company: Past and Present* (New York: Stein and Day, 1979).

10. Tom Barnes, "State Lacks Training Code for Volunteers," *Pittsburgh Gazette* (Aug. 8, 1995). Soyia Ellison, "Growth Leaving Volunteer Fire Departments Burned Out: Industries Pushing Potential Firefighters Out," *Herald-Sun*, Durham, N.C. (Nov. 23, 1995). *U.S. Statistical Abstract*, table 649.

11. The need to raise public awareness is suggested by the finding in national surveys that only one parent in six (and about one student in four) believes violence is increasing in the local schools; "Violence in America's Schools," *World Opinion Update* (Feb. 1995).

12. Estimate based on responses in the Civic Involvement Survey to a question that asked whether people had volunteered during the past twelve months for "a violence prevention effort."

13. Estimate based on a question about volunteering during the past twelve months for "distributing food to the needy."

14. Estimate of 16 million based on a question that asked, "Do you currently participate in any kind of self-help group?" to which 8.3 percent replied yes. Of these, 56 percent said they participate about once a week, 15 percent about once every two weeks, 22 percent about once a month, and 7 percent less often. In my *Sharing the Journey: Support Groups and America's New Quest for Community* (New York: Free Press, 1994), I estimated the number of self-help group members at 8 to 10 million, using more detailed questions that permitted subtracting people who attended Sunday school classes or Bible study groups. In that study 3.6 percent of the public indicated current membership in an "anonymous" group.

15. See, e.g., Robert N. Bellah et al., *Habits of the Heart: Individualism and Commitment in American Life*, rev. ed. (Berkeley and Los Angeles: University of California Press, 1996; Putnam, "Bowling Alone."

16. Mary C. Dufour and Kathryn G. Ingle, "Twenty-Five Years of Alcohol Epidemiology: Trends, Techniques, and Transitions," *Alcohol Health and Research World* 19 (Jan. 1995).

2. THE CHANGING MEANINGS OF INVOLVEMENT

1. William H. Whyte Jr., *The Organization Man* (Garden City, N.Y.: Doubleday, 1956). On Masons as organization men see esp. Lynn Dumenil, *Freemasonry and American Culture, 1880–1930* (Princeton: Princeton University Press, 1984). On the growth of service organizations versus fraternal orders see Clifford Putney, "Service over Secrecy: How Lodge-Style Fraternalism Yielded Popularity to Men's Service Clubs," *Journal of Popular Culture* 27 (1993).

2. "Their ideal of service is a gregarious one—the kind of service you do others

right in the midst of them and not once removed"; Whyte, *Organization Man*, 80. Sinclair Lewis, *Babbitt* (New York: New American Library, 1922), 166.

3. W. Lloyd Warner and Paul S. Lunt, *The Social Life of a Modern Community* (New Haven: Yale University Press, 1941). Whyte attributed the organization men's interest in "belonging" to their having been taught to work together in military units during World War II, their growing representation in managerial and professional positions, the ideology of the human relations school of management, and uncertainties produced by the decline of small towns and tightly knit ethnic communities.

4. Quoted in Harold O. Bahlke, "Rotary and American Culture: A Historical Study of Ideology" (Ph.D. diss., University of Minnesota, 1956), 111–112.

5. Robert Cooley Angell, *The Integration of American Society: A Study of Groups and Institutions* (New York: McGraw-Hill, 1941); Albert Blumenthal, *Small-Town Stuff* (Chicago: University of Chicago Press, 1932); Max Lerner, *America as a Civilization*, vol. 1: *The Basic Frame* (New York: Simon and Schuster, 1957).

6. Charles F. Marden, *Rotary and Its Brothers* (Princeton: Princeton University Press, 1935). Mark C. Carnes, *Secret Ritual and Manhood in Victorian America* (New Haven: Yale University Press, 1989); Max Lerner, "The Joiners," in *America's Voluntary Spirit*, ed. Brian O'Connell (New York: Foundation Center, 1983).

7. David T. Beito, "Mutual Aid, State Welfare, and Organized Charity: Fraternal Societies and the 'Deserving' and 'Undeserving' Poor, 1900–1930," *Journal of Policy History* 5 (1993).

8. Whyte, *Organization Man*, 143. "The organization man does some civic work, but it is largely out of a sense of obligation rather than from any personal impulse. Characteristically, he is involved in civic work at that state of his career when, as a branch manager to the national organization, he is ex officio a leader in the local community." Ibid., 163–164.

9. See, e.g., Anne Firor Scott, *Natural Allies: Women's Associations in American History* (Urbana: University of Illinois Press, 1991); Lori D. Ginzberg, *Women and the Work of Benevolence: Morality and Class in the 19th Century United States* (New Haven: Yale University Press, 1990).

10. Quoted in Mark Sullivan, *Our Times, the United States, 1900–1925*, vol. 2: *American Finding Herself* (New York: Scribner, 1927), 637; Sinclair Lewis went further, observing that women's "husbands objected to their 'wasting time and getting a lot of crank ideas' in unpaid social work"; *Babbitt*, 102.

11. Nancy F. Cott, *The Bonds of Womanhood: Woman's Sphere in New England, 1780–1835* (New Haven: Yale University Press, 1977); Nancy A. Hewitt, *Women's Activism and Social Change: Rochester, New York: 1822–1872* (Ithaca: Cornell University Press, 1984); Theda Skocpol, *Protecting Soldiers and Mothers: The Political Origins of Social Policy in the United States* (Cam-

bridge: Harvard University Press, 1992). Mary I. Wood, *The History of the General Federation of Women's Clubs: The First Twenty-Two Years of Its Organization* (New York: General Federation of Women's Clubs, 1912), 4.

12. William R. Leach, *Land of Desire: Merchants, Power and the Rise of a New American Culture* (New York: Pantheon, 1993). Lerner, "The Joiners," 85: "[Joining a women's club] means a chance to act as culture surrogates for their husbands, who are too busy to keep up with the trends in literature, the arts, or the community services. Americans have learned to take the club-women with a kindly bantering acceptance. . . The jokes about the ladies' club lecture circuits cannot conceal a measure of pride on the part of a new nation in having wives with leisure enough to spend on veneer, like garden clubs, reading and discussion clubs, parent-teacher associations, and child-study clubs."

13. Lerner, "The Joiners".

14. Angell, *Integration of American Society*. Whyte, *Organization Man*, 394–395.

15. Of women's clubs in the 1950s Whyte wrote, "They saw no antithesis; their primary goal was to develop 'citizenship' rather than social activity, but they saw both kinds of participation as indivisible—parts of a satisfying whole"; *Organization Man*, 398. William L. O'Neill, *Everyone Was Brave* (Chicago: Quadrangle Books, 1971).

16. Oral histories are replete with comments like "We always knew everybody and their kids and whose dog was running down the street." Whyte aptly describes the norm of civility: "If misfortune strikes a family, the neighbors are not only remarkably generous but remarkably tactful"; *Organization Man*, 391. Arthur J. Vidich and Joseph Bensman, *Small Town in Mass Society: Class, Power, and Religion in a Rural Community* (New York: Doubleday, 1958), 34, emphasize charity: "In its most typical form neighborliness occurs in time of personal and family crisis—birth, death, illness, fire, catastrophe. On such occasions friends and neighbors mobilize to support those in distress: collections of money are taken, meals are prepared by others, cards of condolence are sent."

17. Among the characteristics of bad neighbors observed by Vidich and Bensman in *Small Town* were keeping to themselves, taking advantage of you, not getting along, showing off, stirring up trouble, thinking they're better than everybody else, being bossy, and cheating. A man from the midwest recalled bad neighbors as "Not speaking, not saying good morning. Kind of aloof. All of the things that happen in modern urban cities. Like there's people that look the other way. That would be being a bad neighbor." Text quotation from Whyte, *Organization Man*, 368.

18. Blumenthal, *Small-Town Stuff*. Studies, such as Whyte's, of geographic propinquity and friendship patterns suggest that people did not go significantly out of their way to become acquainted with neighbors.

19. Michael Harrington, *The Other America: Poverty in the United States* (New York: Macmillan, 1993 [1962]).

20. See Arlene Kaplan Daniels, *Invisible Careers: Women Civic Leaders from the Volunteer World* (Chicago: University of Chicago Press, 1988).

21. Katha Pollitt, "For Whom the Ball Rolls," *Nation* (April 15, 1996), 9–10.

22. The history of the Larimer Woman's Club (a pseudonym) is based on my research in its archives; details about the wider community are drawn from local newspapers and other records.

23. Kevin Sack, "Volunteering Made Easier for Busy Young Workers," *New York Times* (Nov. 25, 1995).

24. The survey was the one I designed and commissioned as part of the research for this book. The other responses were "admire a little" and "wouldn't necessarily admire." Thirty-eight percent said they wouldn't necessarily admire someone who belonged to a club or service organization, while only 4 percent said this about someone who tries to help the poor and 6 percent about someone who knows how to get things organized.

25. E.g., 92 percent of respondents in the Civic Involvement Survey said they were very satisfied or fairly satisfied with "the way neighbors help each other" in their community.

26. Burton A. Weisbrod, *The Nonprofit Economy* (Cambridge, Mass.: Harvard University Press, 1988). The estimate of nonprofit employment is from a question in the Civic Involvement Survey that asked employed respondents whether they worked for "a for-profit organization, such as a business" (70 percent), "a private, non-profit organization, such as a community center or church" (8 percent), or "a tax-supported organization, such as a government agency or school" (14 percent); the remaining 8 percent selected "other."

27. For example, one of the agencies we studied received about 80 percent of its funds from Head Start, HUD, the state's Department of Education, the state's Human Resources Administration, Medicare, the city's Department for the Aging, the federal Ryan White AIDS fund, and the city's housing authority, among others.

28. Paul Leinberger and Bruce Tucker, *The New Individualists: The Generation after the Organization Man* (New York: HarperCollins, 1991), 21.

29. According to a national study conducted in 1993, 65.8 percent of professionals had done volunteer work within the past year, compared with 47.7 percent of the general public; see *America's Independent Sector in Brief* (Washington: Independent Sector, 1996). In my Economic Values Survey, 43 percent of employees of nonprofit organizations said they were "involved in any charity or social service activities, such as helping the poor, the sick or the elderly," compared with 20 percent of for-profit employees and 36 percent of government employees; 50 percent of nonprofit employees said they had "donated time to a volunteer organization" in the past year, compared with 32 percent of for-profit employees and 40 percent of government employees. Nonprofit employees were also the most likely to have done informal volunteering such as visiting someone in the hospital, helped someone through a personal crisis,

or given money to a beggar. Wuthnow, *God and Mammon in America* (New York: Free Press, 1994).

30. In the Civic Involvement Survey 54 percent said that "a person who does volunteer work" is someone they admire a lot; 51 percent had done some kind of volunteer work within the past year.

31. See, e.g., Roy Lubove, *The Professional Altruist* (New York: Atheneum, 1965).

32. Marvin Olasky, *The Tragedy of American Compassion* (Washington: Regnery, 1992).

33. Laurent A. Parks Daloz et al., *Common Fire: Lives of Commitment in a Complex World* (Boston: Beacon, 1996).

34. Virginia A. Hodgkinson and Murray S. Weitzman, *Giving and Volunteering in the United States*, 1996 ed. (Washington: Independent Sector, 1996), find that approximately three-fourths of all volunteering is performed formally in conjunction with nonprofit organizations.

35. Two hours is the median time per week as estimated by the 51 percent of respondents in the Civic Involvement Survey who volunteered within the past year. This figure is lower than that in Independent Sector's Giving and Volunteering Surveys, which permit respondents to identify a number of different domains to which their volunteer activity may be relevant and then to add all the hours for those domains even if a single activity may have contributed to several domains.

36. When asked how many of the people in their neighborhood they knew well, 29 percent of the respondents in the Civic Involvement Survey said at least half, 16 percent said about a quarter, 47 percent said only a few, and 8 percent said they knew nobody.

37. Frank Riessman and Eric Banks, "The Mismeasure of Civil Society," *Social Policy* (Spring 1996); according to the Community Associations Institute, the number of homeowners' associations grew from 45,000 in 1982 to 180,000 in 1993; for distinctions between homeowners' associations and community activism see Gordana Rabrenovic, *Community Builders: A Tale of Neighborhood Mobilization in Two Cities* (Philadelphia: Temple University Press, 1996).

38. Thomas Moore, *Soul Mates: Honoring the Mysteries of Love and Relationship* (New York: HarperCollins, 1994), xvii.

39. As another example, a man in his sixties who has lived in the same house for the past twenty years says he knows none of his neighbors ("it's hot and so everyone just drives into their garage and puts the door down and you never see them"), but he has four friends who stood by him a number of years ago during a crisis and he believes he could still turn to them if something went wrong.

40. An estimate of the growth of the self-help movement, which includes groups for the bereaved, for people with disabilities and health needs, for parents, and for victims of crime and domestic violence, comes from figures compiled by the fifty state-level self-help clearinghouses. In 1976 membership in all such groups was estimated at 5 to 8 million; in 1988, 12 to 15 million; see

"News Summary," *New York Times* (July 16, 1988). Another way of estimating their growth is by comparing a 1984 Harris poll with my 1992 survey. In 1984 only 3 percent of adults said yes when asked, "Are you now participating in a mutual support self-help group for the purpose of aiding you in coping with a specific problem or problems of everyday life?" In 1992, 10 percent of the public were participating in a "small group that meets regularly and that provides caring and support for its members" and described their group as a "self-help group." Although these questions are not strictly comparable, they are consistent with estimates drawn from other sources. Membership in AA (which was founded in 1935 and became a national phenomenon only in the 1950s) grew from approximately 445,000 in 1979 to 980,000 in 1989, to 1,127,471 in 1992; see Mary C. Dufour and Kathryn G. Ingle, "Twenty-five Years of Alcohol Epidemiology," *Alcohol Health and Research World* 19 (Jan. 1995); Bill Marvel, "Religion of Sobriety," *Dallas Morning News* (June 10, 1995). Al-Anon (founded in 1951) grew from 1,500 groups in 1981 to 1,900 (with approximately 500,000 members) in 1990; in 1990 there were 1,300 ACOA (Adult Children of Alcoholics) groups, none of which existed prior to 1982; see Katy Butler, "Adult Children of Alcoholics," *San Francisco Chronicle* (Feb. 20, 1990); Sara Wuthnow, "Working the ACOA Program," in *"I Come Away Stronger": How Small Groups Are Shaping American Religion*, ed. Robert Wuthnow (Grand Rapids, Mich.: Eerdmans, 1994).

41. See, e.g., J. Kleist, "Network Resource Utilization Patterns of Members of Alcoholics Anonymous" (Ph.D. diss., University of Akron, 1990); T. Clark and M. Hughes, *Sickle Cell Mutual Help Groups, a Five Year Study* (Chapel Hill: Psychosocial Research Division, University of North Carolina, 1992); Thomasina Borkman and Maria Parisi, "The Role of Self-Help Groups in Fostering a Caring Society," in *Care and Community in Modern Society: Passing on the Tradition of Service to Future Generations*, ed. Paul G. Schervish, Virginia A. Hodgkinson, and Margaret Gates (San Francisco: Jossey-Bass, 1995).

42. In the Civic Involvement Survey 45 percent thought they could count on their neighbors for help if someone in their family became seriously ill.

43. In the Civic Involvement Survey 70 percent thought "people not caring about each other" was a problem in their community (34 percent said it was a serious problem).

3. POROUS INSTITUTIONS

1. See Peter L. Berger and Thomas Luckmann, *The Social Construction of Reality* (Garden City, N.Y.: Doubleday, 1966).

2. Between 1980 and 1990 the number of Americans who worked entirely from their homes grew from 2.2 million to 3.4 million; Charyl Russell, "How Many Home Workers?" *American Demographics* (May 1996), online.

3. Arlene Skolnick, *Embattled Paradise: The American Family in an Age of Uncertainty* (New York: Basic Books, 1991), 1.

4. U.S. Bureau of the Census, *The American Almanac, 1995–1996: Statistical Abstract of the United States* (Austin: Reference Press, 1996), table 87; Andrew J. Cherlin, *Marriage, Divorce, Remarriage*, rev. ed. (Cambridge, Mass.: Harvard University Press, 1992). Over a longer period, the shift in marital patterns is also dramatic. Of marriages that occurred during the 1920s, approximately 20 percent have resulted in divorce. Of marriages in the 1950s, this proportion is approximately 30 percent. And of marriages in the 1970s or 1980s it exceeds 50 percent. Most divorced people remarry, and many of those who divorce a second time also remarry. The important trend, however, is that the symbolic and legal boundary separating marriage and nonmarriage is being crossed more often; marriage is no longer a bond that is inviolable. Explanations for the rising divorce rate that find greatest empirical support include ones that emphasize economic conditions that require women to participate in the labor force, movement of jobs that undermine the economic status of certain segments of the male population, and geographic mobility or other shifts away from traditional family and community support systems; see Sara McLanahan and Lynne Casper, "Growing Diversity and Inequality in the American Family," in *State of the Union: America in the 1990s*, vol. 2: *Social Trends*, ed. Reynolds Farley (New York: Russell Sage, 1995). These explanations suggest the relatedness of various manifestations of what I am calling porous institutions. McLanahan and Casper also cite evidence that shows these changes are not limited to the United States.

5. *American Almanac*, table 71. Frank F. Furstenberg, "The Future of Marriage," *American Demographics* (June 1996).

6. *American Almanac*, table 60; Reynolds Farley, *The New American Reality: Who We Are, How We Got Here, Where We Are Going* (New York: Russell Sage, 1996).

7. *American Almanac*, table 143.

8.. Theodore Caplow et al., *Recent Social Trends in the United States, 1960–1990* (Montreal: McGill-Queen's University Press, 1991).

9. Median age at first marriage rose from 20.3 for women and 22.8 for men in 1960 to 24.5 for women and 26.7 for men in 1994, and the proportion of women unmarried by their late 20s tripled from 11 percent in 1960 to 33 percent in 1993; Furstenberg, "Future of Marriage"; U.S. Census Bureau, "Age at First Marriage at Record High," Public Information Office Press Release, March 13, 1996. Judith Stacey, *Brave New Families: Stories of Domestic Upheaval in Late Twentieth Century America* (New York: Basic Books, 1990). Marcia Mogelonsky, "The Rocky Road to Adulthood," *American Demographics* (May 1996), online.

10. *American Almanac*, table 656. Economic Values Survey, 1992; my analysis.

11. John A. Byrne, "The Pain of Downsizing," *Business Week* (May 9, 1994); Matt Murry, "Amid Record Profits Companies Continue to Lay Off Employees,"

Wall Street Journal (May 8, 1995). Joe Zeff and Pat Lyons, *The Downsizing of America* (New York: Times Books, 1996). Lester C. Thurow, *The Future of Capitalism: How Today's Economic Forces Shape Tomorrow's World* (New York: Morrow, 1996).

12. According to a 1995 survey of large corporations, two-thirds expected to be making greater use of temporary workers in the next three years; Jan Larson, "Temps are Here to Stay," *American Demographics* (Feb. 1996), online. American Management Association survey reported in Susan Chandler, "Poisoned Ivy," *Business Week* (June 10, 1996).

13. Lawrence Mishel and David M. Frankel, *The State of Working America, 1990–91* (New York: M. E. Sharpe, 1991). Downsizing has also taken place in other areas. Especially in service areas, smaller facilities that can be tailored more to individual needs and to local contexts are now viewed more favorably than large bureaucratic structures. A notable examples is residential facilities for persons with mental retardation. The average number of residents per state-operated facility in 1970 was approximately 1,000; by 1993 it was 42. Private facilities were never as large, but the average number of residents dropped from 9 to 4 between 1977 and 1993; *American Almanac*, table 202.

14. New York Stock Exchange, *Fact Book* (New York: NYSE, 1995). *American Almanac*, tables 860, 869. Seth Godin, ed., *Information Please Business Almanac and Sourcebook* (Boston: Houghton Mifflin, 1996).

15. *American Almanac*, table 874.

16. In a single decade starting in the middle 1980s the number of students in public elementary schools per computer dropped from 79 to 12, and in public high schools, from 52 to 9. Most of the growth in network television occurred earlier, reaching a saturation point by the 1960s. The growth in telecommunications since the 1960s has thus occurred largely through the introduction of new media. Cable television subscriptions climbed from 6.7 percent of households in 1970 to 62 percent in 1994; VCRs rose from 21 percent of households in 1985 to 79 percent in 1994; *American Almanac*, tables 258, 897. Quotation from Ronald Collins, "Clutter," *Columbia Journalism Review* (Nov.–Dec. 1991), 49.

17. *American Almanac*, table 649.

18. Ibid., table 858.

19. Tom Peters, *Liberation Management: Necessary Disorganization for the Nanosecond Nineties* (New York: Fawcett Columbine, 1992), 11, 663.

20. *American Almanac*, table 33. U.S. Census Bureau, "Geographic Mobility: March 1993 to March 1994," P20–485.

21. *American Almanac*, table 1031.

22. Richard Merelman, *Making Something of Ourselves: On Culture and Politics in the United States* (Berkeley: University of California Press, 1984), 38–39.

23. Knight-Ridder survey of registered voters (Jan. 1996), online. Wuthnow, *Acts of Compassion* (Princeton: Princeton University Press, 1991).

24. See Thomas Bender, *Community and Social Change in America* (New Brunswick: Rutgers University Press, 1978).

25. A man in his late twenties who works as a financial analyst spoke for many when he asserted that there is probably too much individualism for the good of our communities, but that "you're just brought up to believe in it." He explained how he has come to think about individualism: "The individual is the preeminent being in the universe. There's always a distinction between me and you. Comity, sharing, cannot truly exist. What I have is mine, and it's mine because I deserve it, and I have a right to it." He looks out for himself, does no volunteer work at the moment, and says he does not rely on his friends.

26. On the historical context of recent immigration see Ronald Takaki, *A Different Mirror: A History of Multicultural America* (Boston: Little, Brown, 1993).

27. *American Almanac*, tables 5, 7, 1364. On the internationalization of markets, finance, and labor, see Rosabeth Moss Kanter, *World Class: Thriving Locally in the Global Economy* (New York: Simon and Schuster, 1995): "The new networks are often loose and fluid. Their membership overlaps with that of other networks, and allies cooperate for only some purposes."

28. *American Almanac*, tables 429, 901.

29. For an illustration of the decline in supervisory capacity see Alan Ehrenhalt, *The Lost City: Discovering the Forgotten Virtues of Community in Chicago of the 1950s* (New York: Basic Books, 1995). In the 1950s, Ehrenhalt argues, Chicagoans were more likely to "play the hand they were dealt," living as they did under the watchful eye of churches, political bosses, employers, and neighbors. The banker Ben Bohac, for example, built up his business by going door to door, visiting his neighbors, taking an active part in civic organizations, and establishing personal bonds that subjected him to his customers' scrutiny. By the 1990s Bohac's bank had been purchased by a downtown firm and then sold to a Dutch conglomerate, making it easier for his customers to choose other banks if they wished.

30. *American Almanac*, table 238.

31. Bennett Harrison, *Lean and Mean: The Changing Landscape of Corporate Power in the Age of Flexibility* (New York: Basic Books, 1994).

32. Jay Belsky, "Etiology of Child Maltreatment: A Developmental Ecological Analysis," *Psychological Bulletin* 114 (1993; Sara McLanahan and Gary D. Sandefur, *Growing Up With a Single Parent* (Cambridge, Mass.: Harvard University Press, 1994). Judith Wallerstein, "The Long-Term Effects of Divorce on Children," *Journal of the American Academy of Child and Adolescent Psychiatry* 30 (1991). Lee Robins and Darrel Regier, *Psychiatric Disorders in America* (New York: Free Press, 1991).

33. Zeff and Lyons, *Downsizing of America*; Mishel and Frankel, *State of Working America*, 268. The number of American families filing for personal bankruptcy grew from 0.3 million in 1982 to 1.1 million in 1996; between 1988 and 1996 the average amount owed by families filing for bankruptcy in-

creased from less than $80,000 to more than $120,000; two of the most frequently cited reasons for filing personal bankruptcy were job loss and divorce; Saul Hansell, "Personal Bankruptcies Surging as Economy Hums," *New York Times* (Aug. 25, 1996).

34. Charles Heckscher, *White-Collar Blues: Management Loyalties in an Age of Corporate Restructuring* (New York: Basic Books, 1996). The problem of health insurance is a familiar example. Without a national health insurance plan, those who earn their livings as temporary workers or as self-employed contractors, and especially those who lose their jobs, can find themselves and their families without medical assistance. Indeed, 15 percent of the population is said to be without health insurance of any kind, and the proportion who did not have continuous coverage in a recent two-year period was nearly 40 percent among those who experienced at least one interruption in their employment status; *American Almanac*, tables 170–171. Average benefits for the entire labor force declined during the 1980s by 14 percent in real terms; Mishel and Frankel, *State of Working America*, 86.

35. Jason DeParle, "Report to Clinton Sees Vast Extent of Homelessness," *New York Times* (Feb. 17, 1994). Christopher Jencks, *The Homeless* (Cambridge, Mass.: Harvard University Press, 1994).

36. U.S. Census Bureau, "Marital Status and Living Arrangements: March 1994," P20–484. *American Almanac*, table 68.

37. Trust in Government Survey conducted by Princeton Survey Research Associates (Jan. 1996). *American Almanac*, tables 127, 308.

38. Zeff and Lyons, *Downsizing of America*; when asked "In recent years, has the amount of time you devote to doing volunteer work increased, decreased, or stayed about the same," 24 percent of the general public said it had increased, 21 percent said it had decreased, and 53 percent said it had stayed the same; of those who said they were worried that someone in their household might be laid off, only 16 percent had increased their volunteering and 26 percent had decreased it; a comparable question about "your involvement or participation in civic or community groups" showed that 21 percent of the general public had increased their participation, 20 percent had decreased it, and 57 percent said it had stayed the same; among those who were worried about layoffs, only 15 percent had increased their participation and 23 percent had decreased it.

39. Juliet Schor, *The Overworked American* (New York: Basic Books, 1992). Mishel and Frankel, *State of Working America*. Wuthnow, *God and Mammon in America* (New York: Free Press, 1994).

40. *American Almanac*, table 638. Economic Values Survey, my analysis of the 557 women in the study who were working full or part time and who had at least one child living at home: 57 percent said they experienced stress at work at least once or twice a week, 39 percent said that lack of time for their family was a source of stress at work, and the same proportion said they had recently been late for work. Only 22 percent said they had a lot of energy left over

when they came home from work. With so many women in the labor force, the category "housewife" now refers to a different kind of woman from in the past, and thus to a different propensity for civic involvement. A generation ago housewives were about as inclined as working women to join voluntary associations, probably because many housewives were middle-class women who had time to be involved in such organizations. In recent years housewives are considerably less likely than working women to be active in civic organizations, probably because they are more likely to be mothers of young children or women without employable skills.

41. This is the case both for holding memberships in voluntary associations and for actually being involved in charity or social service activities. These conclusions are drawn from my analysis of group membership data in the General Social Survey and from my 1992 Economic Values Survey and my 1989 American Values Survey.

42. Partly, this difference is a function of women in professional and managerial positions working longer hours and also being more likely to volunteer. But it is also for this reason that some observers discount the inclusion of women in the labor force as having anything to do with declining civic involvement. See Robert D. Putnam, "Tuning In, Tuning Out: The Strange Disappearance of Social Capital in America," *P.S.: Political Science and Politics* 27 (1995).

43. Among white women working full time in the Economic Values Survey, 44 percent of those with no children at home donated time to a voluntary organization, compared with 35 percent of those who had one child at home and the same percentage of those who had two or more; 40 percent of those who had a lot of energy left after work did so, compared with 28 percent of those who had hardly any energy left; 43 percent of those who controlled their daily schedule did so, compared with 22 percent of those who did not control it. Among part-time workers, those who work fewer hours are more likely to volunteer than those who work more hours, and women with children at home are actually more likely than women without children to volunteer, suggesting that those who have the time do so as a way of supporting activities in which their children are involved. For women working part time, volunteering peaks in their thirties and early forties (when children are in school), whereas for women working full time volunteering does not peak until their late forties and early fifties (when the nest is empty).

44. Lions Clubs figures from Christine Rose, Manager, Membership Operations Department, International Association of Lions Clubs; other trends are discussed in Robert D. Putnam, "Bowling Alone: America's Declining Social Capital," *Journal of Democracy* 6 (Jan. 1995).

45. George Pettinico, "Civic Participation and American Democracy," *Public Perspective* (June–July 1996). *American Almanac*, table 424. My analysis of General Social Surveys conducted nationally in 1974 and 1994.

46. Christopher Jencks, "Who Gives to What?" in *The Nonprofit Sector: A Re-*

search Handbook, ed. Walter W. Powell (New Haven: Yale University Press, 1987), esp. table 18.7.

47. My analysis of General Social Survey data; the figures in the text are based on a variable I constructed which counts membership in all kinds of associations listed except for church-related groups and labor unions. The former category is excluded because it has been shown to be ambiguous to respondents (meaning church membership for some and membership in a group within a church for others) and the latter because of special economic circumstances that had worked against labor organizing.

48. The specific question is "Do you, yourself, happen to be involved in any charity or social service activities, such as helping the poor, the sick, or the elderly?" The percentage responding yes was 26 in 1977, 29 in 1981, 31 in 1984, 36 in 1986, 39 in 1987, 41 in 1989, and 46 in 1991. The surveys were conducted by the Gallup Organization and are available on Public Opinion Online through Lexis-Nexis.

49. See Andrew Kohut, *Trust and Citizen Engagement in Metropolitan Philadelphia* (Washington: Pew Research Center for the People and the Press, 1997).

50. Thirty-nine service clubs founded before 1950 have a median membership of 12,000, whereas the nine founded since 1950 s have a median membership of only 575. Median membership is 6,000 for the six Bible societies founded before 1950, 800 for the eight founded after 1950. Most civil rights organizations have been founded since 1950, but the same pattern is evident: median membership of 50,000 for the five founded before 1950, and of 2,500 for the fifty founded since 1950. An additional thirty-three civil rights groups since 1950 are nonmembership organizations. Labor unions show a similar pattern: for those founded before 1950, a median membership of 50,000; for those founded after 1950, 4,500. Sandra Jaszczak, ed., *Encyclopedia of Associations*, 31st ed. (Detroit: Gale Research, 1996).

51. It is also revealing to consider the strength of dislike for groups having these various characteristics. Most respondents said they would be "very unlikely" to join each kind of group, rather than only somewhat unlikely: 60 percent said they would be very unlikely to join "a group that is part of a large national bureaucracy," 52 percent said this about "a group that expects you to be a member for life," 37 percent about "a group that is run by a small circle of long-time members," 56 percent about "a group that is run by wealthy people," 58 percent about a group that "accepts only men or only women," 80 percent about a group that "has secret rituals," and 90 percent about a group that "has a history of racial discrimination."

52. The data also suggest a relationship between porousness and disliking these characteristics. For instance, controlling for other predisposing social characteristics (education, parents' education, sex, and age), people who say they know relatively few of their neighbors (i.e., who live in a more porous social space) are 33 percent more likely than those who are better integrated into

their neighborhoods to say they would be "very unlikely" to join an organization that expected lifelong membership, 21 percent more likely to say this about a group that was part of a large national bureaucracy, and 56 percent more likely to say it about a group that was run by long-term members; these respondents were only 55 percent as likely as better-integrated respondents to have joined any groups or organizations (based on logit regression analysis).

53. Trust in Government Survey conducted by Princeton Survey Research Associates (Jan. 1996). *America at the Crossroads: A National Energy Strategy Poll* (Washington: Alliance to Save Energy and Union of Concerned Scientists, 1991).

54. Other initiatives include altruistic endeavors like the Creative Coalition, a network of entertainers interested in social issues, and the Smith Family Foundation, which is dedicated to AIDS and HIV issues. New wealth has been the occasion for some of these organizations, for example the Leeann Chin Foundation in Minnesota and the Hall Family Foundation in Kansas City. Some are nonprofit organizations that include a small staff of salaried employees but operate mainly through the volunteer efforts of interested professionals: Cleveland's Free Clinic, which provides health services to people with AIDS, for example, or PULSE, a Philadelphia organization that provides free legal counsel.

55. Matthew Rees, "A Force upon the Plain," *Commentary* (May 1996). Lisa Teachey, "Houston's Gang-Related Crimes," *Houston Chronicle* (June 21, 1996).

4. SAVING THE SUBURBS

1. On particular suburbs in these decades see William H. Whyte Jr., *The Organization Man* (Garden City, N.Y.: Doubleday, 1956); Herbert Gans, *The Levittowners: Ways of Life and Politics in a New Suburban Community* (New York: Columbia University Press, 1967); John R. Seeley, R. Alexander Sim, and Elizabeth W. Loosley, *Crestwood Heights* (New York: Basic Books, 1956).

2. In the 1994 General Social Survey, 60 percent of suburban women listed themselves as working full or part time, 21 percent as keeping house, and 13 percent as retired; my analysis.

3. Mark Baldassare, *Trouble in Paradise: The Suburban Transformation in America* (New York: Columbia University Press, 1986). Growing diversity means that people may be avoiding each other more and thus realizing more acutely that they don't truly live in a community. Among persons most likely to live in suburbs (white college graduates who are registered voters), 67 percent say racial differences play a big role in dividing Americans, 67 percent say the same thing about income differences, and 59 percent say it about divisions between political liberals and conservatives; relatively few emphasize immigration (37 percent), gender differences (28 percent), or religious differences

(18 percent) as a divisive factor; Knight-Ridder 1996 survey. Although only 18 percent of the suburban population in 1990 consisted of nonwhites, the white suburban population increased between 1980 and 1990 by only 9.2 percent, whereas the black suburban population increased by 34.4 percent, the Hispanic population by 69.3 percent, and the other ethnic (mostly Asian American) population by 125.9 percent; William H. Frey, "The New Geography of Population Shifts," in *State of the Union: America in the 1990s*, vol. 2: *Social Trends*, ed. Reynolds Farley (New York: Russell Sage, 1995).

4. Only 35 percent of suburban residents in the 1994 General Social Survey said they had grown up in the same city in which they now lived.

5. In the Civic Involvement Survey, respondents were asked whether their own community was best described as a central-city area, a suburban area, or a small town or rural area; 42 percent said they lived in a suburban area. Other studies confirm high levels of satisfaction with residents' own communities: 86 percent of Americans say they are satisfied with their community as a place to live, and 84 percent are satisfied with the quality of life in their community (yet only 39 percent say they are satisfied with "community in this country"). Respectively, these figures are from the People's Satisfaction with Their Lives and Government Poll conducted by the Gallup Organization in 1995, the Family Circle Family Index Project conducted by Family Circle Magazine in 1993, and a Gallup, CNN, Knight-Ridder survey conducted by the Gallup Organization in 1992. Among suburban residents in the 1994 General Social Survey, 90 percent said they derive at least a "fair amount" of satisfaction from the place they live (69 percent said "quite a bit" of satisfaction). Nor is there evidence that people's perceptions of their own communities have become more negative over the years. For example, a 1973 survey found that 75 percent of Americans were satisfied with the quality of life in their community, and in a 1949 poll 86 percent said they were "reasonably satisfied" with their community; Gallup Polls (Sept. 24, 1973; Jan. 24, 1949).

6. David M. Hummon, *Commonplaces: Community Ideology and Identity in American Culture* (Albany: State University of New York Press, 1980).

7. In the Civic Involvement Survey 45 percent of suburban residents said "too many people moving into the community" was a problem; 74 percent complained about "traffic problems."

8. M. P. Baumgartner, *The Moral Order of a Suburb* (New York: Oxford University Press, 1988), writes of a deadening moral minimalism, tolerance, avoidance, and preference for tranquillity, rather than strong reactions to offenses or a willingness to engage in conflict. In the 1994 General Social Survey, 51 percent of suburban residents said their life was pretty routine or dull. In my interviews, words like "boring," "dull," and "sleepy" were not uncommon.

9. When asked, "Are the people you have contact with through your work mostly from your own community or from other places," 70 percent of employed suburban residents said from other places, 27 percent said from their own community, and the rest were unsure or gave other responses.

10. Only 56 percent of suburban residents who were members of a religious congregation said it was located in their neighborhood.

11. Joel Garreau, *Edge City: Life on the New Frontier* (New York: Doubleday, 1991), found that most of the places he studied did not have formal names, but were identified by such rubrics as "28 and Mass Pike" (near Boston), "the Galleria area" (near Houston), and "287 & 78" (in New Jersey). In the Civic Involvement Survey, 44 percent of suburban residents said they made personal long-distance calls at least once a week.

12. The Civic Involvement Survey asked, "Which of these comes closest to your definition of community: your neighborhood, the town in which you live, the larger region in which you live, or the people you associate with?" Among suburban residents, 38 percent said their neighborhood, 36 percent the town in which they live, 11 percent the larger region, 11 percent the people they associate with, and 3 percent said they couldn't choose or didn't know.

13. Baumgartner, *Moral Order of a Suburb*, writes that the suburb is "a place where comparatively 'weak ties' to other people, rather than strong bonds of enduring and great attachment, typify social relationships," and that suburbanites "tend to be socially anchored only loosely into their atomized and shifting networks of associates. Their high rate of mobility from place to place means that bonds between persons are frequently ruptured and replaced with new and equally temporary ones, so that relationships often have short pasts and futures" (9, 91).

14. Viewing the parade is a good way to understand the civic life of an older suburb like Hillsdale. It begins with a color guard and ends about an hour and a half later with mounted riders from a nearby military academy. In between are representatives of the American Legion, the VFW, and other veterans' organizations, the high school band, the military academy drill team, and lots of fire engines. Every Cub Scout, Boy Scout, and Girl Scout in Hillsdale marches in the parade. So does every Little League team and soccer team. The local Red Cross chapter is represented, as are the library, each volunteer fire company, the Shriners, the synagogue, and most of the churches. Businesses are not permitted to participate unless they have been in town for more than a hundred years, and politicians are discouraged from participating as well. The parade starts at a parking lot at one end of the business district and ends at the war memorial in the park, where a patriotic speech concludes the event.

15. In several of the communities we studied parades are no longer as popular or as filled with local meaning as they once were. Memorial Day parades have been canceled for the first time in a half-century, and in other cases attendance has been sparse compared with the numbers of people who flock to air shows, amusement parks, or the beach. Members of veterans' organizations report that declining memberships make it harder to drum up interest in parades, and some residents complain that the parades have become too

commercialized. One contrasted the solemn occasions of the past with a float in a recent parade that was sponsored by a restaurant featuring scantily clad women. Another said it was hard to do anything civic because Memorial Day is now a favorite time for shopping malls to have sales. Some also mention that visits to cemeteries have declined significantly in recent years as family members become more scattered.

16. Data from the 1996 Knight-Ridder survey of registered voters shed some light on this distance from politics: only 30 percent of white voters with college degrees think the President has a big impact on the average citizen's life; 68 percent think ordinary citizens could have a big influence in Washington if they were willing to do so; yet only 19 percent regularly contact public officials to make their views known. I understand these results to mean that people feel they could influence political leaders if they wanted to, but that they apparently do not feel it is worth their time because what these officials do is unlikely to affect them.

17. Matthew C. Moen, *Transformation of the Christian Right* (Tuscaloosa: University of Alabama Press, 1992); Michael Lienisch, *Redeeming America: Piety and Politics in the New Christian Right* (Chapel Hill: University of North Carolina Press, 1994).

18. In the 1996 Knight-Ridder survey, 25 percent of registered voters thought the government was doing too much to control guns (44 percent thought it was doing too little). Opposition to gun-control was most concentrated among men who had been to college but had not graduated (42 percent thought government was doing too much), and least concentrated among women with college degrees (12 percent).

19. In the Civic Involvement Survey, 27 percent of suburban residents said they use the Internet or electronic mail.

20. Another man who favored using the Internet explained: "I find that people are much more gregarious and have much more courage on the Internet than they do in person. Because you don't have to worry about what your mask is showing. You just write the lie that you're writing." But he was also worried: "I think that in a way, as far as social skills are concerned, there's going to be a problem that's going to plague the 21st century because we don't know how to really talk to each other in real time. It's already happening."

21. In the Civic Involvement Survey, 67 percent of those who said they were very satisfied with their school system also were very satisfied with the overall quality of life in their community, compared with only 20 percent of those who were very dissatisfied with their school system (gamma = .328).

22. National Center for Education Statistics, *National Education Longitudinal Study of 1988, Second Follow-Up* (Washington: U.S. Department of Education, Office of Educational Research and Improvement, 1994), CD-ROM version. Only 13 percent of those parents who felt involved in their neighborhoods said they never took part in school activities, compared with 28 percent

of those who said they "just live here." Among the former, 44 percent had contacted the school to do volunteer work, but among the latter only 25 percent had done so.

23. National Center for Education Statistics, *National Education Longitudinal Study of 1988.*

24. Marlin Levin, *Balm in Gilead: The Story of Hadassah* (New York: Schocken, 1973). *Facts about Hadassah* (New York: Hadassah, 1995).

25. The decline is approximate and may reflect some "pruning" that took place several years ago, but the lack of growth is of concern to local members in view of the fact that the city's Jewish population has increased sufficiently for a new synagogue to be organized.

26. Reinharz quoted in PR Newswire (Nov. 16, 1995), online. Despite repeated phone calls, e-mail and Internet inquiries, and correspondence, it was impossible to secure figures on membership trends for Hadassah. Published figures in recent years are 385,000 or 380,000, leaving the impression that accurate annual figures may not be available. One staff member who asked to remain anonymous said the organization is reluctant to give out figures because "membership is declining."

27. On Hadassah's adaptations to accommodate working women and professionalization see June Sochen, "Jewish Women as Volunteer Activists," *American Jewish History* 70 (1980).

28. Alan E. Pisarski, *Commuting in America* (Washington: ENO Foundation for Transportation, 1987); Robert Cervero, *Suburban Gridlock* (New Brunswick: Rutgers University Press, 1986).

29. Secondary analysis of results of a survey conducted by the *Washington Post* in 1995.

5. AGAINST THE ODDS IN THE INNER CITY

1. In Cleveland, for example, 42 percent of the population have incomes below the poverty line. But inner cities are not the only areas in which poverty is evident: according to the U.S. Census Bureau, only 42 percent of poor people live in central cities; Robert Lavelle, *America's New War on Poverty* (San Francisco: KQED Books, 1995). Between 1970 and 1990 in urban Chicago, for example, the unemployment rate grew from 4.4 to 11.3 percent, the percentage living below the poverty level increased from 14.4 to 21.3 percent, median family income in constant dollars fell by 10 percent, and aggravated assaults increased by more than 300 percent; Don Terry, "Chicago Prepares and Promises No Repeat of 1968," *New York Times* (Aug. 25, 1996).

2. *State of America's Cities* (National League of Cities, 1301 Pennsylvania Avenue NW, Washington, DC 20004, 1995); government statistics quoted in Lavelle, *America's New War on Poverty*, indicate that the inflation-adjusted value of Aid to Families with Dependent Children (AFDC) plus food stamps declined by 26 percent between 1972 and 1992.

3. According to the 1994 General Social Survey, only 5 percent of those who lived in cities and had below-average incomes were members of service organizations—less than half the proportion of suburban residents who held such memberships; my analysis. On the low satisfaction with their communities among residents of central-city areas and low-income neighborhoods in the Civic Involvement Survey, see Table 1 in Methods. Similarly, in a survey among black residents of poor inner-city neighborhoods in Chicago in 1988, only a third of the respondents regarded their neighborhood as a good place to live; in census tracts with large numbers of people with incomes below the poverty level, this proportion was only 18 percent; William Julius Wilson, *When Work Disappears: The World of the New Urban Poor* (New York: Knopf, 1996).

4. John D. Kasarda, "Cities as Places Where People Live and Work: Urban Change and Neighborhood Distress," in *Interwoven Destinies: Cities and the Nation,* ed. Henry G. Cisneros (New York: Norton, 1993); idem, "Inner-City Concentrated Poverty and Neighborhood Distress: 1970–1990," *Housing Policy Debate* 4 (1993); Mark A. Hughes, "Misspeaking Truth to Power: A Geographical Perspective on the 'Underclass' Fallacy," *Economic Geography* 65 (1989); idem, "Formation of the Impacted Ghetto: Evidence from Large Metropolitan Areas: 1970–1980," *Urban Geography* 11 (1990).

5. William Julius Wilson, *The Truly Disadvantaged: The Inner City, The Underclass, and Public Policy* (Chicago: University of Chicago Press, 1987). Douglas S. Massey and Mitchell L. Eggers, "The Ecology of Inequality: Minorities and the Concentration of Poverty, 1970–1980," *American Journal of Sociology* 95 (1990); Douglas S. Massey, Andrew B. Gross, and Kumiko Shibuya, "Migration, Segregation, and the Concentration of Poverty," *American Sociological Review* 59 (1994); Roderick J. Harrison and Claudette E. Bennett, "Racial and Ethnic Diversity," in *State of the Union: America in the 1990s,* vol. 2: *Social Trends,* ed. Reynolds Farley (New York: Russell Sage, 1995).

6. From logistic regression analyses, where the dependent variable was saying that crime was a serious problem, the odds ratios were 1.94 for residents of central city versus other areas, 2.01 for residents of low-income neighborhoods versus other neighborhoods, and 1.99 for nonwhite versus white respondents. Thus the odds of perceiving crime as a serious community problem were approximately eight times greater among inner-city low-income minorities than among suburban or small-town average-income whites. The comparable odds ratios for drug abuse were 2.08, 2.04, and 1.58; for problems in the schools, 1.58, 1.65, and 1.20; and for a lack of jobs, 1.64, 2.10, and 2.21. All coefficients (except 1.20) were significant at or beyond the .05 level of probability.

7. Wilson, *When Work Disappears,* 19.

8. See, e.g., Elijah Anderson, "Neighborhood Effects on Teenage Pregnancy," in *The Urban Underclass,* ed. Christopher Jencks and Paul E. Peterson (Wash-

ington: Brookings, 1991); Christopher Jencks and Susan E. Mayer, "The Social Consequences of Growing Up in a Poor Neighborhood," in *Inner City Poverty in the United States*, ed. L. E. Lynn Jr. and M. G. H. McGeary (Washington: National Academy of Sciences, 1990).

9. Wilson, *When Work Disappears*, ch. 3; Delbert S. Elliott et al., *Beating the Odds: Overcoming Adversity in High-Risk Neighborhoods* (Chicago: University of Chicago Press, 1997). Peter F. Nardulli, Jon K. Dalager, and Donald E. Greco, "Voter Turnout in U.S. Presidential Elections: An Historical View and Some Speculation," *P.S.: Political Science and Politics* 29 (1996): as a ratio of voter turnout to eligibility, "relative propensity to vote" declined from a postwar high of 1.08 among residents of main center cities in 1948 to a low of .82 in 1992 (a 24 percent decline), compared with a decline from 1.13 to 1.05 (7 percent) in suburbs of main center cities.

10. My analysis of data from General Social Surveys.

11. Characteristics of residents of poor neighborhoods that coincide with these perceptions include unemployment at twice the rate, large families (seven or more members) at triple the rate, and self-care or mobility limitations at twice the rate of other areas; U.S. Census Bureau, "Census Bureau Study Focuses on Residents of Poverty Areas" (Public Information Office Press Release, July 31, 1995).

12. My analysis of the 1994 Independent Sector Survey of Giving and Volunteering.

13. National Center for Education Statistics, *National Household Education Survey, 1993: School Safety and Discipline*; my analysis of data from the subset of approximately 5,500 parents of high school students. National Center for Education Statistics, *National Education Longitudinal Study of 1988*; my analysis. The respective figures for having contacted the school about doing volunteer work were 44 percent and 31 percent.

14. Robert I. Lerman and Martin Rein, *Social Service Employment: An International Perspective* (New York: Russell Sage, 1997); see also Julian Wolpert, "Fragmentation in America's Nonprofit Sector," in *Care and Community in Modern Society: Passing on the Tradition of Service to Future Generations*, ed. Paul G. Schervish, Virginia A. Hodgkinson, and Margaret Gates (San Francisco: Jossey-Bass, 1995).

15. Michael O'Neill, *The Third America: The Emergence of the Nonprofit Sector in the United States* (San Francisco: Jossey-Bass, 1989); Kay Lehman Schlozman and John T. Tierney, *Organized Interests and American Democracy* (New York: Harper and Row, 1986); Kay Lehman Schlozman, "Voluntary Associations in Politics: Who Gets Involved?" in *Representing Interests and Interest Group Representation*, ed. William Crotty, Mildred A. Schwartz, and John C. Green (Lanham, Md.: University Press of America, 1994).

16. Henry G. Cisneros, *Higher Ground: Faith Communities and Community Building* (Washington: Department of Housing and Urban Development,

1996). My analysis of the 1994 Independent Sector Survey of Giving and Volunteering.

17. Among residents of low-income, inner-city neighborhoods in the Civic Involvement Survey who went to local churches, 41 percent said their church had fewer than 200 members and 69 percent said theirs had fewer than 300 members; among suburban residents, only 20 percent attended churches of fewer than 200 members, and 32 percent attended churches of fewer than 300 members. On the role of churches in generating civic skills see Sidney Verba, Kay Lehman Schlozman, and Henry E. Brady, *Voice and Equality: Civic Voluntarism in American Politics* (Cambridge, Mass.: Harvard University Press, 1995).

18. See Nancy Ammerman, *Congregations and Communities* (New Brunswick: Rutgers University Press, 1996); James P. Wind and James M. Lewis, eds., *American Congregations*, 2 vols. (Chicago: University of Chicago Press, 1994).

19. Wolpert, "Fragmentation in America's Nonprofit Sector," 476: "Higher poverty rates in center cities . . . imply that considerable assistance is needed from suburban residents to sustain the nonprofit institutions concentrated in the center city. City nonprofits will be even harder pressed financially if suburbanization leads to greater loosening of ties to these institutions."

20. Mara B. Adelman and Lawrence R. Frey, *The Fragile Community: Living Together with AIDS* (Mahwah, N.J.: Erlbaum, 1996).

6. SURVIVING IN SMALL-TOWN AMERICA

1. When asked where they would like to live, nearly half the American public say they would move to a small town or rural area if they could, while only a quarter would prefer a suburb and 10 percent would move to a large city; CBS News–*New York Times* Poll (April 1991), online. When asked in the Civic Involvement Survey, "If you could live anywhere, would you rather live in a central city area, a suburban area, or in a small town or rural area," 54 percent chose the third alternative. Other evidence shows that small towns are growing. Nationally, three out of four nonmetropolitan counties gained population between 1990 and 1994. This increase reversed a long trend of population decrease caused by low fertility rates and a shift away from agricultural jobs. Kenneth M. Johnson and Calvin L. Beale, "The Rural Rebound Revisited," *American Demographics* (July 1995).

2. In the Civic Involvement Survey, respondents who lived in small towns or rural areas were more likely than others to say their work contacts were mostly with people from their own community; still, 56 percent said these contacts were mostly with people from other places.

3. Interviewees speak glowingly of being able to park in front of the barbershop, amble across the street to the bakery, or walk their children to school. People

who have fought traffic in cities and suburbs before settling in small towns are especially fond of these amenities. As one woman who had fled the city to live in a tiny hamlet put it, "Business here can be done on foot in a very small area."

4. In the Civic Involvement Survey, 31 percent of the residents of small towns said that "people not caring enough about each other" was a serious problem in their community, compared with 34 percent of the total sample.

5. Albert Blumenthal, *Small-Town Stuff* (Chicago: University of Chicago Press, 1932).

6. Yvonne M. Vissing, *Out of Sight, Out of Mind: Homeless Children and Families in Small-Town America* (Knoxville: University Press of Kentucky, 1996). Town council members and other officials, such as school board and planning board members, appear to be perceived as more important in small towns than elsewhere because people know them personally, and also because the central concerns of small-town residents are often taxes, roads, open space, and new developments. Residents vote for local officials largely on the basis of these issues. Indeed, our interviews in small towns revealed considerable interest in local politics, much like that observed in the 1950s by Arthur J. Vidich and Joseph Bensman, *Small Town in Mass Society: Class, Power, and Religion in a Rural Community* (New York: Doubleday, 1958), 111: "Politics is a dominant theme of village life. Every man, from the politically impotent to the controlling figures of the community, talks politics. Longstanding issues such as town and village relations, past issues, dead issues, irrevocable decisions such as school consolidation and settled problems solved by time alone—all these in addition to local current affairs are discussed and rediscussed."

7. Vidich and Bensman, ibid., emphasize such outside influences in the 1950s as price-support programs for milk producers and trade with larger towns.

8. In the Civic Involvement Survey, 31 percent of all residents of small towns and 39 percent of those who had lived at their present address for less than a year said they had grown up in suburbs or cities.

9. The Civic Involvement Survey asked, "Are you personally acquainted with any political officials?" Controlling for other factors, residents of small towns were 1.505 times as likely as residents of suburbs to say yes. Other factors in the logit regression model that were significantly associated (positively or negatively) with saying yes were being male (1.473), being African American (0.614), being under age 35 (0.649), being age 50 or over (1.658), being unemployed (0.423), and having attended college (2.689); variables that were not significant were living in a central-city area, living in a low-income neighborhood, having an income below $25,000, and being Hispanic.

10. See Evelyn Brooks Higginbotham, *Righteous Discontent: The Women's Movement in the Black Baptist Church, 1880–1920* (Cambridge, Mass.: Harvard University Press, 1993).

11. Approximately 16 million Americans engage in quilting, some 5 percent of

whom are dedicated quilters who account for half of the $1.6 billion market for quilting materials; Diane Crispell, "Quilting Isn't Quitting," *American Demographics* (April 1995), online.

12. On moral order in a small town see Kai T. Erikson, *Everything in Its Path: Destruction of Community in the Buffalo Creek Flood* (New York: Simon and Schuster, 1976); Anthony F. C. Wallace, *Rockdale: The Growth of an American Village in the Early Industrial Revolution* (New York: Norton, 1978).

7. THE GOOD CITIZEN

1. In the Civic Involvement Survey, 90 percent said it was essential or very important to "be a person of strong moral character" in order to be a good citizen; this was a higher figure than for voting, contacting public officials, helping the poor, doing volunteer work, or being a member of a club or service organization.

2. Charles Taylor, *Sources of the Self: The Making of the Modern Identity* (Cambridge, Mass.: Harvard University Press, 1989); James Sellers, *Public Ethics: American Morals and Manners* (New York: Harper and Row, 1970). Amy Gutmann, *Democratic Education* (Princeton: Princeton University Press, 1987); Adam Seligman, "Animadversions upon Civil Society and Civic Virtue in the Last Decade of the Twentieth Century," in *Civil Society: Theory, History, Comparison*, ed. John A. Hall (London: Polity, 1995). Thomas Lickona, *Educating for Character* (New York: Bantam, 1991).

3. This interview was conducted by Kathleen Joyce.

4. In Florida, for example, the Federation of Garden Club Circles has seen a decline in membership from 33,000 in 1979 to 23,000 in 1996; Nanette Holland, "Club Members Seek New Role in Society," *Tampa Tribune* (Aug. 31, 1996).

5. The trade-off between exploring one's inner self and participating in service organizations was evident as one man talked about his informal group as his community: "We start to grapple with what it really means to be us, both as individuals and as a human species, and I like playing with those dark, scary corners of myself. That I don't get as a member of the Shriners or the Kiwanis or any of those things, because those things are organized in such a way you never really get to the nitty gritty or what it is or what it's about to be you and what does that mean."

8. THE QUESTION OF TRUST

1. Tom W. Smith, "Factors Relating to Misanthropy in Contemporary American Society," GSS Topical Report no. 29 (Chicago: NORC, 1996), concludes that there is "definitely some evidence of a rise in misanthropy." In answer to the General Social Survey question, "Generally speaking, would you say that most people can be trusted or that you can't be too careful in dealing with

people," 46 percent chose the trusting response in 1972, but only 34 percent did so in 1994. In another set of General Social Survey questions, trust declined from 47 percent in 1973 to 37 percent in 1994, and in yet another set, from 40 percent in 1975 to 32 percent in 1994. Confidence in institutions or in the leaders running major institutions is also sometimes taken as a measure of trust; surveys yield conflicting patterns but point generally toward erosion. In Harris surveys, the proportion of the public expressing a great deal of confidence in these institutions declined significantly between 1976 and 1995: the military, from 61 to 43 percent; the U.S. Supreme Court, from 50 to 32 percent; major educational institutions, from 61 to 27 percent; medicine, from 73 to 26 percent; major companies, from 55 to 21 percent; the press, from 29 to 11 percent; Congress, from 42 to 10 percent; and the executive branch of the federal government, from 41 to 9 percent. "Confidence in Institutions," *World Opinion Update*, April 1995.

2. See Adam B. Seligman, *The Problem of Trust* (Princeton: Princeton University Press, 1997); Francis Fukuyama, *Trust: The Social Virtues and the Creation of Prosperity* (New York: Free Press, 1995); Robert D. Putnam, *Making Democracy Work: Civic Traditions in Modern Italy* (Princeton: Princeton University Press, 1993); James S. Coleman, *Foundations of Social Theory* (Cambridge, Mass.: Harvard University Press, 1990).

3. Civic Involvement Survey. The question was, "Does each of the following statements describe you, personally, very well, fairly well, not very well, or not at all?" The statements were, "I often feel like I have too much to do," "I change my mind fairly often," "Sometimes I don't trust myself," and "I have trouble fulfilling my responsibilities." Percentages in the text are those who responded "very well" or "fairly well."

4. In the Civic Involvement Survey, only 48 percent of those who said the statement "Sometimes I don't trust myself" described them very well or fairly well agreed with the statement "Most people can be trusted," compared with 65 percent of those who said it did not describe them very well and 67 percent of those who said it did not describe them at all. Controlling for a number of other factors (central-city residence, small-town residence, low-income neighborhood, income below $25,000, being male, being African American, being Hispanic, under age 35, age 50 or over, unemployed, and having attended college), those who said they sometimes don't trust themselves were .536 (based on logit regression) times as likely as others to say most people can be trusted. For the statement "Sometimes I have trouble fulfilling my responsibilities," the comparable coefficient was .642 (both significant at or beyond the .05 level of probability). The other variables that predicted low levels of trust were income, being male, being African American, being Hispanic, under age 35, unemployed, and not having attended college.

5. Robert N. Bellah et al., *Habits of the Heart: Individualism and Commitment in American Life*, rev. ed. (Berkeley and Los Angeles: University of California Press, 1996); Steven M. Tipton, *Getting Saved from the Sixties: Moral Mean-*

ing in Conversion and Cultural Change (Berkeley and Los Angeles: University of California Press, 1982); Kenneth J. Gergen, *The Saturated Self: Dilemmas of Identity in Contemporary Life* (New York: Basic Books, 1991).

6. In the Civic Involvement Survey, being very unlikely to trust "somebody who is running for political office" was positively associated in logit regression models with living in a central-city area and being male, and negatively associated with having attended college. Twenty-five percent of respondents were personally acquainted with one or more political officials. They were slightly more likely than other respondents to say they would be very likely or fairly likely to trust somebody who was running for political office, but the difference was not statistically significant; even among those who were acquainted with officials, 41 percent said they would be unlikely to trust somebody running for office.

7. Eric M. Uslaner, "Faith, Hope, and Charity: Social Capital, Trust, and Collective Action," Department of Government and Politics, University of Maryland, 1996.

9. THE LARGER PICTURE

1. In a recent survey, 86 percent of American women aged 18–55 agreed with the statement "I get plenty of support and help from my family and friends" (as did 91 percent in the United Kingdom, 90 percent in Spain, 82 percent in Germany, 79 percent in France, and 69 percent in Italy); "Women and Society," *World Opinion Update* (April 1996).

2. In the Civic Involvement Survey, 67 percent said they could count on close personal friends for help if someone in their family was seriously ill. Married respondents were asked how many people had attended their wedding. In the highest socioeconomic group the average number of guests was 142 for people aged 25–34, 149 for those 35–44, 135 for those 45–54, and 82 for those 55 and over; in the middle socioeconomic group the respective figures were 107, 130, 115, and 96; and in the lowest socioeconomic group, 119, 108, 107, and 69. Since most younger people have married more recently than older people, a reasonable inference is that wedding attendance has remained stable or perhaps increased. A multiple regression analysis supports this conclusion: the standardized regression coefficients are −.021 for being under age 35, −.134* for being 50 and older, −.001 for being male, −.204* for ever having been divorced, −.050 for parents' financial status, .127* for having attended college, −.070* for having an income below $25,000, and .062 for having at least one parent who graduated from college (* indicates significance at or beyond the .05 level). Attendance at funeral services has declined slightly, but attendance at wakes has increased, perhaps suggesting the importance of being able to attend at times that fit into work and family schedules; Funeral and Memorial Information Counsel, *1995 Study of American Attitudes toward Ritualization and Memorialization* (McLean, Va.: Wirthlin Group, 1995);

Allied Industry Joint Committee, *American Attitudes and Values Affected by Death and Deathcare Services* (McLean, Va.: Wirthlin Group, 1990).

3. Many men we interviewed emphasized what has been termed the domestic male. One older man said he regretted the time his church had taken away from his family: "I was at church three, four nights a week when I was raising my boys, plus working and traveling. I was just never there. Really, there's significance here. I think churches should allow married men and women to be there for all the worship services and then on one extra-curricular activity a week. That's it. And the rest of the time you belong at home with your children."

4. Only 36 percent of respondents in the Civic Involvement Survey had lived at their present address more than ten years. Approximately 100 million long-distance calls are placed every Mother's Day, and 155 million Mother's Day cards are purchased annually. Even more dramatic are the 2.65 billion Christmas cards sent annually, a figure that rose by 35 percent in a recent five-year period. The average American receives approximately 30 greeting cards each year. Fully 97 percent of Americans celebrate their birthdays with other people, 90 percent receive at least one birthday card, and one person in two gets 10 or more; Camala Brown, "Cakes, Cards, and Candles," *American Demographics* (March 1995), online. Mark Granovetter, "The Strength of Weak Ties," *American Journal of Sociology* 78 (1973).

5. See Seymour Martin Lipset, Martin Trow, and James Coleman, *Union Democracy: The Internal Politics of the International Typographical Union* (Garden City, N.Y.: Doubleday, 1956); Robert D. Putnam, *Making Democracy Work: Civic Traditions in Modern Italy* (Princeton: Princeton University Press, 1993); Sidney Verba, Kay Lehman Schlozman, and Henry E. Brady, *Voice and Equality: Civic Voluntarism in American Politics* (Cambridge, Mass.: Harvard University Press, 1995).

6. "People's Satisfaction with Their Lives and Government," *World Opinion Update* (July 1995); when asked "How satisfied are you with the way democracy works in this country," 64 percent of Americans said very or somewhat satisfied, compared with 62 percent in Canada, 55 percent in Germany, 43 percent in France, 40 percent in the United Kingdom, and 35 percent in Japan. A 1995 survey asked Americans, "In general, does the United States government usually represent the interests of the American people or the narrow concerns of special interest groups?"; 30 percent said the American people, and 63 percent said special interest groups; *World Opinion Update* (May 1995).

7. One practical suggestion for how to cultivate vertical relationships came from a middle-class woman: "I think too many times people try to get involved politically, like on national elections and things like that, and that's their first involvement and sometimes you get really squashed, stepped on, because you're just a little peon down here. Nobody knows you. You're not important to anybody. You're just licking envelopes for a presidential campaign. It's the

stuff that's nearest and dearest to you that's better to get involved in. It gives you a real feel for what's going on around you politically and government wise and it's a way that you can not only be involved but make a contribution."

8. Among those in the Civic Involvement Survey who said they had done any volunteer work in the past year, 77 percent said their organizations received funds from individual donors; 25 percent said foundations were a source of funds; 32 percent said state or local government; and 21 percent said their organizations received funds from the federal government.

9. I am grateful to Jean Cohen, who has written perceptively on the role of law in civic participation in several yet-unpublished papers.

10. Thirty-nine percent of volunteers said their organizations received funds from corporations. On corporations and social activism see Charles Perrow, *The Radical Attack on Business* (New York: Harcourt, Brace, Jovanovich, 1972); David Vogel, *Fluctuating Fortunes: The Political Power of Business in America* (New York: Basic Books, 1989).

11. Membership in the National Council of Corporate Volunteerism doubled between 1985 and 1994 to 1,200 companies; Catherine Romano, "Pressed to Service," *Management Review* (June 1994).

12. Marilyn Jackson-Beeck and Jeff Sobal, "The Social World of Heavy Television Viewers," *Journal of Broadcasting* 24 (1980). Robert D. Putnam, "The Strange Disappearance of Civic America," *American Prospect* (Winter 1996) (http://epn.org/prospect/24/24putn.html). Pippa Norris, "Does Television Erode Social Capital? A Reply to Putnam," *P.S.: Political Science and Politics* 29 (1996). Using national survey data, Norris found that number of hours per week viewing television was negatively correlated at statistically significant levels with seven measures of civic participation (voting, doing campaign work, making campaign contributions, contacting officials, protesting, being a member of an organization, and engaging in informal community activity); but in multiple regression models including controls for education, age, gender, race, employment status, and income, only two of these relationships remained significant (and both were weak). Norris also examined specific kinds of viewing (such as watching public television or news programs), and concluded that television can have positive as well as negative effects on civic participation.

13. Legal definitions of incivility have also changed profoundly; see Kenneth Cmiel, "The Politics of Civility," in *The Sixties: From Memory to History*, ed. David Farber (Chapel Hill: University of North Carolina Press, 1994).

14. Consider the multiple languages, sources, and aspects of the self revealed in these comments: (1) "I don't want to feel beholden or made to do activities that I don't feel like doing. Like stuffing envelopes or going door to door to collect money or whatever might be needed." (2) "I think the thing that would most interest me now would be to be part of a garden group, but I'm not sure there is such a thing in my community." (3) "I'm excessively busy and I really treasure my moments when I can crash." (4) "I see too many

people, so that it makes me feel not wanting to party and see people socially. I see so many people every day in my job." (5) "I haven't the energy for [good works] or even the inclination. I don't want anything more to do with neediness." (6) "I have a vague dream that when I retired and wanted to do something voluntary I would go and rock babies in the hospital, just because it would give me pleasure to hold these lovely little sweethearts. To be connected to babies again."

Index